WORLD MISSION

An Analysis
of the World Christian Movement

SECOND EDITION
Full revision of the original work

Cross-Cultural Considerations

Part Three of a Manual in Three Parts

Jonathan Lewis, Ph.D., Editor

WILLIAM CAREY LIBRARY
Pasadena, California

Published by: William Carey Library, P.O. Box 40129, Pasadena, CA 91114, telephone (818) 798-0819

ISBN 0-87808-239-5
Printed in the United States of America

Editor: Jonathan Lewis, Ph.D.
Assistant Editors: Meg Crossman and Stephen Hoke, Ph.D.
Technical Editor: Susan Peterson
Assistants: Joe Varela and Patrick Roseman
Illustrators: John Devine and Dawn Lewis

Acknowledgments

Many of the articles and excerpts in this manual are found in the mission anthology *Perspectives on the World Christian Movement: A Reader* (revised edition), edited by Ralph Winter and Steven Hawthorne and published by William Carey Library. We are heavily indebted to the editors of this anthology for their encouragement in the production of this course. We would especially like to thank Dr. Ralph Winter for his inspiration and genius as the originator of this course, and we recognize his tireless efforts on behalf of the unreached peoples of the world. A special note of appreciation also goes to the *Perspectives* course office in Pasadena, California, which has cooperated fully in the re-edition process, in the hope of greater compatibility with their popular extension course.

My heartfelt thanks go to my assistant editors, Meg Crossman and Dr. Stephen T. Hoke. Meg's advocacy and use of the *World Mission* manuals in the Arizona *Perspectives* courses provided a wealth of insights for improving the material. Her contributions are reflected primarily in the first two volumes. Steve Hoke, veteran missions lecturer, was of invaluable help in improving the third volume. His knowledge, insights, and ready assistance are very much appreciated. Most of the credit for the technical production of this work goes to Susan Peterson. Her long hours of formatting, proofreading, indexing, and producing the figures and tables speak eloquently for themselves. We gratefully acknowledge Joe Varela and Pat Roseman, who assisted Susan in these tasks. We have kept many of John Devine's and Dawn Lewis's illustrations from the first edition. Thank you all for your marvelous help. May it advance the expansion of God's kingdom to the ends of the earth.

Jonathan Lewis, Editor
January 1994

Other Course Materials by the Editor

- *World Mission Leader's Guide*. An aid to those who want to organize and conduct a study group utilizing these manuals. It includes suggestions for promotion and organization of the course, as well as sample answers to each of the questions in the texts. An appendix gives useful helps on group dynamics. Available from William Carey Library.

- *Misión Mundial: Un Análisis del Movimiento Cristiano Mundial* (3 volumes).

- *Guia para el tutor del grupo de estudio de: Misión Mundial* (3 volumes).

- *Video de Misión Mundial* (3 videos, 5 hours total).

  The Second Edition of the Spanish manuals, accompanying leader's guide, and the lecture videos are available from Unilit, 1360 N.W. 88th Ave., Miami, FL 33172.

  Please contact the publisher for other language editions under production.

- *Working Your Way to the Nations: A Guide to Effective Tentmaking*. A 12-lesson course for use by local churches in guiding the preparation of cross-cultural "tentmaking" missionaries. Available from William Carey Library. Editions of this strategic course in Korean, Spanish, and Portuguese are under production.

PART 3

CROSS-CULTURAL CONSIDERATIONS

89993

Preface to the Second Edition

We live in a rapidly changing world. These changes affect the way the advancing World Christian Movement perceives its mandate and carries out its task. The Second Edition of *World Mission* has tried to analyze these trends and incorporate their discussion into the text. Two Thirds World missions, reaching rapidly expanding cities, mission to the world's poor and destitute, the 10/40 window, strategic partnerships, church/mission tension—these and other current issues are woven into the discussion of the biblical, historical, strategic, and cross-cultural foundation of missions, improving and strengthening these basic themes.

The editors have worked closely with the *Perspectives* office at the U.S. Center for World Mission in Pasadena, California, to assure that these manuals are suited for students participating in their extension courses. Questions have been improved, and the research assignment has been redesigned to enhance the application of the end-product. Useful indexes and an appendix have also been added.

Organization and Use of This Manual

World Mission: An Analysis of the World Christian Movement is a manual that can be used by study groups in a formal or informal educational setting. The manual is in three parts, each being a separate unit.

- **Part One, The Biblical/Historical Foundation**, examines the roots of world mission, including its origin and its development through the ages.

- **Part Two, The Strategic Dimension**, defines the remaining mission task and the strategies necessary to reach the unreached.

- **Part Three, Cross-Cultural Considerations**, explores the challenge of cross-cultural communication of the gospel.

Each of the 15 chapters of this manual is divided into three study units. Each unit develops a distinct concept and relates it to the material studied in preceding units. Questions interspersed throughout the text direct the reader's attention to key points and stimulate reflection on the readings.

Each chapter ends with two sections of questions. The first section, **Integrative Assignment**, is designed to help the reader assimilate the material studied. The questions invite the student to do further research and encourage the development of the student's abilities to communicate what is learned. Study groups should use these questions for group discussion. In Part Two of the manual, an "Unreached Peoples" research project is incorporated into the Integrative Assignment. This fascinating project will require extra time and effort from the student.

The second section of questions, **Questions for Reflection**, asks for a response to personal and spiritual issues raised by the readings. We recommend that each student enter his or her thoughts either in the workbook or in a personal diary. We also suggest that a devotional time be provided during each group session to share these comments.

CHAPTER 11

Mission and Culture

In order to have an effective cross-cultural ministry, missionaries must first of all be students of culture—that is, of the way a particular people organize their world. *Culture is an integrated system of beliefs (about God or reality or ultimate meaning), of values (about what is true, good, beautiful, and normative), of customs (how to behave, relate to others, talk, pray, dress, work, play, trade, farm, eat, etc.), and of institutions which express these beliefs, values, and customs (government, law courts, temples or churches, family, schools, hospitals, factories, shops, unions, clubs, etc.), which binds a society together and gives it a sense of identity, dignity, security, and continuity.*[*]

Effective missionaries identify with the culture. Through an intimate knowledge of the people, missionaries see the world as the people see it and experience life as they do. We have no better example of this identification than Jesus Christ Himself. He left His home in glory to become a vulnerable, dependent human infant. He knew hunger and thirst, poverty and oppression. He experienced rejection, anger, and loss. He wept. His experience of human nature gave Him the tremendous insight He manifested during His earthly sojourn (Heb. 2:17) and provided a relational platform for powerful ministry.

Like Christ, cross-cultural missionaries must seek to understand the people they hope to reach with the gospel. They must strive to gain the people's perspective on life and to identify wholeheartedly with them. In a unique way, cross-cultural missionaries stand as intercessors and advocates for the unreached group with whom they are identified (1 Pet. 2:9). This chapter will address issues surrounding successful identification and other aspects of cross-cultural interaction. We will also consider how missionaries function as "agents of change" within a culture.

---

[*] Lausanne Committee for World Evangelization. (1978). *The Willowbank report: Gospel and culture* (Lausanne Occasional Papers No. 2, p. 7). Wheaton, IL: Author.

I. Identification

When we think of identification, images of Hudson Taylor in native Chinese dress and a braided pigtail come to mind. Heart-to-heart identification, however, is much more than adopting dress and customs. It is the result of a sequence of actions based on attitudes. Entering a culture with an open, trusting, and accepting outlook is the first step. Responding to the inevitable cultural differences with humility, as a learner, is a second step.

There are three dimensions to this work: (1) We must come to a knowledge of all aspects of the people's culture; (2) we must participate with them in their lifestyle; and (3) we must demonstrate genuine empathy with them. *The ultimate goal of identification is not to see how much like the other culture one can become, but how profoundly and effectively one can learn to* **communicate** *with those of the other culture.* In the following article, anthropologist William D. Reyburn shares additional insights which he has gained through his personal quest for genuine identification.

❏ *Identification in the Missionary Task* *

William D. Reyburn **

A steady downpour of rain had been falling from late afternoon until long after dark. A small donkey followed by a pair of men slowly made its way down the slippery sides of the muddy descent which wound into the sleepy town of Baños, high in the Ecuadorean Andes. No one appeared to pay any attention as the two dark figures halted their burro before a shabby Indian hostel. The taller of the two men stepped inside the doorway where a group of men sat at a small table drinking *chicha* by candle light. No sooner had the stranger entered the room than a voice from behind the bar called out, "*Buenas*

* Reyburn, W. D. (1978). Identification in the missionary task. In W. A. Smalley (Ed.), *Readings in missionary anthropology II* (pp. 746-760). Pasadena: William Carey Library.

** William D. Reyburn has served the United Bible Societies as a translations consultant in South and Central America, Africa, Europe, and the Middle East. During 1968-1972 he served as translations coordinator of the UBS, based in London.

noches, meester." The man in the rain-soaked poncho turned quickly to see a fat-faced woman standing half concealed behind the counter. "*Buenas noches, señora,*" he replied, lifting his hat slightly. Following a short exchange of conversation the man and barmaid reappeared outside and led the donkey through a small gate to a mud stable. The two men removed their load and carried it to a stall-like room beside the stable where they were to spend the night.

I sat down on the straw on the floor and began pulling off my wet clothes. I kept hearing the word *meester* which I had come to dislike intensely. Why had that funny little woman there in the semi-darkness of the room addressed me as *meester*? I looked at my clothes. My hat was that of the poorest *cholo* in Ecuador. My pants were nothing more than a mass of patches held together by still more patches. On my dirty mud-stained feet I wore a pair of rubber tire *alpargatas* the same as any Indian or *cholo* wore. My red poncho was not from the high class Otavalo weavers. It was a poor man's poncho made in Salcedo. It had no fancy tassels and in true *cholo* fashion there were bits of straw dangling from its lower edge, showing that I was a man who slept with his burro on the road. But why then did she call me *meester*, a term reserved for Americans and Europeans? At least she could have addressed me as *señor*, but no, it had to be *meester*. I felt as though my carefully devised disguise had been stripped from me with the mention of that word. I kept hashing it over and over in my mind. It wasn't because she detected a foreign accent, because I had not as yet opened my mouth. I turned to my Quechua Indian companion, old Carlos Bawa of Lake Colta. "Carlos, the lady knew I am a *meester*. How do you think she knew, Carlitos?"

My friend sat huddled in the corner of the room with his legs and arms tucked under his two ponchos. "I don't know, *patroncito.*" Looking up quickly at Carlos, I said, "Carlos, for three days I have been asking you not to call me *patroncito*. If you call me that, people will know I am not a *cholo*." Carlos flicked a finger out from under the collar of his woolen poncho and touching his hat brim submissively replied, "I keep forgetting, *meestercito.*"

Disgusted and aching in my rain-soaked skin, I felt like the fool I must have appeared. I sat quietly watching the candle flicker as Carlos dozed off to sleep in his corner. I kept seeing the faces of people along the road we had walked for the past three days. Then I would see the face of this woman in Baños who had robbed me of what seemed like a perfect disguise. I wondered then if perhaps I hadn't been taken for a European even earlier. I was hurt, disappointed, disillusioned, and to make things worse I was dreadfully hungry. Reaching into our packsack I pulled out the bag of *machica* flour my wife had prepared for us, poured in some water, and stirred the brown sugar and barley mixture with my finger and gulped it down. The rain was letting up now, and from a hole in the upper corner of the room I could see the clouds drifting across the sky in the light of the moon. A guitar was strumming softly out in the street, and in the stall next to us a half dozen Indians had just returned from the stable and were discussing the events of their day's journey.

> *I asked myself again and again what it meant to be identified with this old Quechua Indian who was so far removed from the real world in which I lived.*

Blowing out the candle, I leaned up against the rough plank wall and listened to their conversation, then eventually fell asleep. It was some hours later when I was startled awake from the noise of our door creaking open. I got to my feet quickly and jumped behind the opening door waiting to see what was going to happen. The door quietly closed and I heard old Carlos groan as he settled down onto his mat to sleep. Carlos was returning, having gone out to relieve himself. My companion had been warning me for several days that Indians often rob each other and I should always sleep lightly. It was quiet now, deathly silent. I had no idea what time it may have been, as a watch was not suitable for my *cholo* garb. I lay on the floor thinking about the meaning of identification. I asked myself again and again what it meant to be identified with this old Quechua Indian who was so far removed from the real world in which I lived.

I was traveling the Indian markets of the Ecuadorean Andes in order to know what really lay hidden in the hearts of these Quechua Indians and Spanish-speaking *cholos*. What was the real longing in their hearts that could be touched? I wanted to know what it was that drunkenness seemed to satisfy. Was the Quechua Indian really the sullen withdrawn personality that he appeared to be before his *patrón*? Was he so adjustable to life conditions that his attitude could incorporate most any conflict without upsetting him seriously? Was he really a good Catholic, a pagan, or what kind of a combination? Why underneath was he so opposed to outward change? What was he talking about and worrying over when

> **A major aspect of the missionary task is the search for a connection or point of contact.**

he settled down at night in the security of his own little group? I was after the roots that lay behind the outward symbols which could respond to the claims of Christ. The answer to questions like these would form the basis for a missionary theology, a relevant communication to these people's lives. I could see no purpose in putting the Christian proposition before a man unless it was made in such a way that it forced him to struggle with it in terms of surrender to the ultimate and most basic demand that could be placed upon him. In order to know what had to be addressed to the depths of his being, I had to wade down to it through what I was convinced were only outward displays of a deeper need in his heart.

A major aspect of the missionary task is the search for a *connection* or *point of contact*. The proclamation of the gospel aside from such a contact point is a proclamation which skirts missionary responsibility. This is simply the process in which the one who proclaims the good news must make every effort to get into touch with his listener. Man's heart is not a clean slate that the gospel comes and writes upon for the first time. It is a complex which has been scrawled upon and deeply engraved from birth to death. The making of a believer always begins with an unbeliever. Clearly this is the job of the Holy Spirit. However, this does not remove man from his position of responsibility. It is man in his rational hearing and understanding that is awakened to belief. It is the conquering of man's basic deceit that allows the Holy Spirit to lay claim to him and to make of him a new creature. A man must be aware that he stands in defiance of God's call before he can be apprehended by God's love. Before an enemy can be taken captive he must stand in the position of an enemy.

1. Why wasn't the author's attempt to pass as a cholo successful?

_____

_____

_____

2. What does the author identify as a major responsibility of the missionary in communicating the gospel?

_____

_____

The forms of identification

Missionary identification may take on many different forms. It may be romantic or it may be dull. It may be convincing or it may appear as a sham. The central point is that identification is not an end in itself. It is the road to the task of gospel proclamation. Likewise the heart of the controversial matter of missionary identification is not how far one can go but rather what one does with the fruits of identification. Going native is no special virtue. Many missionaries in the humdrum of their daily routine about a school or hospital have awakened men's hearts to the claim of the gospel.

Identification is not an end in itself. It is the road to the task of gospel proclamation.

Some so-called identification is misoriented and tends to create the impression that living in a native village or learning the native tongue is automatically the "open sesame" of the native's heart. It is not the sheer quantity of identification that counts; it is rather the purposeful quality that comprehends man as a responsible being seeking to be in touch with his reality. The limitations for knowing what is this contacted reality are great. The practical obstacles for missionary identification are many. In the pages that follow we shall attempt to outline some of these as we have lived in them and to evaluate the effects of the lack of missionary identification and participation.

The force of unconscious habit

Without doubt the nature of the obstacle to identification is the fact that one has so well learned one's own way of life that he practices it for the most part without conscious reflection. In the case described above, the old Quechua Indian Carlos Bawa, the donkey, and I had been traveling across the plateau of the Andes spending the days in the markets and the nights cramped into tiny quarters available to itinerant Indians and *cholos* for approximately 10 cents U.S. We had made our way from Riobamba to Baños, a three-day trek by road, and no one except an occasional dog appeared to see that all was not quite normal. It was not until stepping into the candle-lit room of the inn at Baños that I was taken for a foreigner (at least it so appeared). I suspect that it bothered me a great deal because I had created the illusion for a few days that I was finally on the inside of the Indian-*cholo* world looking about and not in the least conspicuous about it. When the innkeeper addressed me as *meester*, I had the shock of being rudely dumped outside the little world where I thought I had at last gained a firm entrance.

The following morning I went to the lady innkeeper and sat down at the bar. "Now, tell me, *señora*," I began, "how did you know I was a *meester* and not a local *señor* or a *cholo* from Riobamba?" The fat little lady's eyes sparkled as she laughed an embarrassed giggle. "I don't know for sure," she replied. I insisted she try to give me the answer, for I was thoroughly confused over it all. I went on. "Now suppose you were a detective, *señora*, and you were told to catch a European man dressed like a poor *cholo* merchant. How would you recognize him if he came into your inn?" She scratched her head and leaned forward over the counter. "Walk outside and come back in like you did last night." I picked up my old hat, pulled it low on my head, and made for the door. Before I reached the street she called out, "Wait, *señor*, I know now what it is." I stopped and turned around. "It's the way you walk." She broke into a hearty laugh at this point and said, "I never saw anyone around here who walks like that. You Europeans swing your arms like you never carried a load on your back." I thanked the good lady for her lesson in posture and went out in the street to study how the local people walked. Sure enough, the steps were short and choppy, the trunk leaning forward slightly from the hips and the arms scarcely moving under their huge ponchos.

Knowing that the squatting position with the poncho draped from ears to the hidden feet was more natural, I squatted on the street corner near a group of Indians and listened to them chat. They continued with their conversation and paid no attention to my presence. Two missionaries whom I knew very well emerged from a hotel doorway nearby. I watched them as they swung their cameras about their shoulders and discussed the problem of over-exposure in the tricky Andean sunlight. A ragged *cholo* boy sitting beside me scrambled to his feet, picked up his shoe-shine box, and approached the pair. He was rebuffed by their nonchalant shaking of the head. As they continued to survey the brilliant market place for pictures, the shoe-shine boy returned to his spot beside me. Sitting down he mumbled, "The *señores* who own shoes ought to keep them shined." I leaned toward the boy and beckoned for his ear. He bent over his shoe box as I whispered to him. The boy then jumped back to his feet and started after the pair who were crossing the street. On the other side they stopped and turned to him as he said, "The evangelicals are not respected here unless we see their shoes are shined." One man lifted a foot and rubbed his shoe on his pants cuff, while the other settled down for a toothbrush, spit and polish shine.

I arose, passed within three feet of my friends, and took up a listening post in the heart of the busy market, where I sat until my legs began to ache. As I got up to my feet I yawned and stretched, and as I began to walk away I noticed I had drawn the attention of those sitting about me. Again I had behaved in a way that felt so natural but in a way which was not like the local folks do. In front of me an old woman dropped a bag of salt. I unthinkingly reached down to help her, and it was only by a bit of providential intervention that I was saved from being hauled off to jail for attempting to steal.

This extremity of identification or disguise may appear as one way of overdoing a good thing. However, only a missionary among the withdrawn highland Quechuas can really appreciate how difficult it is to talk with these people in a situation of equality. I simply could not accept the Quechua's response as being valid and representing his real self as long as he was talking to the *patrón*. I wanted to hear him without a *patrón* present, and I wanted to be addressed stripped of that feudal role which I was sure completely colored our relationship. I found that the submissive, sluggish Indian whom I had known in my role of *patrón* became a scheming quick-witted person who could be extremely friendly, helpful, or cruel depending upon the situation.

3. What did the author learn about the Quechuas which he might not have learned if he had not pursued an extreme identification with them?

_____

_____

_____

Limits of identification

Perhaps the most outstanding example in which I was reminded of the limitations of identification occurred while we were living in a mud-and-thatch hut near Tabacundo, Ecuador. We had moved into a small scattered farming settlement near the Pisque River about a kilometer from the United Andean Mission for whom we were making a study. My wife and I had agreed that if we were to accomplish anything at the UAM we would have to settle among the people and somehow get them to accept us or reject us. We were accepted eventually but always with reservations. We wore nothing but Indian clothes and ate nothing but Indian food. We had no furniture except a bed made of century plant stalks covered with a woven mat exactly as in all the Indian houses. In fact, because we had no agricultural equipment, weaving loom, or granary, our one-room house was by far the most empty in the vicinity. In spite of this material reduction to the zero point, the men addressed me as *patroncito*. When I objected that I was not a *patrón* because I owned no land, they reminded me that I wore leather shoes. I quickly exchanged these for a pair of local made *alpargatas* which have a hemp fiber sole and a woven cotton upper. After a time had passed I noticed that merely changing my footwear had not in the least gotten rid of the appellation of *patroncito*. When I asked again the men replied that I associated with the Spanish townspeople from Tabacundo. In so doing I was obviously identifying myself with the *patrón* class. I made every effort for a period to avoid the townspeople, but the term *patroncito* seemed to be as permanently fixed as it was the day we moved into the community.

The men had been required by the local commissioner to repair an impassable road connecting the community and Tabacundo. I joined in this work with the Indians until it was completed two months later. My hands had become hard and calloused. One day I proudly showed my calloused hands to a group of men while they were finishing the last of a jar of fermented *chicha*. "Now, you can't say I don't work with you. Why do you still call me *patroncito*?" This time the truth was near the surface, forced there by uninhibited alcoholic replies. Vicente Cuzco, a leader in the group, stepped up and put his arm around my shoulder and whispered to me. "We call you *patroncito* because you weren't born of an Indian mother." I needed no further explanation.

4. What limit to identification confronted the author? Can you think of other limits which may be beyond a missionary's control?

_____

_____

_____

Ownership of a gun

Living in an African village caused us to become aware of the effect of other formative attitudes in our backgrounds. One of these in particular is the idea of personal ownership. While living in the south Cameroun village of Aloum among the Bulu in order to learn the language, we had been received from the first day with intense reception and hospitality. We were given Bulu family names; the village danced for several nights, and we were loaded with gifts of a goat and all kinds of tropical foods.

We had been invited to live in Aloum, and we were not fully prepared psychologically to understand how such an adoption was conceived within Bulu thinking. Slowly we came to learn that our possessions were no longer private property but were to be available for the collective use of the sublcan where we had been adopted. We were able to adjust to this way of doing because we had about the same material status as the others in the village. Their demands upon our things were not as great as their generous hospitality with which they provided nearly all of our food.

Then one night I caught a new vision of the implication of our relation to the people of Aloum. A stranger had appeared in the village, and we learned that Aloum was the home of his mother's brother. It was the case of the nephew in the town of his maternal uncle, a most interesting social relationship in the patrilineal societies in Africa. After dark when the leading men in the village had gathered in the men's clubhouse, I drifted over and sat down among them to listen to their conversations. The fires on the floor threw shadows which appeared to dance up and down on the mud walls.

> *Slowly we came to learn that our possessions were no longer private property but were to be available for the collective use of the sublcan where we had been adopted.*

Finally silence fell over their conversations, and the chief of the village arose and began to speak in very hushed tones. Several young men arose from their positions by the fires and moved outside to take up a listening post to make sure that no uninvited persons would overhear the development of these important events. The chief spoke of the welcome of his nephew into his village and guaranteed him a safe sojourn while he was there. After these introductory formalities were finished, the chief began to extol his nephew as a great elephant hunter. I was still totally ignorant of how all this affected me. I listened as he eulogized his nephew's virtue as a skilled hunter. After the chief finished, another elder arose and continued to cite cases in the nephew's life in which he had displayed great bravery in the face of the dangers of the jungles. One after another repeated these stories until the chief again stood to his feet. I could see the whites of his eyes which were aimed at me. The fire caused little shadows to run back and forth on his dark face and body. "Obam Nna," he addressed me. A broad smile exposed a gleaming set of teeth. "We are going to present our gun to my nephew now. Go get it."

I hesitated a brief moment but then arose and crossed the moonlit courtyard to our thatch-covered house, where Marie and some village women sat talking. I kept hearing in my ears: "We are going to present our gun... our gun...." Almost as if it were a broken record stuck on the plural possessive pronoun, it kept repeating in my ears, "*ngale jangan... ngale jangan....*" Before I reached the house I had thought of half a dozen very good reasons why I should say no. However, I got the gun and some shells and started back to the clubhouse. As I reentered the room I caught again the sense of the world of Obam Nna. If I were to be Obam Nna, I should have to cease to be William Reyburn. In order to be Obam Nna, I had to crucify William Reyburn nearly every day. In the world of Obam Nna I no longer owned the gun as in the world of William Reyburn. I handed the gun to the chief and, although he didn't know it, along with it went the surrender of a very stingy idea of private ownership.

5. How did the Bulu concept of ownership differ from the author's?

_____

_____

_____

6. What had to happen to "William Reyburn" in order for him to become "Obam Nna"? Why?

_____

_____

_____

Symbolic value of food

Another problem in village participation is the matter of food and water. However, this is not the problem most people think it is. We found while living in Paris that our French friends were often scandalized at the things which we ate. One of the most offensive of these was cheese with pie. I have seen Frenchmen grimace as if in agony upon seeing us combine these two foods.

I have stayed among the Kaka tribe on the open grasslands of the eastern Cameroun and have made studies among them. The life of these people is quite different from the jungle Bulu of the south. Life on the savanna is more rigorous and results in a different adjustment to natural conditions. Food is much less abundant, and cassava is the main staple. Unlike the Bulu who have adopted many European ways, the Kaka are more under the influences of Islam, which filter down from their cattle-raising Fulani neighbors to the north.

I had gone into the village of Lolo to carry out some studies relative to the translation of the book of Acts and had taken no European food, determined to find what the effects of an all-Kaka diet would be. I attempted to drink only boiled water, but often this was entirely impossible. I found that the simple mixture of cassava flour and hot water to form a mush was an excellent sustaining diet. On one occasion over a period of six weeks on this diet I lost no weight, had no diarrhea, and suffered no other ill effects. All of this food was prepared by village women, and I usually ate on the ground with the men wherever I happened to be when a woman would serve food. On several occasions when I was not in the right place at the right time, it meant going to bed with an empty stomach. I carefully avoided asking any woman to prepare food especially for me, as this had a sexual connotation which I did not care to provoke.

Once I had been talking most of the afternoon with a group of Kaka men and boys about foods people eat the world over. One of the young men got his Bulu Bible and read from the 10th chapter of Acts the vision of Peter who was instructed to kill and eat "all manner of four-footed beasts of the earth, and wild beasts, and creeping things, and fowls of the air." This young Kaka who had been a short while at a mission school said, "The Hausa people don't believe this because they won't eat pigs. Missionaries, we think, don't believe this because they don't eat some of our foods either." I quite confidently assured him that a missionary would eat anything he does.

That evening I was called to the young man's father's doorway, where the old man sat on the ground in the dirt. In front of him were two clean white enamel pans covered by lids. He looked up at me and motioned for me to sit. His wife brought a gourd of water which she poured as we washed our hands. Then flicking wet fingers in the air to dry them a bit, the old man lifted the lid from the one pan. Steam arose from a neatly rounded mass of cassava mush. Then he lifted the lid from the other pan. I caught a glimpse of its contents. Then my eyes lifted and met the unsmiling stare of the young man who had read about the vision of Peter earlier in the afternoon. The pan was filled with singed caterpillars. I swallowed hard, thinking that now I either swallowed these caterpillars, or I swallowed my words and thereby proved again that Europeans have merely adapted Christianity to fit their own selfish way of life. I waited as my host scooped his shovel-like fingers deep into the mush, then with a ball of the stuff he

pressed it gently into the caterpillar pan. As he lifted it to his open mouth I saw the burned and fuzzy treasures, some smashed into the mush and others dangling loose, enter between his teeth.

My host had proven the safety of his food by taking the first portion. This was the guarantee that he was not feeding me poison. I plunged my fingers into the mush, but my eyes were fixed on the caterpillars. I wondered what the sensation in the mouth was going to be. I quickly scooped up some of the creeping things and plopped the mass into my mouth. As I bit down the soft insides burst open, and to my surprise I tasted a salty meat-like flavor which seemed to give the insipid cassava mush the ingredient that was missing.

We sat silently eating. There is no time for conversation at the Kaka "table," for as soon as the owner has had his first bite male hands appear from every direction and the contents are gone. As we sat eating quickly the old man's three wives with their daughters came and stood watching us from their kitchen doorways. They held their hands up and whispered busily back and forth: "White man Kaka is eating caterpillars. He really has a black heart." The pans were emptied. Each one took a mouthful of water, rinsed his mouth and spat the water to one side, belched loudly, said, "Thank you, Ndjambie" (God), arose and departed into the rays of the brilliant setting sun. My notes on that night contain this one line: "An emptied pan of caterpillars is more convincing than all the empty metaphors of love which missionaries are prone to expend on the heathen."

7. Why was it important that the author eat the caterpillars?

_____

_____

_____

Ideological insulation

There are other obstacles to missionary participation in native life which arise from background as well as local Christian tradition. It does not take a folk or primitive people long to size up the distance which separates themselves from the missionary. In some cases this distance is negligible, but in others it is the separation between different worlds. Missionaries with pietistic backgrounds are prepared to suspect that everything the local people do is bad and that therefore, in order to save them, they must pull them out and set up another kind of life opposed to the original one. This process seldom if ever works, and when it does the result is the creation of a society which consists of converted souls but no converted life. The missionary under these circumstances takes the path of least resistance, keeps himself untouched by the world, and of course does not get into touch with the world in order to save it.

8. What negative effect can an insulated or "sheltered" Christian background have on identification?

_____

_____

_____

Freedom to witness

The Christian church sealed off from the world becomes unintelligible to the world it attempts to reach. It is like the father who can never remember how to be a child and therefore is looked upon as a foreigner by his children. Missionary participation and identification are not produced by a study of anthropology but by being freed through the Spirit of the Lord to witness to the truth of the gospel in the world.

Christianity calls men into a brotherhood in Christ, but at the same time Christians often negate that call by separating mechanisms which run the gamut from food taboos to racial fear. The Christian gospel is foreign enough to the self-centeredness of man's view of the universe. However, before this misconception of the self can be corrected, there is a barrier that must be penetrated. In Christian terminology it is the cross which leads man from his walled-up self out into the freedom for which he was intended. There is yet another foreignness which must be overcome through sacrifice of one's own way of

> *The Christian church sealed off from the world becomes unintelligible to the world it attempts to reach.*

thinking and doing things. Christianity cannot be committed to one expression of civilization or culture. The missionary task is that of sacrifice. Not the sacrifice of leaving friends and comfortable situations at home, but the sacrifice of reexamining one's own cultural assumptions and becoming intelligible to a world where he must not assume that intelligibility is given.

A missionary theology asks this question: "At what points in this man's heart does the Holy Spirit challenge him to surrender?" The missionary task is to ferret out this point of contact through identification with him. The basis of missionary identification is not to make the "native" feel more at home around a foreigner nor to ease the materialistic conscience of the missionary but to create a *communication* and a *communion* where together they seek out what Saint Paul in 2 Corinthians 10:5 calls the "arguments and obstacles"—"We destroy arguments and every proud obstacle to the knowledge of God, and take every thought captive to obey Christ." This is the basis for a missionary science, the biblical foundation of a missionary theology, and the *raison d'être* of the missionary calling in which one seeks, even in the face of profound limitations, to identify oneself in the creation of new creatures in a regenerate communion.

9. What is the ultimate purpose of identification?

_____

_____

_____

We don't have to be cross-cultural missionaries to appreciate the value of identification in Christian witness. Even within the context of our home churches, identification is an essential element for growth. Unfortunately, little importance is given to this dynamic. The new believer usually goes from having almost exclusively non-Christian friends to having almost all Christian friends within six months of conversion. Seldom are the natural bridges of identification exploited to bring those other friends to Christ.

Among the many reasons for this phenomenon is the fact that people gravitate toward those with whom they feel most comfortable. Without a conscious effort to reverse this trend, evangelism becomes a difficult and confrontive experience for most. Rather than being based on genuine interest and friendship, evangelism easily turns into an impersonal rhetorical (even combative) exercise with strangers.

For the missionary, this problem may be compounded. The missionary must not only break out of the evangelical subculture and accompanying Christian jargon, but also overcome the barriers encountered in reaching another culture. Without successful identification, the missionary runs the risk of failure in communicating the gospel.

II. Understanding Culture

One of the dimensions of identification is knowledge of the target culture. In order to gain such knowledge, one needs a basic understanding of the conceptual tools used in *cultural anthropology* (the study of cultures). Learning about a culture doesn't guarantee acceptance into it, but it does help to promote the process of identification and adaptation.

The following article by Lloyd E. Kwast describes a method of viewing a culture by visualizing it as four concentric layers. As with an onion, each layer must be peeled back to reveal the layer beneath. The author applies an interesting "man from Mars" technique to peel back the layers of culture found in a North American classroom setting.

❑ *Understanding Culture* *

Lloyd E. Kwast **

What is a culture, anyway? For the student just beginning the study of missionary anthropology, this question is often a first response to a confusing array of descriptions, definitions, comparisons, models, paradigms, etc. There is probably no more comprehensive word in the English language than the word "culture" or no more complex a field of study than cultural anthropology. Yet a thorough understanding of the meaning of culture is prerequisite to any effective communication of God's good news to a different people group.

The most basic procedure in a study of culture is to become a master of one's own. Everyone has a culture. No one can ever divorce himself from his own culture. While it is true that anyone can grow to appreciate various different cultures and even to communicate effectively in more than one, one can never rise above his own or other cultures to gain a truly supracultural perspective. For this reason, even the study of one's own culture is a difficult task. And to look objectively at something that is part of oneself so completely is nearly impossible.

One helpful method is to view a culture, visualizing several successive "layers," or levels of understanding, as one moves into the real heart of the culture.*** In doing so, the "man from Mars" technique is useful. In this exercise one simply imagines that a man from Mars has recently landed (via spaceship) and looks at things through the eyes of an alien space visitor.

Behavior

The first thing that the newly arrived visitor would notice is the people's *behavior*. This is the outer and most superficial layer of what would be observed by an alien. What activities would he observe? What is being done? When walking into a classroom, our visitor may observe several interesting things. People are seen entering an enclosure through one or more openings. They distribute themselves throughout the room seemingly arbitrarily. Another person enters dressed quite differently than the rest, moves quickly to an obviously prearranged position facing the others, and begins to speak.

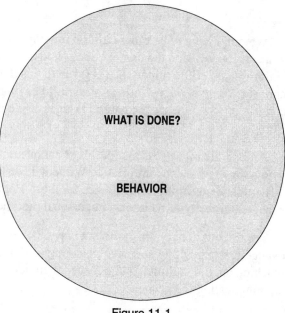

WHAT IS DONE?

BEHAVIOR

Figure 11-1

* Kwast, L. E. (1992). Understanding culture. In R. D. Winter & S. C. Hawthorne (Eds.), *Perspectives on the world Christian movement: A reader* (rev. ed.) (pp. C3-C6). Pasadena: William Carey Library.

** Lloyd Kwast taught for eight years in a college and theological school in Cameroon, West Africa, under the North American Baptist General Missionary Society. He has been the Chairman of the Department of Missions at Talbot Theological Seminary. He is currently a Professor at the Biola University School of Intercultural Studies and is Director of the Doctor of Missiology Program there.

*** This four-layer model was first introduced by G. Linwood Barney in an unpublished manuscript entitled *The supracultural and the cultural: Implications for frontier missions.* For the original version of this manuscript, see Barney, G. L. (1973). The supracultural and the cultural: Implications for frontier missions. In R. P. Beaver (Ed.), *The gospel and frontier peoples* (pp. 48-55). Pasadena: William Carey Library.

As all this is observed, the question might be asked, "Why are they in an enclosure? Why does the speaker dress differently? Why are many people seated while one stands?" These are questions of *meaning*. They are generated by the observations of behavior. It might be interesting to ask some of the participants in the situation why they are doing things in a certain way. Some might offer one explanation; others might offer another. But some would probably shrug and say, "It's the way we do things here." This last response shows an important function of culture, to provide "the patterned way of doing things," as one group of missionary anthropologists defines it. You could call culture the "super glue" which binds people together and gives

> **Culture is the "super glue" which binds people together and gives them a sense of identity and continuity which is almost impenetrable.**

them a sense of identity and continuity which is almost impenetrable. This identity is seen most obviously in the way things are done—behavior.

10. What is the "most basic procedure" in the study of culture? Why?

_____

_____

_____

Values

In observing the inhabitants, our alien begins to realize that many of the behaviors observed are apparently dictated by similar choices that people in the society have made. These choices inevitably reflect the issue of cultural *values*, the next layer of our view of culture. These issues always concern choices about what is "good," what is "beneficial," or what is "best."

If the man from Mars continued to interrogate the people in the enclosure, he might discover that they had numerous alternatives to spending their time there. They might have been working or playing instead of studying. Many of them chose to study because they believed it to be a better choice than play or work. He discovered a number of other choices they had made. Most of them had chosen to arrive at the enclosure in small four-wheel vehicles, because they view the ability to move about quickly as very beneficial. Furthermore, others were noticed hurrying into the enclosure several moments after the rest had entered and again moving out of the room promptly at the close of the meeting. These people said that using time efficiently was very important to them. Values are "pre-set" decisions that a culture makes between choices commonly faced. They help those who live within the culture to know what "should" or "ought" to be done in order to "fit in" or conform to the pattern of life.

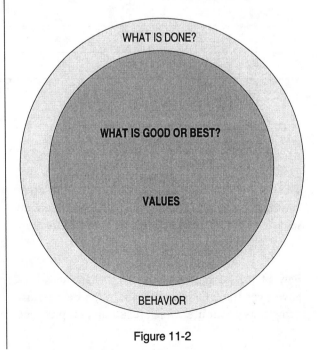

Figure 11-2

Beliefs

Beyond the questions of behavior and values, we face a more fundamental question in the nature of culture. This takes us to a deeper level of understanding, that of cultural *beliefs*. These beliefs answer for that culture the question: "What is true?"

Values in culture are not selected arbitrarily, but invariably reflect an underlying system of beliefs. For example, in the classroom situation, one might discover upon further investigation that "education" in the enclosure has particular significance because of their perception of what is true about man, his power to reason, and his ability to solve problems. In that sense culture has been defined as "learned and shared ways of perceiving" or "shared cognitive orientation."

Interestingly, our alien interrogator might discover that different people in the enclosure, while exhibiting similar behavior and values, might profess totally different beliefs about them. Further, he might find that the values and behaviors were opposed to the beliefs which supposedly produced them. This problem arises from the confusion within the culture between operating beliefs (beliefs that

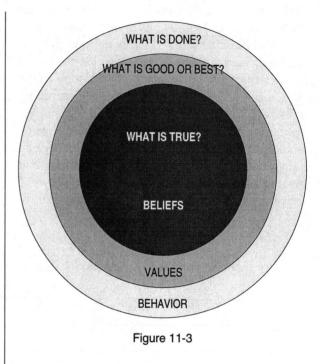

Figure 11-3

affect values and behavior) and theoretical beliefs (stated creeds which have little practical impact on values and behavior).

11. *How do values affect one's behavior? How do they interact with beliefs?*

_____

_____

_____

Worldview

At the very heart of any culture is its *worldview*, answering the most basic question: "What is real?" This area of culture concerns itself with the great "ultimate" questions of reality, questions which are seldom asked but to which culture provides its most important answers.

Few of the people our man from Mars questions have ever thought seriously about the deepest assumptions about life, which result in their presence in the classroom. Who are they? Where did they come from? Is there anything or anyone else occupying reality that should be taken into consideration? Is what they see really all there is, or is there something else or something more? Is right now the only time that is important? Or do events in the past and the future significantly impact their present experience? Every culture assumes specific answers to these questions, and those answers control and integrate every function, aspect, and component of the culture.

This understanding of worldview as the core of every culture explains the confusion many experience at the level of beliefs. One's own worldview provides a system of beliefs which are reflected in his actual values and behavior. Sometimes a new or competing system of beliefs is introduced, but the worldview remains unchallenged and unchanged, so values and behavior reflect the old belief system. Sometimes people who share the gospel cross-culturally fail to take the problem of worldview into account and are therefore disappointed by the lack of genuine change their efforts produce.

This model of culture is far too simple to explain the multitude of complex components and relationships that exist in every culture. However, it is the very simplicity of the model which commends it as a basic outline for any student of culture.

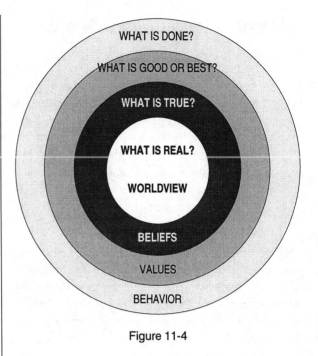

Figure 11-4

12. What is at the core of a culture and what is its impact on the society as a whole?

_____

_____

_____

Understanding the concept of "layers" of culture can be a valuable tool in understanding a particular culture. The model provides a skeleton upon which the missionary can build in studying a people. Using this guide, the missionary can peel back the layers and can identify points of contact where the gospel may have a significant impact.

Culture Shock

It's inevitable. To one degree or another, those who work overseas experience *culture shock*. This feeling of disorientation is *normal* and should be anticipated by the cross-cultural worker. In the following article, Stephen Hoke gives us some insight into this phenomenon.

❏ *Coping With Culture Shock*

Stephen T. Hoke *

We are all creatures of our own culture. As we grow up, we nail together a raft of familiarity that helps us ride the waves of change in our own society. Year after year, plank by plank, we develop a coping strategy for life. It may be a rough-hewn vessel, but we have each mastered the cultural cues for our own sea of life. We even enjoy scanning the broad horizons as long as our feet are firmly planted on the raft of what we have come to know as "normal."

Culture shock sums up all the complicated emotions that we feel when the pieces of our raft begin to separate. Up until this time, the planks of the familiar were so firmly fastened together that we were unconscious of them. Now, as they float away, we look longingly after each one.

Culture shock can make most missionaries feel like quitting, but when understood, it can become a positive learning experience. There are four stages to this phenomenon: Romance, Reaction, Recognition, and Resolution. If we know what to expect, we can creatively deal with our own feelings and the new world that confronts us.

Romance

At first, adjusting to a new culture looks easy. In the first weeks, there are a few discomforts, but nothing a little flexibility can't handle. You're mainly an enthusiastic spectator, absorbing the sights and forming impressions. You find yourself saying things like, "This raw fish isn't so bad—you just have to have a positive attitude" … and you almost believe you're telling the truth.

Reaction

The second stage can best be described as a reaction to reality. It is a time of growing—growing irritation and hostility! Daily activities that you used to take for granted now seem like insurmountable problems. The frustration leads to a potential crisis when you realize that it's not going to be "like home." At this point, you may cling desperately to your own cultural norms, or the opposite—"go native" and completely renounce your own culture and values. Neither response is healthy, but the difficulty in seeing a third alternative just adds to your frustration.

Recognition

The first sign of your recovery from the *reaction* stage is a return of your sense of humor. As you enter the third stage, this returned sense of humor is accompanied by a recognition of communication cues in people's faces, actions, and tones. Developing some language facility, you can communicate more effectively. You begin to build a new raft of familiarity. Having become more accustomed to the food, sounds, and nonverbal behaviors, you have fewer headaches and upset stomachs, and you feel less confused, uncertain, and lonely.

Resolution

The fourth stage is one of nearly complete recovery and adjustment. Some call it becoming "bicultural." You are able to function in two cultures with confidence. You may even find that there are many customs, sayings, and attitudes which you enjoy and, in fact, call your own. You possess an awareness of how another culture feels from the standpoint of the insider. You almost forget that you were once a foreigner.

---

* Dr. Stephen T. Hoke has a lifetime of experience in cross-cultural ministry and Christian missions. Raised by missionary parents in Japan for 15 years, he has taught missions at Seattle Pacific University, was Associate Director of Training for World Vision, and served as President of L.I.F.E. Ministries (Japan). He has authored 30 popular articles on missions and has been involved in the training of over 1,000 people for cross-cultural service in 11 countries. He is presently Vice President of Training with Church Resource Ministries in California.

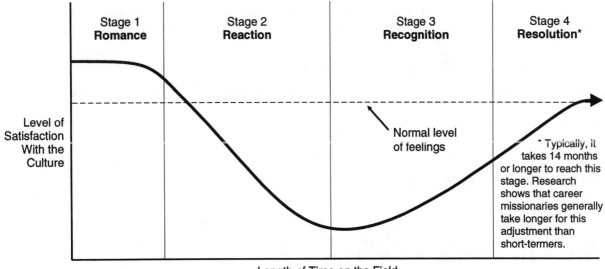

Figure 11-5. Stages of Culture Shock

13. *How can understanding culture shock and its symptoms help an individual overcome the problem?*

_____

_____

_____

_____

Becoming Bicultural

When one adapts to a new culture, he or she becomes a bicultural person. Sometime during this process, the concept that there is really only one way to live is shattered. One begins to deal with cultural variety—with the recognition that people build cultures in different ways and that they invariably believe in the superiority of their own ways. We call this attitude *ethnocentrism*. One understands that aside from showing some curiosity, people are generally not interested in learning other culturally determined ways of doing things. Bicultural individuals have moved from a philosophy which assumes uniformity, to one that recognizes and affirms diversity. Their outlook in relating to others begins to change, and they may find they feel most comfortable with other bicultural people.

Bicultural people really live in two worlds. They are part of two cultures and are never fully adjusted when they are in one or the other. They may eventually feel more comfortable in their adopted culture than in their native one, but inside they are still part of both. No matter which culture they are in, they will always seek little details, such as food or news, which reaffirm the other part of themselves. Their happiest moments may come when they are moving from one culture to the other after a long absence.

14. *Most long-term missionaries become bicultural and raise bicultural children. What kind of stress are these missionary kids likely to experience due to their biculturalness?*

_____

_____

_____

Cross-Cultural Differences*

Anthropologists have discovered that profound differences exist between cultures. Not only are these differences noted on the superficial behavioral level of dress, food, language, and actions, but at every level these differences are marked. Values, beliefs, and worldview vary greatly from culture to culture.

This variation can be graphically illustrated by the confusion and conflict which may ensue when persons from distinct cultures establish a meeting time. When a North American makes an appointment for 10:00 a.m., he expects the other person to show up within five minutes of that time. If the person shows up at 10:15, he is "late" and an apology is in order. If he is 30 minutes late, he had better have a very good excuse. If he is 45 minutes late, he might as well not show up, and he has committed a rather serious offense.

In parts of Arabia, people have a different concept of time. When an appointment is made for 10:00 a.m., only a servant is expected to show up at that time—in obedience to his master. The proper time for others to meet is from 10:45 to 11:15, demonstrating independence and equality. This system works well since equals would expect the meeting to take place about 10:45. The problem occurs when a North American sets up a meeting with an Arab, and neither one is sensitive to the other's concept of time. If the American is left waiting, he will be offended. At the same time, the Arab will probably think that the American is acting like a servant.

* This section is summarized from Hiebert, P. G. (1976). Culture and cross-cultural differences. In A. F. Glasser et al. (Eds.), *Crucial dimensions in world evangelization* (pp. 45-60). Pasadena: William Carey Library.

Paul G. Hiebert is Professor of Missions and Anthropology and Chairman of the Missions and Evangelism Department at Trinity Evangelical Divinity School. He previously taught anthropology and South Asian studies at Fuller Theological Seminary's School of World Mission. Hiebert served as a missionary in India with the Mennonite Brethren Board and has also been a Professor of Anthropology at the University of Washington in Seattle. He is the author of *Cultural Anthropology*, *Anthropological Insights for Missionaries*, and *Case Studies in Mission* with Frances H. Hiebert.

15. *How could conflicts over time, such as the one described above, be avoided?*

_____

_____

_____

Cross-Cultural Misunderstandings

When people from two distinct cultures come into contact with each other, conclusions about one culture are often drawn based on the other person's cultural assumptions. The North American may think that the Arab has no sense of propriety or time when he shows up 45 minutes "late" for an appointment, but this, obviously, is not true.

Cultural misunderstandings often arise out of actions done subconsciously. This principle is illustrated in the way people use physical space when they stand talking to each other. North Americans usually stand at a distance of about a meter and a half when discussing general matters. When they want to discuss a more personal matter, they usually approach to within one meter's distance and lower their voices. Latin Americans generally stand within one meter's distance in discussing general matters and closer for personal ones.

Misunderstandings arise when a North American meets a Latin American. The Latin may move within a meter's distance in order to converse. The North American, feeling a bit uneasy at this distance, may move back a step. The Latin, feeling that he is now having to talk "across the room," steps within his range again. As the conversation progresses (or breaks down), the Latin may get the impression that North Americans are cold and distant, and the North American may get the impression that Latin Americans are pushy and too familiar.

16. *What assumptions should we make about the behavior of people from another culture?*

_____

_____

_____

The primary task in entering a new culture is to become an observer of its ways. Behavior should never be judged on the basis of our own cultural assumptions and background. We should assume that what is being done in another culture is normal and should seek to understand why. Misunderstandings arise out of ignorance of another culture.

Ethnocentrism

Each of us grows up in the center of our own world. We are "egocentric" by nature. Only as we mature do we begin to cross the gap between "me" and "you" in order to understand another's viewpoint. We also grow up in the center of a particular culture and learn its "right" ways. We look with suspicion on other practices and customs, believing them to be improper or inferior. This *ethnocentrism* is based on the natural tendency to judge the behavior of people on the basis of our own cultural assumptions.

Westerners generally believe that the "proper" manner of eating is with forks and spoons. They may be repulsed by people in India and the Middle East when they eat with their fingers. This "improper" manner of eating is viewed quite differently from the Indian's perspective. As one Indian put it, "You see, we wash our hands carefully, and besides, they have never been in anyone else's mouth. But look at these spoons and forks and think about how many other people have already had them inside their mouths!"

If cross-cultural misunderstandings are based on a lack of knowledge about another culture, ethnocentrism is based on feelings and values. It is not enough just to understand the other culture. If identification is to take place, the feelings which distinguish "them" from "us" must be dealt with. When "they" become part of the circle we consider "our kind of people," then we have successfully dealt with our ethnocentrism.

17. *How do you think one can best deal with the feelings produced by ethnocentrism?*

_____

_____

_____

Bible Translation

Missionaries are often called to do Bible translation work, particularly when attempting to reach an unreached people group. Translation is a difficult task because there is no word in one culture that carries exactly the same meaning in another culture. The same forms do not carry the same meaning from language to language. Words are symbols to which cultural values and meaning are always attached. We may find words which represent the same object, but the underlying meaning of that object will vary from culture to culture.

Hiebert illustrates a typical problem of Bible translation with the following example:

> How do you translate "lamb of God" (John 1:29) into Eskimo in which there is no word for or any experience of animals we call sheep? Do you make up a new word and add a footnote to describe the creature that has no meaning in their thinking? Or do you use a word such as "seal" that has much the same meaning in their culture as "lamb" does in Palestine? Obviously cultural differences raise problems when we translate a message from one language and culture to another.*

Translators in the past have not always understood the problem of meaning, and the result has been translations which are poorly received. More recently, when translating Scripture, translators have been concerned with producing "dynamic equivalent" translations which attempt to preserve the meaning, even if the form must be different. In some cases, when a translation problem arises, other forms with an equivalent meaning in that culture can be substituted. At other times, it may seem wisest to create a new word and teach its meaning. Both alternatives have their drawbacks. If a term is substituted, the translator runs the risk of distorting the Scripture message in some way. If a new word is created, it will not be understood right away and may require generations before its meaning is clearly assimilated.

---

* Hiebert, P. G. (1976). Culture and cross-cultural differences. In A. F. Glasser et al. (Eds.), *Crucial dimensions in world evangelization* (p. 54). Pasadena: William Carey Library.

Translation work requires a great deal of technical skill. The translated Word, however, is essential to the long-range building of the church. If the church is to mature and establish firm roots, its leadership must become intimately acquainted with God's Word and shape their worldview by it.

18. *In the Hindu worldview, gods often become men. This belief presents a problem in speaking of Christ's incarnation. The choice of a Hindu word for incarnation could be interpreted to mean that Christ was the incarnation of one of their pantheon of gods. How would you deal with this problem?*

_____

_____

_____

Cultural differences are of importance to the missionary, who must go through culture shock, learn to overcome misunderstandings and ethnocentric feelings, and translate the message so that it is understood. There are several other implications of cultural differences on the missionary task as well.

The Gospel and Culture

A clear distinction between the gospel and *culture* must be made. If this distinction is not made, one runs the risk of making one's culture the message. Democracy, capitalism, pews and pulpits, organizational systems and rules, and formal dress on Sundays are some of the cultural "baggage" which has often been attached to the gospel message. Rejection of Christianity is often based on rejection of the foreign cultural load that is placed on the message, rather than the message itself.

This distinction is not easily made. People cannot think without conceptual categories and symbols, so the message must be put in some cultural form in order to be understood and communicated. However, we must be careful not to add our own cultural expressions to the biblical message. Forms and symbols must be adapted from the target culture instead.

Failure to distinguish between biblical and cultural messages can lead to confusion. Different cultures will give differing moral values to certain behaviors and, even within the culture, these values may change with time. At one time in North America, for example, the practice of coloring the lips with lipstick was considered "sin" by many in the church. Today there are few North Americans who consider this widespread cultural practice sinful. In this case, the culture has changed, and so has its moral evaluation of a certain practice. We need to recognize that each culture defines certain behaviors as sinful, and that as a culture changes, so do its definitions of which behaviors are sinful.

This does not mean that there are no moral absolutes. The Bible is definite and prescriptive about many moral issues, and these principles must be made clear. However, a word of caution is in order. There are some biblical norms, such as greeting one another with a holy kiss (1 Thess. 5:26), which seem to be directed at specific cultural situations and may not apply to cultures universally.

19. How can the attachment of cultural "baggage" to the gospel be minimized?

_____

_____

_____

Syncretism vs. Indigenization

Syncretism occurs when a cultural form or symbol has been adapted to Christian expression in a culture but carries with it attached meanings from the former belief system. For example, a traditional heathen feast may be adapted for use by Christians, but some of the forms may continue to carry occult connotations. The old meanings can severely distort or obscure the intended Christian meaning. The fear of syncretism has been one of the reasons missionaries have not always been open to adapting cultural forms to the gospel.

When the adaptation of cultural forms is done carefully, indigenization rather than syncretism occurs. Indigenization is successful when a culture finds ways of expressing Christian meaning through the adaptation or creation of forms which are consistent with the culture. Meaning is preserved without the burden of foreign cultural baggage.

20. Each of the following cultural practices could be assimilated successfully by an indigenous church, yet each one has the potential to lead to syncretism. In each case, what signs of syncretism would you look out for?

a. Traditional sacrifice of a pig or chickens before a wedding ceremony.

b. Using native rhythms and dances in worship.

c. Painting pictures of Christ that look like one's ethnic race.

_____

_____

_____

Conversion and Unforeseen Side Effects

Cultural traits are always linked together. Changes in one or more of these traits can lead to unforeseen changes in other areas of the culture. For example, the people in one African village let their village become dirty when they became Christians. When they accepted Christ as Lord, they no longer feared the evil spirits that they believed hid in refuse. They felt, therefore, that there was no longer any need to keep the village clean.

Most cultural traits fill a need or perform an important function within a culture which contributes to the culture's existence. When a cultural trait is altered or eliminated, care must be taken that a vacuum is not left. A cultural substitute must be found, or the results can be tragic. Where polygamy has been practiced, for example, believers have often been asked to give up all but one wife. Generally, no arrangement has been made for the abandoned wives. The only recourse left to these women is to enter a life of prostitution or slavery. These are ethical questions which must be taken into consideration.

We have seen that during the process of acculturation, missionaries face a number of challenges. They must pass through culture shock, deal with ethnocentric feelings, overcome misunderstandings, and translate the message in such a way that it is understood with the meaning that is intended. Later on, they must make sure they do not attach cultural baggage to the message, guard against syncretism, and anticipate cultural side effects of conversion. No occupation is more challenging!

III. Missionary: Agent of Change

Missionaries have come under severe attack by secular humanists, anthropologists, and the media for "destroying" cultures. Are they guilty as charged? The following article by Don Richardson was written in response to the widely diffused notion that missionaries are agents of cultural imperialism.

❏ *Do Missionaries Destroy Cultures?* *

Don Richardson **

When Fray Diego de Landa, a Catholic missionary accompanying Spanish forces in the New World, discovered extensive Maya libraries, he knew what to do. He burned them all, an event, he said, the Maya "regretted to an amazing degree, and which caused them much affliction." The books, in his opinion, were all of "superstition and lies of the devil." And so, in 1562, the poetry, history, literature, mathematics, and astronomy of an entire civilization went up in smoke. Only three documents survived de Landa's misguided zeal.

Magnificent totem poles once towered in Indian villages along Canada's Pacific coast. By 1900 virtually all such native art had been chopped down, either by missionaries who mistook them for idols, or by converts zealously carrying out the directives of missionaries.

These incidents and many more show that we missionaries have sometimes acted in a culture-destroying manner. Whether through misinterpreting the Great Commission, pride, culture shock, or simple inability to comprehend the values of others, we have needlessly opposed customs we did not understand. Some, had we understood them, might have served as communication keys for the gospel!

---

* Richardson, D. (1992). Do missionaries destroy cultures? In R. D. Winter & S. C. Hawthorne (Eds.), *Perspectives on the world Christian movement: A reader* (rev. ed.) (pp. C137-C143). Pasadena: William Carey Library.

** Don Richardson pioneered work for Regions Beyond Missionary Union (RBMU) among the Sawi tribe of Irian Jaya in 1962. Author of *Peace Child*, *Lords of the Earth*, and *Eternity in Their Hearts*, Richardson is now Minister-at-Large for RBMU. He speaks frequently at missions conferences and Perspectives Study Program classes.

The world has been quick to notice our mistakes. Popular authors like Herman Melville, Somerset Maugham, and James Michener have stereotyped missionaries as opinionated, insensitive, neurotic, sent to the heathen because they were misfits at home.

Michener's austere Abner Hale, a missionary in the novel *Hawaii*, became the archetype of an odious bigot. Hale shouts hellfire sermons against the "vile abominations" of the pagan Hawaiians. He forbids Hawaiian midwives to help a missionary mother at the birth of "a Christian baby." The mother dies.

Hale even forbids Hawaiians to help his wife with housework lest his children learn the "heathen Hawaiian language." His wife works herself into an early grave.

When Buddhist Chinese settle in Hawaii, Michener has Hale barging into their temples to smash their idols.

Interesting literary grist, to be sure.

Unfortunately for naive readers, "Abner Hale" came to mean "missionary." We've been carrying him on our backs ever since.

Anthropologist Alan Tippett of the Fuller Seminary School of World Mission once researched hundreds of early missionary sermons stored in the Honolulu archives. None had the ranting style Michener suggests as typical. Critics seem to suggest, naively, that if only missionaries stayed home, primitive people would be left undisturbed to fulfill the myth of Rousseau's "noble savage."

Impact of secular forces

The fact is, commercial exploiters or other secular forces have already wrought havoc with indigenous cultures on an awesome scale. Livingstone was preceded by Arab slave traders. Amy Carmichael was preceded by victimizers who dragged boys and girls away to temples, where they faced the terrors of child prostitution.

Secular forces such as these have sometimes destroyed entire peoples. In North America not only the famous Mohicans but also the Hurons and possibly as many as 20 other Indian tribes were pushed into extinction by land-hungry settlers. Pioneers on one occasion sent a tribe wagonloads of gift blankets known to be infected with smallpox.

In Brazil only 200,000 Indians remain from an original population estimated at 4 million. In the past 75 years more than one tribe per year has disappeared.

Readers may assume that Brazil's missing tribes have been absorbed into society, but this is not the case. Thousands have been brutally poisoned, machine-gunned, or dynamited from low-flying aircraft. Other thousands succumbed to a slower, more agonizing death by apathy. As encroachment caused their cultures to disintegrate, Indian men have even been known to cause their wives to miscarry. They refused to bring children into a world they could no longer understand.

Concern is widespread today—and justly so—for endangered animal species. But hundreds of our own human species are in even greater danger!

Prior to 1858, India's Andaman Islands were the home of at least 6,000 pygmy negritoes. Then the British established a penal colony in the islands and victimization began. Today a scant 600 negritoes remain.

Similar tragedies are unfolding throughout the Philippines, Asia, and Africa.

Concern is widespread today—and justly so—for endangered animal species. But hundreds of our own human species are in even greater danger! A yearly loss of 10 linguistically distinct tribes may be a conservative figure.

Only a few of the world's governments have established agencies to protect their ethnic minorities. Brazil, the Philippines, and India are three examples.

Secular agencies, however, suffer from severe budget restrictions. Furthermore, other arms of government may interfere with the programs.

For example, not long after Brazil's National Foundation for the Indian established Xingu National

Park as a reserve for endangered tribes, roadbuilders obtained permission to blast a modern highway through the center of it! As a result two of Xingu's "protected" tribes were destroyed by measles and influenza introduced by construction crews.

Clearly, the "enlightened" policy of "leave-them-alone" isn't working.

What then can halt their march toward extinction?

Grants, land, and secular welfare programs may help on the physical level (though sometimes godless officials introduce alcoholism or other vices, undermining whatever good their programs may accomplish).

But the greatest danger to aboriginals is one that such programs cannot deal with—the breakdown of the aboriginal's sense of "right" relationship with the supernatural. Every aboriginal culture acknowledges the supernatural and has strict procedures for "staying right" with it. When arrogant outsiders ridicule a tribe's belief, or shatter its mechanisms for "staying right," severe disorientation sets in.

The greatest danger to aboriginals is one that secular welfare programs cannot deal with—the breakdown of the aboriginal's sense of "right" relationship with the supernatural.

Tribesmen believe they are under a curse for abandoning the old ways. They become morose and apathetic, believing they are doomed to die as a people.

Materialistic social workers or scientists cannot help such people. The tribesmen sense even an unspoken denial of the supernatural, and become even more depressed.

21. What is the greatest current threat to indigenous cultures?

_____

_____

Effects of spiritual encouragement

Who then can best serve such people as spiritual ombudsmen?

None other than the very ones popularly maligned as the number one enemy: the Bible-guided, Christ-honoring missionary.

Consider some case histories:

The Wai Wai

Less than a generation ago, according to Robert Bell of the Unevangelized Fields Mission, Brazil's Wai Wai tribe had been reduced to its last 60 members. This had come about largely through foreign diseases, and by the Wai Wai custom of sacrificing babies to demons to try to prevent those diseases.

Then a handful of UFM missionaries identified themselves with the tribe, learned their language, gave it an alphabet, translated the Word of God, and taught Wai Wai to read. Far from denying the supernatural world, the missionaries showed the Wai Wai that a God of love reigned supreme over it. And that God had prepared for them a way of "staying right" on a far deeper level than they had ever dreamed of.

The Wai Wai now had a rational—even delightful—basis for not sacrificing babies to demons, and the tribe began to grow. Today the Wai Wai are fast becoming one of Brazil's most populous tribes. And optimistic Wai Wai Christians are teaching other dwindling groups of Indians how to cope with the 20th century through faith in Jesus Christ.

Repentance and faith in Jesus Christ can solve many of the survival problems of endangered peoples.

The help given to the Wai Wai, furthermore, is only a very recent example of a long heritage of helping beleaguered peoples.

Native Americans

Near Stockbridge, in what is now Massachusetts, early American missionary John Sargent and his associates established a community to preserve Indian rights, preparing them for survival among encroaching Europeans.

Before ethnocentrism was named as a social evil, and before the birth of anthropology as a science, Sargent and his helpers unpatronizingly tilled the soil side by side with their Indian friends. Practicing what anthropologists now call "directed change," they also shared their Christian faith. The Indians received it as their own.

That faith, and the love of their spiritual paracletes, sustained the tribe through more than a century of suffering. Greedy settlers soon decided that the land was too good for "mere Indians" and evicted them. After protesting unsuccessfully, Sargent obtained guarantees of land further west.

A few years later the community was uprooted again by other settlers. And again. Fifteen times they were forced to move. Each time the missionaries moved with them, wresting concessions for new land and holding the community together.

At last the community settled in Michigan, where it was allowed to rest, and survives to this day. As a side benefit, such missionary experiments helped convince scholars that a science of anthropology was necessary.

In both cases just cited, missionaries introduced culture change, but not arbitrarily and not by force. They brought only changes required by the New Testament or required for the survival of the people. Often the two requirements overlap (for example, the cessation of Wai Wai child sacrifices).

The Sawi

Once an interviewer regaled me (perhaps facetiously) for persuading the Sawi tribe in Indonesia to renounce cannibalism.

"What's wrong with cannibalism?" he asked. "The Sawi practiced it for thousands of years. Why should they give it up now?"

I replied, "Can a people who practice cannibalism survive in the world today? No, they cannot. The Sawi are now citizens of the Republic of Indonesia. The Indonesian Republic does not permit its citizens to eat other people. Therefore, part of my task was to give the Sawi a rational basis for voluntarily renouncing cannibalism before the guns of the police decided the issue."

On another level Sawi culture entertained a dark compulsion to venerate dead relatives by handling, or even eating, the rotting flesh of their corpses. Yet when the Sawi received the Christian teaching of the resurrection, they immediately abandoned such procedures, almost with a sigh of relief. The gospel cured them of this strange compulsion.

The Sawi are among perhaps 400 black-skinned Melanesian tribes just emerging from the stone age in Irian Jaya. Thirteen years ago the Netherlands ceded Irian Jaya (then New Guinea) to Indonesia. Today, an estimated 100,000 Indonesians have migrated to Irian Jaya. Will the tribal people be prepared to cope with their more enterprising migrant neighbors? Or will they become extinct?

Ethnic crises of this magnitude are far too sensitive to be left to the dubious mercy of purely commercial interests. Missionaries whose hearts overflow with the love of Christ are the key.

Scattered throughout Irian Jaya, more than 250 evangelical missionaries (all too few) are ministering the gospel to both races. Knowledgeable in Indonesian as well as many of Irian's 400 tribal languages, they are helping members of clashing cultures understand each other. With the sympathetic help of the Indonesian government, they are optimistic that major culture shock may be averted.

Already, through faith in Christ, tens of thousands of Irianese have begun a smooth transition into the 20th century.

Surely ethnic crises of this magnitude are far too sensitive to be left to the dubious mercy of purely commercial interests. Missionaries whose hearts overflow with the love of Christ are the key.

22. In what ways do Christian missionaries act as benign agents in cultural transition?

_____

_____

_____

The issue is not whether missionaries do or should change cultures. Missionaries, by the very nature of their work, are agents of change. They are but one of many political, ideological, and economic forces which are continually exerting influence on societies around the world. The more relevant question is, Which of these many agents has the people's best interest at heart?

In the following article, David Hesselgrave demonstrates why Christianity is the only world force which has at heart the preservation of the best in human cultures.

❑ *Christ and Culture* *

David J. Hesselgrave **

When God created man and man's environment, He pronounced everything "very good" (Gen. 1:31). God gave man a *Cultural Mandate* which entailed certain rulership over his environment (Gen. 1:26-30). God, however, did not withdraw from the scene. Nor did He cease to be God. Rather, He continued to provide for and fellowship with His creatures. How long that blissful state continued we do not know, but it was interrupted by the fall. And the fall left its mark on creation, creature, and culture (Gen. 3:14-19). Man's hope rested on the promise of the "seed of woman" who would bruise the serpent's head.

Subsequently, mankind collectively failed as miserably as Adam and Eve had failed individually, with the result that God pronounced judgment upon man, beast, and land (Gen. 6:6-7). Following the flood, Noah and his family received promises and a *Social*

Mandate that was to apply to them and their progeny down through the generations (Gen. 8:21–9:17).

The significance of this simple and sublime story in the first chapters of Genesis must be carefully probed but can never be completely fathomed. It forms the basis of a theology of culture that is amplified throughout sacred Scripture. Man's relationship to God precedes and proscribes all other relationships. In this sense true religion is prior to culture, not simply a part of it. In listening to the usurper and choosing to disobey God, man invited the impress of sin upon all that he was and all he touched. The fall did not result in the eradication of the image of God in the creature nor in the countermanding of all cultural prerogatives. But it did interpose another and false authority over man, and it did mar man's person and productions. Only under Christ can man be redeemed and his culture renewed.

_____

* Hesselgrave, D. J. (1978). *Communicating Christ cross-culturally* (pp. 80-82). Grand Rapids: Zondervan.

** After 12 years of service in Japan under the Evangelical Free Church, David J. Hesselgrave became Professor of Missions at the School of World Mission and Evangelism at Trinity Evangelical Divinity School in Deerfield, Illinois. He later served as Director of the School of World Mission and Evangelism, and is now the Professor Emeritus of Mission. He is also the Executive Director of the Evangelical Missiological Society. Hesselgrave is the author of *Planting Churches Cross-Culturally* and *Communicating Christ Cross-Culturally*.

23. How was human culture affected by the fall?

_____

_____

_____

The *Gospel Mandate* (Matt. 28:18-20) requires that missionaries teach other men to observe all that Christ has commanded. In teaching, missionaries touch culture—and happily so—for *all culture needs transformation in motivation if not in content.* If anything at all is apparent in our world, it is that God has ordained culture but has not been allowed to order culture. Satan is indeed "the god of this world" (2 Cor. 4:4). Therefore, as Calvin insisted, believers must work to make culture Christian (i.e., under Christ) or at least conducive to (i.e., allowing the maximum opportunity for) Christian living. As J. H. Bavinck puts it, the Christian life *takes possession* of heathen forms of life and thereby makes them new:

> Within the framework of the non-Christian life, customs and practices serve idolatrous tendencies and drive a person away from God. The Christian life takes them in hand and turns them in an entirely different content. Even though in external form there is much that resembles past practices, in reality everything has become new, the old has in essence passed away and the new has come. Christ takes the life of a people in His hands, He renews and reestablishes the distorted and deteriorated, He fills each thing, each word, and each practice with a new meaning and gives it a new direction.*

The missionary is involved in this process directly and indirectly. He may attempt to stay above the culture line and deal only with matters of the soul. But that effort is as hopeless as is the effort of the social scientist to eliminate God from his world and explain Christianity in cultural terms only. In the

---

The missionary cannot communicate Christianity without concerning himself with culture because, though Christianity is supracultural in its origin and truth, it is cultural in its application.

---

first place, the missionary cannot communicate without concerning himself with culture because communication is inextricable from culture. Just as Christ became flesh and dwelt among men, so propositional truth must have a cultural incarnation to be meaningful. In the second place, the missionary cannot communicate *Christianity* without concerning himself with culture because, though Christianity is supracultural in its origin and truth, it is cultural in its application.

24. In what way is Christianity supracultural?

_____

_____

_____

_____

* Bavinck, J. H. (1960). *An introduction to the science of missions* (D. H. Freeman, Trans.) (p. 179). Philadelphia: The Presbyterian and Reformed Publishing Co.

Only Christ can heal cultures. The missionary's role is to be an agent of that healing. By carrying out Christ's redemptive mission, the missionary stimulates change which allows a people to experience their greatest fulfillment within their own culture. In the following excerpt, Dale Kietzman and William Smalley offer an explanation of the role of the church and the missionary in culture change.

❏ *Introducing Cultural Change* *

Dale W. Kietzman and William A. Smalley **

The important thing for the missionary to note is that change is almost always initiated by someone within the cultural community. Even though the idea may have been sparked by contact with another culture, it still must be introduced from within to be accepted. The alternative to this scheme is change forced upon a people through superior might, whether moral or physical. This is the sort of change that missions have often been responsible for and that resulted in such unfortunate reaction.

The real agent of the Holy Spirit in any society for the changes in the culture of that society is the church, the body of believers (*not* necessarily the organized church of any particular denomination). The church is the salt working through the whole dish. It is that part of the society which has a new relationship to God—yet it reacts in terms of the attitudes and presuppositions of that society. It understands, in an intuitive, unanalyzed way, motives and meanings as the missionary cannot. It must make the decisions.

25. Who are the real agents of Christian change within a culture?

_____

_____

_____

The missionary's basic responsibility is to provide the material upon which the native Christian and church can grow "in grace and knowledge" to the point where they can make reliable and Spirit-directed decisions with regard to their own conduct within the existing culture. This involves a complete freedom of access to the Word of God, with such encouragement, instruction, and guidance in its use as may be necessary to obtain a healthy and growing Christian community.

* Kietzman, D. W., & Smalley, W. A. (1978). The missionary's role in culture change. In W. A. Smalley (Ed.), *Readings in missionary anthropology II* (pp. 527-529). Pasadena: William Carey Library.

** Dale W. Kietzman, a member of Wycliffe Bible Translators since 1946, worked with the Amahuaca Indians of Peru. He served in a number of administrative roles, including United States Division Director. He also served as President of World Literature Crusade/Every Home for Christ and more recently as Chairman of the Communications Division at the William Carey International University. Kietzman is author of numerous articles and books on mission subjects and on the Indians of South America.

William A. Smalley is Professor Emeritus of Linguistics at Bethel College in St. Paul, Minnesota. He worked for 23 years for the United Bible Societies and continues as a consultant to the Bible Societies in his retirement. He was also active in the formation of the Toronto Institute of Linguistics. He was editor of the journal *Practical Anthropology* from 1955 to 1968 and is editor of *Readings in Missionary Anthropology* and numerous other articles.

The missionary's role in culture change, then, is that of a catalyst and of a source of new ideas, new information. It is the voice of experience, but an experience based on his own culture for the most part and therefore to be used only with care and understanding. Part of the value of anthropological study, of course, is that it gives at least vicarious experience in more than one cultural setting, for by study in this field the missionary can gain awareness of the much wider choice of alternatives than his own culture allows.

It is the church which is the legitimate agency in which the missionary should work. It is the people who must make the decisions based on the new ideas which they have received. It is they who must reinterpret old needs and expressions, examined now in the light of their relationship to God and to their fellow men in Christ Jesus.

26. What is the missionary's role in culture change?

_____

_____

_____

Missionaries are agents of culture change, and no one should be under the illusion that they are not. Neither should anyone think that missionaries are the only ones who occupy that role. Rather, there are several competing forces contributing to change in societies all over the world. Missionaries are God's agents of redemption, and as such, they can introduce the healing presence of Christ into cultures that have been twisted by the fall of man. They function as catalysts, stimulating the true agent of change within the culture—the church—to initiate the changes which are necessary.

Summary

As Christ found it necessary to identify with mankind in order to minister salvation and become our high priest, so missionaries must seek to identify with those to whom they go in order to minister to them effectively. The objective, however, is not to see how much missionaries can identify, but to use that identification to find points of contact within the culture whereby the gospel can take root. Identification, then, is the means by which missionaries can discover effective ways to communicate the gospel.

The first task missionaries have upon entering a new culture is to become students of that culture. A basic knowledge of anthropology will help them penetrate the four levels at which cultures are organized, i.e., the people's behavior, values, beliefs, and worldview. In the process of acculturation, missionaries will experience culture shock, will need to deal with their ethnocentrism, must overcome misunderstandings, and must translate the message in a way which preserves the intended meaning while being understood. They must not attach cultural baggage to the message. While striving for indigenization, they must guard against syncretism and negative cultural side effects.

Recognizing that they are agents of culture change, missionaries must understand their proper role. This is a key to the successful indigenization of the church. Missionaries act as catalysts within the culture. They are resource persons to the church, and the church is the real agent of the Holy Spirit in bringing change to a culture.

Integrative Assignment

In this assignment, you will develop an entry strategy for those who will be establishing a presence among the unreached group. You will also try to answer the question: *What will be the result?*

WORKSHEET #5: IDENTIFYING WITH THE TARGET GROUP

A. Establishing a Presence

1. How will you establish a presence among your target group? What entry strategy will the team use?

_____

_____

_____

2. What is the most appropriate language to use for evangelization of these people? Why?

_____

_____

_____

3. How will the team go about learning the language and culture?

_____

_____

4. How will they identify with the people?

_____

_____

_____

5. What need(s) will you be addressing? How will the love of Christ and the power of the gospel be demonstrated to the target group?

_____

_____

_____

B. Proclaiming the Good News

6. What cultural values, structures, or practices are the greatest hindrances to the gospel?

_____

_____

_____

7. What cultural values, beliefs, structures, or practices might provide a bridge for the gospel?

_____

_____

_____

8. What social structures will influence your evangelistic efforts?

_____

_____

_____

9. What will precede your sharing of the gospel message? How and with whom will you first share it?

_____

_____

_____

10. What will characterize the corporate expression of this people group's faith in Christ? Are there cultural practices or structures which could be reinterpreted and incorporated into Christian lifestyle or worship?

_____

_____

_____

11. What culturally appropriate media (literature, audio or video cassettes, radio, etc.) will you use for evangelism and for teaching converts?

_____

_____

_____

WRITTEN REPORT

In this report, you will describe how your team will establish a presence among the people and will anticipate how the team will go about learning the language and adapting to the culture. You will also describe how initial evangelization might proceed and will try to foresee possible problems and opportunities for the growing church.

Questions for Reflection

In his article, "Identification in the Missionary Task," William Reyburn states that in order to be Obam Nna, he "had to crucify William Reyburn nearly every day." What does he mean by this? Meditate on Galatians 2:20 and Luke 9:23. Write your thoughts below.

CHAPTER 12

Becoming a Belonger

The task of cross-cultural evangelism is challenging! The missionary must first deal with personal adjustment to the new culture and identify with the people. The gospel must then be presented in such a way that the people not only understand it, but can respond to the message. When a young church emerges, the missionary must assume the role of mentor and guide, encouraging the church to develop its own cultural expression while guarding against syncretism. Not all missionaries succeed.

Getting off to a good start is extremely critical to long-term effectiveness. The first few days among the target people can determine the course of a missionary's ministry for years to come. Attitudes are formed, and pivotal emotional ties are often made during this beginning period. In this chapter, we will examine the importance of entry strategies, the significance of initial roles, and expectations regarding these roles. We will also explore how lifestyle and related attitudes affect the missionary's acculturation and long-term effectiveness.

I. Bonding

The first few weeks in a new country or among a different people are critical to a missionary's adaptation. Intellectual preparation is important to meet the challenges of a new situation, but there is a critical emotional process in those first days which will indelibly stamp the response of the missionary to the target people. In the following article, Thomas and Elizabeth Brewster explain what this process entails and make suggestions for the successful initiation of a new missionary.

❑ *Bonding and the Missionary Task: Establishing a Sense of Belonging* *

E. Thomas Brewster and Elizabeth S. Brewster **

"And the Word became flesh and dwelt among us" (John 1:14).

We have a new little boy who was born into our home just a few months ago. In preparing for his natural childbirth at home, we were introduced to the concept of bonding.

In the animal world it is called imprinting. Most of us remember the picture in our college psychology books of the psychologist Konrad Lorenz being followed by ducklings. At the critical time, right after hatching, Lorenz and the ducklings were alone together and, from then on, they responded to him as though he were their parent. The imprinted duck experiences a sense of belonging to the man.

More recent studies supporting the concept of bonding have been carried out with a variety of animals, including goats, calves, and monkeys. In each case,

the infant and mother have an early period of sensitivity right after birth. If mother and infant are together at that time, a close bond results which can withstand subsequent separations.

But if infant and mother are separated immediately after birth, the infant can become attached to a surrogate—a cloth doll, a different adult animal, or even a human. If infant and mother are later reunited, one or both may reject the other or at least not respond to the other with normal attachment.

Studies of human infants and mothers show the importance of bonding. Apparently, just after birth, divinely designed psychological and physiological factors in the newborn uniquely prepare him to become bonded with his parents. Certainly the excitement and adrenaline levels of both the child and his parents are at a peak. The senses of the infant are being stimulated by a multitude of new sensations. The birth is essentially an entrance into a new culture with new sights, new sounds, new smells, new positions, new environment, and new ways of being held. Yet, at that particular time, he is equipped with an extraordinary ability to respond to these unusual circumstances.

People who support home birth are concerned about the bonding process between parents and the infant. An important collection of research studies by Klaus and Kennell*** is widely read. It is pointed out that the non-drugged newborn is more alert during the first day than at any time during the next week or two. This was our experience, as our son was full of

* Brewster, E. T., & Brewster, E. S. (1982). *Bonding and the missionary task: Establishing a sense of belonging.* Pasadena: Lingua House.

** E. Thomas and Elizabeth S. Brewster have been a husband-wife team specializing in helping missionaries develop effective techniques for learning any language and adapting to the broader culture of which the language is a part. Tom was teaching at Fuller Theological Seminary when he died in 1985. Betty Sue is part-time Assistant Professor for Language and Culture Learning at Fuller's School of World Mission. Their work has taken them to more than 75 countries, and they have helped train over 2,500 missionaries. Their textbook *Language Acquisition Made Practical (LAMP)* has been widely acclaimed for its innovative approach and pedagogical creativity.

*** Klaus & Kennell. (1976). *Maternal infant bonding.* St. Louis: Mosby Co.

interest and curiosity for his first six hours, then, after sleeping, he continued very alert for a few more hours.

These alert hours are the critical time for bonding to occur—for a sense of belonging to be established.

Typical American hospital birth is not conducive to normal bonding for two reasons. Hospital-born babies are usually drugged—groggy from a variety of medications typically given to the laboring mother. Neither the baby, nor mother then, has an opportunity to experience the period of acute alertness immediately after birth.

The other reason normal bonding does not occur within the hospital establishment is that the baby is typically snatched away from his family and straightway placed in the isolation of the nursery.

When normal bonding does not occur, rejection can result. It has been demonstrated, for example, that child abuse occurs far more frequently with children who were born prematurely and then isolated from the mother for even a few days while being kept in incubators.*

Our desire to be intimately together as a family and away from institutional commotion in order to maximize the bonding opportunity for all three of us (father included) was a major reason for choosing home birth.

1. What is the main point the authors make about "bonding"?

_____

_____

_____

The missionary analogy

There are some important parallels between the infant's entrance into his new culture and an adult's entrance into a new, foreign culture. In this situation the adult's senses, too, are bombarded by a multitude of new sensations, sights, sounds, and smells—but he, too, is able to respond to these new experiences and even enjoy them. Just as the participants in the birth experience, his adrenaline is up and his excitement level is at a peak. Upon arrival, he is in a state of unique readiness, both physiologically and emotionally, to become a belonger in his new environment. But then....

Just as the infant is snatched away by the hospital establishment and put into the isolation of the nursery, so the newly arrived missionary is typically snatched away by the expatriate missionary contingency and, thus, isolated from his new language community.

He is ready to bond—to become a belonger with those to whom he is called to be good news. The timing is critical. Ducklings do not become imprinted at any old time. Imprinting occurs at the critical time. Bonding best occurs when the participants are uniquely ready for the experience.

> *The way the new missionary spends his first couple of weeks in his new country is of critical importance if he is to establish a sense of belonging with the local people.*

The way the new missionary spends his first couple of weeks in his new country is of critical importance if he is to establish a sense of belonging with the local people.

---

* Klaus & Kennell (1976). *Maternal infant bonding* (pp. 2-10). St. Louis: Mosby Co.

It is not uncommon for a baby to become bonded with hospital personnel instead of with his own parents. The baby then cries when with the mother and is comforted by the nurse. New missionaries, too, tend to become bonded to the other expatriates rather than to the people of the new society. It happens subtly, maybe while the newcomer is subject to the hospitality of an orientation time.

When his sense of belonging is established with the other foreigners, it is then predictable that the missionary will carry out his ministry by the "foray" method—he will live isolated from the local people, as the other foreigners do, but make a few forays out into the community each week, returning always to the security of the missionary community. Without bonding he does not have a sense of feeling at home within the local cultural context. Thus, he does not pursue, as a way of life, significant relationships in the community. When normal bonding is not established, rejection of the people, or even abuse, can

---

When normal bonding is not established, rejection of the people, or even abuse, can occur.

---

occur—it is often reflected in the attitude behind statements like, "Oh, these people! Why do they always do things this way?" or, "Somebody ought to teach them how to live!" or, "Won't these people ever learn?"

2. What kind of ministry approach may the non-bonded missionary have?

_____

_____

_____

Implications of bonding for the missionary task

A missionary is one who goes into the world to give people an opportunity to belong to God's family. He goes because he himself is a belonger in this most meaningful of relationships. His life should proclaim: "I belong to Jesus who has given me a new kind of life. By my becoming a belonger here with you, God is inviting you through me to belong to Him."

The missionary's task thus parallels the model established by Jesus, who left heaven, where He belonged, and became a belonger with humankind in order to draw people into a belonging relationship with God.

We are convinced that the normal missionary newcomer is ready physiologically, emotionally, and spiritually to become bonded with the people of his new community. Fulfillment of this unique readiness must be initiated at the time of arrival. The timing is critical.

During his first couple of weeks, the newcomer is uniquely able to cope with and even enjoy the newness of a foreign country and its language. There have been months or even years of planning, and his anticipation, excitement, and adrenaline are now at a peak.

The newcomer who is immediately immersed in the local community has many advantages. If he lives with a local family, he can learn how the insiders organize their lives, how they get their food and do their shopping, and how they get around with public transportation. During the first couple of months, he can learn much about the insiders' attitudes and how they feel about the ways typical foreigners live. As he experiences an alternative lifestyle, he can evaluate the value of adopting it for himself and his own family. On the other hand, the missionary whose first priority is to get settled can only settle in his familiar Western way, and once this is done he is virtually locked into a pattern that is foreign to the local people.

Culture shock is predictable for the missionary who has not bonded with the local people of his new community but is much less likely for the bonded person. The one who feels at home does not experience culture shock.

In our first culture it comes naturally for us to do things in a way that works. We know which way to look for traffic as we step off the curb, how to get a bus to stop for us, how to pay a fair price for goods or services, how to get needed information, etc., etc.

But in a new culture, the way to do things seems to be unpredictable. As a result, newcomers experience a disorientation which can lead to culture shock.

The new missionary who establishes his sense of belonging with other missionary expatriates has his entry cushioned by these foreigners. It is generally thought that this cushioning is helpful for the adjustment of the newcomer, whose arrival is often planned to coincide with a field council pow-wow.

We would like to suggest, however, that this cushioning is an unfortunate disservice, because during the first two or three weeks the newcomer would have been especially able to cope with the unpredictable situations encountered in the new culture. Indeed, he might even revel in all the variety. But the critical first few days are the only time such a response is likely. The way these days are spent is, therefore, of crucial importance—and cushioning is the last thing he needs.

The first prayer letter the cushioned missionary sends from the field will typically describe his airport meeting with the local missionaries, the accommodations provided by them, and the subsequent orientation by these expatriates. After writing about how he has been accepted by the other missionaries (one of his high priorities), he will invariably close

with something like: "Our prayer request at this time is that we will be accepted by the local people." A noble desire, but a concern that is being expressed about three weeks too late!—and now without a viable strategy to achieve the goal. The initial blush of life in the new environment is now gone.

The individual who hopes to enter another culture in a gradual way will probably fail to do so, and he may never enjoy the experience of belonging to the people or having them care for him.

Better to plunge right in and experience life from the insiders' perspective. Live with the people, worship with them, go shopping with them, and use their public transportation. From the very first day it is important to develop many meaningful relationships with local people. The newcomer should communicate early his needs and his desire to be a learner. People help people who are in need! Then, when potentially stressful situations come up he can, as learner, secure help, answers, or insight from these insiders. (The one who is being cushioned gets outsiders' answers to insiders' situations, and his foreignness and alienation are thereby perpetuated.)

The individual who hopes to enter another culture in a gradual way will probably fail to do so, and he may never enjoy the experience of belonging to the people or having them care for him.

A couple who have chosen to be isolated from Western people during their first months in a Muslim context wrote us about the victories they have experienced:

> My husband and I knew before we left that we would have different types of adjustments. I knew the hardest time for me would be at first, and he felt that his hard times would occur after he had been here a while. So it has been. I really had a hard time leaving our family. But after I started getting out with the people here, my homesickness faded. The

local community has so warmly received us. At Christmas, 125 of these friends came to our Christmas celebration. And during that season, the closeness of our interpersonal relationships amazed us.

The Lord has blessed our work here, and my husband is discipling two Muslim converts. We really have been alone in many ways. We supported each other, but at times the burdens seemed so big, and we didn't have anyone else to talk to or look to for advice. But I suppose that is why we have such good national friends.

Bonding is the factor that makes it possible for the newcomer to have "such good national friends." Of course there will be stressful situations, but the bonded newcomer, experiencing the wonder of close relationships, is able to derive support from the network of the local friendships he has developed. This, in turn, facilitates the acquisition of the insiders' ways and gives a sense of feeling at home. The one who feels at home may feel discouraged or even melancholy for a time, and some cultural stress is to be expected, but it may not be necessary to experience culture shock. Culture shock, like severe post-partum blues, may be a problem of the structure more than a problem of individuals.

3. Why does bonding help minimize culture shock?

_____

_____

_____

It is significant to note that the new Muslim converts mentioned in the letter above are the result of the ministry of relative newcomers. At a time when other missionaries might typically be experiencing the cushioning and isolation of a language school, those who are bonded and carrying out their language learning in the context of relationships in the new community also have the opportunity to pursue the development of their new ministry from the earliest days of language learning. A few years ago the authors supervised the initial language learning for a team of 11 newcomers in Bolivia. We published an article describing that project in the April 1978 *Evangelical Missions Quarterly*:

… Over 30 people came to know Christ as a result of the involvement ministry that these new language learners were able to develop during those (first) three months. Many of these were either members of families with whom we were living, or were on a route of regular listeners. In both cases, as a result of the personal relationships that they had developed, they were able to follow up and

disciple the new believers. Little wonder that this was a fulfilling experience for these new language learners (p. 103).

Insights gained through relationships can help to ensure, right from the beginning, that the wheels of ministry are not only turning but that they are on the ground and moving in a direction that makes sense to the local people.

> **Bonding and effective interpersonal ministry are realistic even for short-termers, and should be encouraged and facilitated.**

Bonding and effective interpersonal ministry are realistic even for short-termers, and should be encouraged and facilitated. (The rapid international expansion of Mormonism is virtually all being carried out by short-termers, most of whom immediately move in with a local family and become belongers in the community. We were recently told by a Cantonese man from Hong Kong that the missionaries there who have learned the language best are Mormons!)

Only a minimum of the target language is needed to initiate bonding relationships. For example, we recently received a letter with the following comment:

> The best thing that happened to me was on the first day when you challenged us to take the little we knew how to say and go talk with 50 people. I didn't talk with 50; I only talked with 44. But I did talk with 44.

(The "text" she was able to say that first day was limited to a greeting and an expression of her desire to learn the language; then she could tell people that she didn't know how to say any more but she would see them again. She then closed with a thank you and a leave-taking.) The ice was broken on her very first day, and from then on, she was able to begin to feel at home in her new community.

Having local friendships is essential for feeling at home. A report developed by a mission for whom we recently consulted on a language learning project compared the 18 maximumly involved learners with a control group of missionaries who had been through language school. The report revealed that the individuals of the control group (the resident missionaries) each had an average of one close national friend, while each of the learners—after only 11 weeks—had a minimum of 15 close local friendships. Since each learner had had contacts with dozens of local people, there were at least 1,000 nationals who had had positive experiences with the learners during the weeks of the project. The report continued: "Who knows how all of this low-level public relations will ultimately benefit [the mission]; it is highly improbable that it will be detrimental. 'Maximum involvement' language learning is where it's at."

4. Why does bonding offer great potential for immediate ministry?

_____

_____

_____

Normal language acquisition is essentially a social activity, not an academic one. As a result, gaining proficiency in the language is normal for the person who is deeply contexted and has his sense of belonging in the new society. But language study will often be a burden and frustration for the one who is bonded to other foreign missionaries. It is therefore important to facilitate an opportunity for new missionaries to become bonded with (and hence belongers in) their new community. New missionaries should be challenged with the bonding objective and prepared to respond to the opportunity to become a belonger.

Preparation should include an orientation to the importance of bonding, with a commitment to do so. A few sentences of the new language that will be helpful for entry purposes could be learned. Also, skills should be developed in how to carry on language learning in the context of community relationships.*

Then, most important, from his first day he should be encouraged to totally immerse himself in the life of the new community. He should be permitted to choose to remain in isolation from other missionaries for his first few months. He should seek to

---

* A recent study by Stephen M. Echerd (an in-house mission report) included a comparison between learners who had been trained in advance and others who developed skills after arriving in the country: "Those in the group who had previous exposure to LAMP (Language Acquisition Made Practical) made 11.78 time units of progress compared to 5.82 time units of those who had no previous exposure—more than double!"

worship with the people, away from churches where missionaries lead or congregate.

Our observation is that experienced but non-bonded missionaries can be a primary obstacle to the new missionary who wishes to pursue the bonding goal. We have, therefore, occasionally even recommended that a new missionary arrive about three weeks before the other missionaries expect him.

Experienced but non-bonded missionaries can be a primary obstacle to the new missionary who wishes to pursue the bonding goal.

One learner wrote:

> The bonding concept motivated me to fly into Singapore early with no prior contacts or housing set up. This is what I wrote in my journal: I discovered it was actually good to be alone when breaking into a new culture— it especially adds to the expectation of what God will do! Even though I was fearful and lonely at times, I was much hungrier and eager and able to hear His voice and discern His will. And, of course, I found many who were willing to help me.

If a newcomer is going to successfully establish himself as a belonger, live with a local family, and learn from relationships on the streets, a prior decision and commitment to do so is essential. Without such a prior commitment it doesn't happen.

When we have accompanied missionary learners at the time of their entry into other countries, we have found that a prior preparation of perspectives and expectations is helpful. We therefore expect all participants in projects we supervise to meet four conditions:

1. Be willing to live with a local family.

2. Limit personal belongings to 20 kilos.

3. Use only local public transportation.

4. Expect to carry out language learning in the context of relationships that the learner himself is responsible to develop and maintain.

A willingness to accept these conditions tells a lot about an individual's attitude and flexibility.

With a prepared mentality, a newcomer is freed to creatively respond to the bonding and learning opportunities that surround him. We have seen that with a prior decision to do so, it is almost always possible to live with a local family (although non-bonded senior missionaries are typically pessimistic). Our experience is that the new missionary—whether single, married, or even with children—can successfully live with a local family immediately upon arrival. (Live-in options may be multiplied with sleeping bags.) We have seen newcomers find their own families by learning to say something like: "We want to learn your language. We hope to find a family to live with for about three months, and we will pay our expenses. Do you know of a possible family?" It would be unusual to say this "text" to 50 people without getting at least some positive response—a mediator to help you or a family to live with.

---

5. Why is bonding important for the language learner?

_____

_____

_____

We do not intend to imply that immediate and total immersion in a new culture is without risk. There is no other time with so much stress and danger as birth; and entry into a new culture has its own accompanying stress and risk factors. It is likely, however, that the stress and risk components themselves are essential to the formation of the unique chemistry that makes imprinting and bonding possible.

And there is another side to the risk question. If one doesn't take the initial risk and seek to establish himself comfortably with the new society, then he is opting for a long-term risk. It seems that one or the other cannot be avoided. The problem of missionary casualties suggests that there is a heavy price to be paid by those who fail to become belongers. Probably half do not return for a second term, and some who stay, despite ineffectiveness, may be greater casualties than those who go back home.

Indeed it is not easy to live with a family, make friends with numerous strangers, and learn the language, but neither is it easy to continue as a stranger without close friendships and without knowing cultural cues, living a foreign lifestyle with all the time, effort, and alienation that that entails.

Once the new learner is securely established as a belonger, he need not relate exclusively with the local people—he has not rejected either America or Americans. The bonded missionary will probably continue to live and minister with the local people, but after the first few weeks it might not be detrimental from the bonding perspective for him to participate in occasional activities with other expatriates. It might even be helpful for him to spend Saturday evenings with other learners or a supervisor (and, of course, he may seek to listen to the Super Bowl with other Americans).

The question has been raised: "What about missionaries who go to the field as a team?" A team is a team because its members share certain commitments. As a group they can decide that each will become bonded in the local culture, and they can encourage each other in the pursuit of that goal. For the initial months, a sharing time each week or so should be sufficient to maintain their commitments to each other.

The concept of bonding implies a bicultural individual with a healthy self-image. Bonding and "going native" are not the same thing. "Going native" generally implies the rejection of one's first culture—a reaction which is seldom seen and which may not

be possible for normal, emotionally stable individuals. Nor is being bicultural the same as being schizophrenic. The schizophrenic is a broken, fragmented self. But the bicultural person is developing a new self—a new personality.

The bonding strategy and the development of this new acculturated personality can be symbolized and greatly facilitated by taking on a new name, preferably an insider's name. For each of us our name is closely associated with our view of who we are—our self-image. As we join a new culture our goal is to develop a new self—a bicultural self. We need a new self that will feel at home with the people of our new culture. We need a "self" that is relatively free of our adult inhibitions, a self that will free us to fill the potential of our new roles and responsibilities.

> *The bonding strategy and the development of this new acculturated personality can be symbolized and greatly facilitated by taking on a new name, preferably an insider's name.*

In the Scriptures we have the record of many people whose names were changed to fit their changed circumstances. The Lord changed some: Abram, Sarai, Jacob to Israel, Solomon to Jedidiah, Pashhur to Magor-Missabib ("The man who lives in terror," Jer. 20:3), and Simon to Cephas which translated means Peter. Daniel and his friends were given Babylonian names: Belteshazzar, Shadrach, Meshach and Abednego. Naomi chose to be called Mara, and Saul became Paul.

We too experience the significance of changed names in various ways: Women symbolize the belonging relationship of marriage by taking on the husband's name (we know a couple who both took a new last name—Doulos, the Greek word for servant—when they were married); movie stars develop a new image behind a new name; in orthodox churches, vows to God are often accompanied by the novitiate receiving a new name. Even cities and countries are changing their names as they become free from colonialism or choose to identify with a different perspective.

Recent changes include Zaire, Zimbabwe, Ghana, Bangladesh, Sri Lanka, Istanbul, and Harare. The English world calls the islands Falklands, while they are Malvinas to Spanish speakers.

Names mean a lot. Some missionaries used to require converts to take on "Christian" names: Fred, Mary, etc.! Mzee Jomo Kenyatta's first name was Kamau Ngengi. As a child in a Christian school he was required to choose a Western name. He wanted John Peter but was forbidden to choose two, so he ingeniously chose for himself Johnstone, and got the "Peter" in anyway. The name "Kenyatta" came later and served him well as the father of his newly independent country.

The new name with its newly developing personality does not have an established self-image to protect, and it can therefore be free to behave in uninhibited, creative, and childlike ways; it can make mistakes and try, try again.

It will be much easier to develop a bicultural self-image if a new name is adopted, around which the new personality can grow. We personally know many missionaries who have been given a local name as a result of talking about it with the people: Rafik (Friend) in Urdu, Dimakatso (Wonderful Surprise) in Tswana, and "Sara Child" (One who belongs to us) in Sara. Often an adaptation of one's own name is sufficient if it is appropriate as an insider's name in the new society: Tomas, Marcos, etc. In some societies the use of a local kinship name might be best.

The new name with its newly developing personality does not have an established self-image to protect, and it can therefore be free to behave in uninhibited, creative, and childlike ways; it can make mistakes and try, try again. With his newly developing personality the individual can feel at home in his second culture. For the Christian missionary, the process of becoming bicultural can begin with the recognition that God in His sovereignty does not make mistakes in creating us with our first ethnicity. Yet in His sovereignty He may step in and touch us on the shoulder, as it were, and call us to go and be good news to a people of a different ethnicity.

To become a belonger in a legal sense, through formal immigration, might also be considered by some serious missionaries. Immigration need not imply a rejection of one's first country, but rather acceptance of a new one. Throughout history, people have immigrated for political, economic, religious, and marriage reasons. The challenge of reaching a people for Christ should have the potential to similarly motivate some of Christ's bond-servants. The missionary's heavenly citizenship should lift him above the provincialism and ethnocentrism of a continuing allegiance to a country where, in obedience to Christ, he no longer lives. This "recovered pilgrim spirit" was the challenge presented by Joseph F. Conley in a recent Regions Beyond editorial (December, 1979):

> For most North American missionaries, North America is home. That is where he goes when he's sick, and when the going gets too rough he can always return to blend in with the scenery. Tomorrow the quick retreat may be cut off. We may be forced to relive those days when missionaries went abroad, never expecting to return. Many governments which refuse entry to missionary expatriates, hold the door open to naturalized citizens of colonizing communities. The Moravians led the way in this as they set up Christian colonies around the world.
>
> Surrender of treasured national citizenship admittedly calls for a rare variety of commitment. But is that unthinkable? To such our Lord's words will find new and glowing exegesis, "He that hath forsaken lands... for My sake... shall receive an hundredfold and shall inherit everlasting life."

6. *What are the risks involved in bonding? How do these compare to the risk of not becoming bonded?*

_____

_____

_____

_____

The bonded missionary, because he is a belonger, has the opportunity to gain an empathic understanding of insiders' ways, their feelings, desires, attitudes, and fears. He can listen with sensitivity to their otherwise hidden values, concerns, and motives. Thus he can acquire insights and adopt habits of lifestyle and ministry that will enable him to be good news from the perspective of local people in order to draw them into a belonging relationship with God.

Bonding is therefore a perspective many missionaries may choose to value and a goal they may choose to pursue. Making this kind of significant cultural adjustment is not easy, but it is possible, especially if initiated at the critical time for bonding.

In summary, we have observed that the newcomer goes through a critical time for establishing his sense of identity and belonging during his first few weeks in a new country. If he becomes a belonger with expatriates, he may always remain a foreigner and outsider. But at this crucial time has the unique opportunity to establish himself as a belonger with insiders, in order to live and learn and minister within their social context.

The bonding approach suggested by the Brewsters is certainly not the norm for missionaries. The more typical approach includes a period of language study at a language school or institute, followed by introduction to the culture by fellow expatriate missionaries, and finally settling in at the site of future ministry. Although this approach is "standard" and may be more secure initially, it has long-range consequences which may handicap the effectiveness of the missionary. Without bonding, identification will tend to be superficial, and effective communication of the gospel will suffer.

The quote by Joseph Conley in the preceding article suggests that it may be time for North Americans to consider emigration as an avenue for mission involvement. Missionaries from developing nations may also want to consider this option. In fact, the sending of colonizing Christian communities, like those of the Moravians, may very well be one of the most viable options for missions from countries with weak economies.

II. Roles and Expectations

We have spoken of the need to approach the missionary task with flexibility, innovation, and right attitudes. Now let us consider viable missionary roles in the approach to learning language and culture. In the following article, Donald Larson provides a straightforward description of practical and effective roles the missionary can assume.

❑ *The Viable Missionary: Learner, Trader, Story Teller* *

Donald N. Larson **

When my interest in the mission of the Christian church first awakened, I was too old to be acceptable to my denomination as a candidate. But for the past 20 years I have worked behind the scenes in mission, helping people to deal with the problems of language and culture learning. From this position off-stage, I have observed missionaries, sending agencies, local missionary communities, and national Christians and non-Christians in several fields. From these observations I have concluded that there is often a wide gap in the missionary's conception of his role and how it is viewed by the non-Christians of his adopted community. The purpose of this paper is to examine this gap and propose ways and means of closing it.

By way of example, I recently met a young man heading for a short term of missionary service in Southeast Asia and asked him what he was going to be doing there. He replied in all seriousness that he was "going to teach the natives to farm." I pressed him with a question: "Don't they know how to farm there?" He thought for a moment and then replied, "Well, I really don't know. I haven't got a very clear picture of things yet." Imagine what the non-Christian of his adopted community would think of him if they should hear him say such things! Whether this young man knows it or not, these Asians were farmers long before the Pilgrims landed at Plymouth Rock and even long before there were Christians anywhere.

Unfortunately, such statements as those made by the young man are not limited to short-termers. Career missionaries are sometimes unaware of the experience, background, and worldview of the members of their host communities and how they themselves are viewed. This gap between missionaries and non-Christians in their local communities generates communication problems of many different kinds.

7. What attitude was reflected by the young man who was going to Southeast Asia "to teach the natives to farm"?

_____

_____

_____

* Larson, D. N. (1978, April). The viable missionary: Learner, trader, story teller. *Missiology: An International Review, 6*, 155-163.

** Donald N. Larson is Senior Consultant for Cross-Cultural Learning at Link Care Missions. He was Professor of Anthropology and Linguistics at Bethel College in St. Paul, Minnesota, and Director of the Toronto Institute of Linguistics. He formerly served as Director of the Inter-Church Language School in the Philippines.

Typical encounter models

In an encounter with the missionary, whom he views as an outsider, the local non-Christian tends to view their relationship in one of three ways. He uses the schoolhouse, the marketplace, and the courtroom as backdrops to his encounters with the missionary. As if they were at school, he sees the missionary as teacher and himself as student. The purpose of their encounter is to transmit information to be learned. As if they were in the marketplace, he sees the missionary as seller and himself as buyer. The purpose of their encounter is to buy and sell something. As if in the courtroom, he sees the missionary as an accuser and himself as the accused. Their encounter deals with judgment. In the schoolhouse the teacher says, "I will teach you something." In the marketplace the merchant says, "I have something to sell you." In the courtroom the judge says, "I will measure you by this standard." Depending on the scene, the national views his need differently. In the schoolhouse he asks himself whether he needs to learn what the teacher has to teach. In the marketplace he asks himself whether he needs to buy what the merchant has to sell. In the courtroom he asks himself whether he needs to take the judge's accusation seriously.

But can an outsider teach or sell or accuse an insider? Does the non-Christian need what the missionary presents? Is the missionary able to communicate the gospel through the roles of seller, teacher, or accuser? Are they effective? These are serious questions.

Of course, there are other ways to look at the non-Christian's encounter with the missionary than through the three analogies used above.

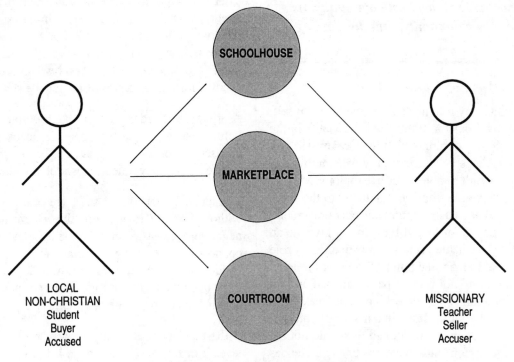

LOCAL
NON-CHRISTIAN
Student
Buyer
Accused

SCHOOLHOUSE

MARKETPLACE

COURTROOM

MISSIONARY
Teacher
Seller
Accuser

Figure 12-1. Typical Encounter Models

8. Why do you think the effectiveness of the typical encounter models is limited? On what premise are they based?

_____

_____

_____

Viable role dimensions

The typical missionary today may be paying too little attention to the viability of his role. If I were volunteering for missions today and hoped to be productive and happy, I would make certain that my role were viable from four perspectives: (1) the community in which I reside, (2) its missionary residents, (3) the agency that sends me, and (4) myself.

> **The new missionary must look for roles that are simultaneously legitimate to these four parties: me, my host community, its missionary community, and the sending agency.**

To elaborate, my role must allow me to be myself, to be my own person. It must also be viable in the local missionary community. If the local missionary community doesn't recognize my role and its importance, I won't be able to survive for long. My role must also be viable from the standpoint of the sending agency. I need their support and encouragement. I cannot survive for long if they do not give me an important place in their community. Finally, my role must be viable from the point of view of the local community. I do not want to parade myself around in this community as some kind of a freak, or a misfit, or a spy, or useless. This matter of community viability is often overlooked. It should not be. It is important, for I must have positive experiences in order to continue. Local residents must feel good about my presence in their community. My contribution must reinforce and complement the ongoing missionary program. The sending agency must have a solid rationale underlying its programs and the opportunities it provides for me.

So the new missionary must look for roles that are simultaneously legitimate to these four parties: me, my host community, its missionary community, and the sending agency.

To the non-Christian, the roles of teacher, seller, or accuser may or may not be viable. The non-Christian may expect the outsider to learn the insider's viewpoint before he can teach effectively about the outside. He may expect him to survive on the level of insiders and depend on the local market before he can sell important goods. He may expect him to measure himself by their own laws before he accuses insiders in terms of an outside standard.

A principle of order seems to be important: learner before teacher, buyer before seller, accused before accuser. An outsider may have to follow this order before he can be viable in these roles to the insider.

Outsiders cannot live on the edge of a community without coming to the attention of insiders in a negative way. The term "outsider" has negative connotations. So the missionary must become an insider, at least to some extent, if he hopes to avoid these negative reactions to his presence and become a valuable person in the community.

If the insider is reluctant to learn from an outside teacher or buy from an outside seller or accept the accusations of an outside accuser, the outsider cannot hope to accomplish much until he finds new roles or redesigns the old ones.

9. *Why is it important that the missionary's role be "viable" from the standpoint of the four parties mentioned above?*

_____

_____

_____

Three roles

As I see it, there are three roles that the missionary can develop in order to establish viability in the eyes of the national non-Christian: learner, trader, and story teller. I would first become a learner. After three months I would add another: trader. After three more months, I would add a third: story teller. After three more months, while continuing to be learner, trader, and story teller, I would begin to develop other roles specified in my job description.

> *From his position as an outsider, the missionary must find a way to move toward the center if he hopes to influence people.*

Let me elaborate. From his position as an outsider, the missionary must find a way to move toward the center if he hopes to influence people. Some roles will help him to make this move. Others will not. His first task is to identify those which are most appropriate and effective. Then he can begin to develop ways and means of communicating his Christian experience through these roles in which he has found acceptance.

1. Learner

More specifically, as learner, my major emphasis is on language, the primary symbol of identification in my host community. When I try to learn it, they know that I mean business—that they are worth something to me because I make an effort to com-municate on their terms. I learn a little each day and put it to use. I talk to a new person every day. I say something new every day. I gradually reach the point where I understand and am understood a little. I can learn much in three months.

I spend my mornings with a language helper (in a structured program or one that I design on my own) from whom I elicit the kinds of materials that I need to talk to people in the afternoons. I show him how to drill me on these materials and then spend a good portion of the morning in practice. Then in the afternoon I go out into public places and make whatever contacts are natural with local residents, talking to them as best I can with my limited proficiency—starting the very first day. I initiate one conversation after another, each of which says both verbally and nonverbally, "I am a learner. Please talk with me and help me." With each conversation partner, I get a little more practice and a little more proficiency, from the first day on.

At the end of my first three months, I have established myself with potentially dozens of people and reached the point where I can make simple statements, ask and answer simple questions, find my way around, learn the meaning of new words on the spot, and most importantly, experience some measure of "at-homeness" in my adopted community. I cannot learn the "whole language" in three months, but I can learn to initiate conversations, control them in a limited way, and learn a little more about the language from everyone whom I meet.

10. *How does Larson suggest that afternoons be spent? Why does the "learner" role require more than just a structured classroom experience?*

_____

_____

_____

2. Trader

When my fourth month begins, I add a role—that of trader, trading experience and insight with people of my adopted community—seeing ourselves more clearly as part of mankind, not just members of different communities or nations. I prepare for this role by periods of residence in as many other places as I can, or vicariously, through course work in anthropology and related fields. I also come equipped with a set of 8″ x 10″ photos illustrating a wide range of ways to be human.

During the second three months I spend mornings with my language helper learning to talk about the photos in my collection. Thus I build on the language proficiency developed in the first months. I practice my description of these pictures and prepare myself as best I can to answer questions about them. Then in the afternoon I visit casually in the community, using the photos as part of my "show and tell" demonstration. I tell as much as I can about the way others live, how they make their livings, what they do for enjoyment, how they hurt, and how they struggle for survival and satisfaction.

At the end of this second phase, I establish myself not only as a learner but as one who is interested in other people and seeks to trade one bit of information for another. My language proficiency is still developing. I meet many people. Depending upon the size and complexity of the community, I establish myself as a well-known figure by this time. I become a bridge between the people of the local community and a larger world—at least symbolically.

3. Story teller

When I begin my seventh month, I shift emphasis again to a new role. Now I become a story teller. I spend mornings with my language helper. Now my object is to learn to tell a very simple story to the people whom I meet and respond to their inquiries as best I can. The stories that I tell are based on the wanderings of the people of Israel, the coming of Christ, the formation of God's new people, the movement of the church into all the world and ultimately into this very community, and finally, my own story of my encounter with Christ and my walk as a Christian. During the mornings I develop these stories and practice them intensively. Then in the afternoon I go into the community, as I have been doing for months, but now to encounter people as story teller. I am still language learner and trader, but I have added the role of story teller. I share as much of the story with as many people as I can each day.

At the end of this third phase, I have made acquaintances and friends. I have had countless experiences that I will never forget. I have left positive impressions as learner, trader, and story teller. I am ready for another role, and another and another.

11. *What does Larson "trade"? What is the key concept of the trader role?*

_____

_____

_____

12. *Why are the "learner" and "trader" roles essential to development of the "story teller" role?*

_____

_____

_____

Viability reconsidered

With this profile in mind, let's examine this activity in the light of our earlier discussion of viability. Figure 12-2 helps to focus on the issues. In this figure, the plus sign (+) means that the role is unquestionably viable. The question mark (?) means that some further discussion and clarification are probably necessary before viability can be established.

From the standpoint of local residents, an outsider who is ready, willing, and able to learn probably has an entree. Furthermore, the average person in these communities probably has a natural curiosity about people in other places. This curiosity can probably be tapped and traded by a sensitive approach. Finally, story telling and the reporting of incidents is common in every community. Everyone does it. Of course, there are rules which must be respected. I assume that someone who has already established himself as learner and trader can share stories and experiences of his own with other people. Local residents will probably listen and perhaps even help him to get it told.

> *From the standpoint of local residents, an outsider who is ready, willing, and able to learn probably has an entree.*

I find these roles viable. I enjoy learning and know how to go about it. I have a general understanding of different ways that people live and appreciate the possibilities inherent in the trader role. I love to tell stories and enjoy listening to them, especially when the teller is deeply involved in them himself.

	DIMENSIONS			
ROLES	LOCAL RESIDENTS	MISSIONARY COMMUNITY	SENDING AGENCY	MISSIONARY
LEARNER	+	?	?	+
TRADER	+	?	?	?
STORY TELLER	+	+	+	+

Figure 12-2. Viability of Roles of Learner, Trader, Story Teller

But from the standpoint of the sending agency and the local community, these roles may be questionable. Of the three, the story teller role is perhaps the easiest one to develop, though one often finds missionaries to be sermonizers, theologizers, or lecturers—not story tellers. The viability of the learner role is open to question. A new missionary, expected to be a learner as far as the affairs of his local missionary organization are concerned, is not always given the time or encouraged to get to know local residents intimately. The viability of the trader role is largely untested, though I believe that sending agencies and local missionary communities should consider its importance carefully.

Why not exploit the learner role to the fullest? Most people who live as aliens sooner or later realize its importance. Why not get the new missionary off on the right foot—especially if it has increasing payoff in his second and third phases? Furthermore, the learner role symbolized a number of important things to local residents that are important in the communication of the gospel. The learner's dependence and vulnerability convey in some small way the messages of identification and reconciliation that are explicit in the gospel. Coming to be known as a learner can certainly do the local missionary

community no harm. It may be able to do some good.

The viability of the trader role is perhaps more difficult to establish—partly because of its newness. It seems to be too "secular." Yet from the community's standpoint, a secular role may be much more natural and acceptable for the alien. Coming as some sort of "sacred specialist," the outsider generates all sorts of questions, objections, and barriers. But there is still another consideration: this role reinforces the idea of the gospel as something for all people. Except for anthropologists, demographers, and a few other specialists, Christians probably have a wider understanding of human variation than any other group of people, simply because of our multi-ethnic, multi-racial, and multi-lingual characteristics. The trader role complements the more formal presentation of the gospel through the sharing of essentially "secular knowledge" about people of the world.

There are obvious implications here for the selection, orientation, and evaluation of missionaries. A discussion of them, however, is beyond the scope of this paper.

13. *As the missionary pursues "learner" and "trader" roles, which of the four parties mentioned earlier will need to be convinced of the viability of these roles?*

_____

_____

_____

14. *Which role has an assumed viability in everyone's eyes? Why?*

_____

_____

_____

Conclusion

We face a difficult situation today as the star of colonialism continues to fall and as the star of maturing national churches continues to rise. Missionaries become more and more frustrated as the viability of their role is questioned. We must take this situation seriously. The biblical mandate challenges the Christian to become one with those to whom he brings the Word of Life. Furthermore, history shows that vulnerability and flexibility are themselves powerful witnesses to the working of the Spirit within man. Finally, if the mission movement is to continue, new roles must be added and old ones must be redesigned.

Any new missionary can prepare himself in rather simple and straightforward fashion to meet the demands of these three roles. Insofar as these roles are viable from the point of view of the local community, the new missionary should begin with them. Unfortunately, sending agencies and local missionary communities may not be ready to buy these ideas. The let's-get-on-with-the-job mentality militates against getting bogged down in learning, trading, and story telling. But this get-on-with-the-job mentality needs to be challenged; for if it implies roles that insulate the missionary from local residents, alternatives must be developed.

Some months ago, at a language and culture learning workshop in East Africa, a missionary asked me if I knew anything about elephants. When I replied that I did not, she asked more specifically if I knew what happens when a herd of elephants approaches a water hole that is surrounded by another herd. I replied that I did not know what would happen. She then proceeded to explain that the lead elephant of the second group turns around and backs down toward the water hole. As soon as his backside is felt by the elephants gathered around the water hole, they step aside and make room for him. This is then the signal to the other elephants that the first herd is ready to make room for them around the hole.

> *This get-on-with-the-job mentality needs to be challenged; for if it implies roles that insulate the missionary from local residents, alternatives must be developed.*

When I asked what point she was trying to make, she stated simply and powerfully, "We didn't back in." The continuing movement of mission in the world today may require missionaries to "back in" to their host communities. The roles of learner, trader, and storyteller may not be appropriate in a headfirst approach, but they may be necessary in an approach which emphasizes "backing in."

15. *Why would some consider "backing in" a waste of time? What is your opinion?*

_____

_____

_____

The LAMP Approach

For most missionaries, the first activity on the mission field will be language learning. Since most of the world's 5,000+ languages are not taught formally, many missionaries will need to use an alternative method. This may be a blessing in disguise, since the alternative to formal study is learning the language directly from the target people—an activity which is conducive to bonding.

Drs. Tom and Elizabeth Brewster have tackled the challenge of structuring field language learning. Over the years, they have developed an approach known as Language Acquisition Made Practical

(LAMP). This system enables most missionaries to acquire a language using lay helpers. The Brewsters have personally helped missionaries in over 75 countries learn languages in a way which also aids their overall adaptation to the culture. Rather than focusing on a specific language, the approach adapts principles of language learning that are universal, enabling the user to learn any language.

The Brewsters published their approach in a manual called *Language Acquisition Made Practical: Field Methods for Language Learners* (available from Lingua House, 135 North Oakland, P.O. Box 114, Pasadena, CA 91101). We, of course, cannot outline the entire manual. However, we would like to provide you with some of the theory behind the approach. If you or your missionaries need to use field methods for language learning, it is advisable to contact Lingua House directly for the LAMP manual and other resources. The following quotation is from the preface of LAMP:

> It can be done!
>
> You can successfully learn a new language if three conditions are met:
>
> > a. You live where the new language is spoken.
> >
> > b. You are motivated to learn the new language.
> >
> > c. You know how to proceed with language learning, step by step and day by day.
>
> The first condition can be met simply by moving to an area where the language is spoken. An even more ideal situation would be for you to live in the home of a family that speaks the language.
>
> Motivation—the second condition—is an act of the will. Some language learners make the mistake of equating motivation with enthusiasm. For them, when their enthusiasm is up, their "motivation" is up. But enthusiasm is an emotion. It ebbs and flows in relation to how you feel or how the world is treating you. In reality, motivation is not an emotion, so don't tie it to your emotions. Motivation is a determination which results in a decision of the will—"I will learn."*

The LAMP manual attempts to provide the learner with the step-by-step, day-by-day procedure for acquiring the target language. It assumes that the first two conditions have been met, that is, that the learner is able to live where the language is spoken by a native population and that sufficient internal and external motivation is sustained throughout the language learning process. If the first two conditions are met, then by properly implementing the methods prescribed in the manual, the language learner will be guided in successful acquisition of the language.

The Nature of Language Learning

The main activity usually associated with learning a language is study. This intellectual activity is often centered in a classroom where the structure of the language is analyzed and learned, vocabulary is memorized, and the language learner gradually learns to produce phrases and sentences. Students using this approach often feel frustrated when they are put in a situation where they must actually use the language. Although they may have studied for several years, they often find they can't carry on a conversation with a native speaker.

---

* Brewster, E. T., & Brewster, E. S. (1976). *Language acquisition made practical: Field methods for language learners* (p. 1). Colorado Springs: Lingua House.

That language "study" is not essential to language learning is evidenced by the fact that millions of illiterate people throughout the world speak two or more languages fluently. These people often cannot even read their own names, but they have learned second and third languages because they have used them. Their "school room" has been the marketplace, the streets, and the homes of the community. Thus it can be seen that language acquisition is more a performance skill than a cognitive skill. As an activity, it is more closely related to practicing football than to studying history. Mastery of a language can only be achieved through disciplined, consistent practice and use.

The Fun of Language

Millions of people around the world learn second languages in a "natural" way. In fact, all of us learned our first language apart from any conscious effort. Children learn language through experimentation and play. In their first efforts, they produce sounds which they repeat over and over, often to the delight of their parents. This practice carries over to the first objects they learn to identify and their first experimentation with putting a string of words together. Their early attempts are seldom "correct" from an adult's standpoint, but children are not self-conscious about their "mistakes" and usually receive much positive reinforcement for their efforts.

Children seem to make a game of learning language. Besides repeating sounds, words, and phrases over and over, they experiment with different ways of saying the same thing. They seem to talk just for the pleasure of hearing themselves. When they learn the question forms, they seem to ask questions just for the joy of getting a response (which often drives their parents to distraction). Fascination with language and the lack of self-consciousness are the greatest assets in acquiring a language. These motivate the learner to practice and use what is acquired in a natural and unforced manner.

16. How are the greatest assets a child brings to language learning inhibited by adult behavior?

_____

_____

_____

Most adults subconsciously resist the idea of becoming "childlike" to learn a language. Yet, for the missionary, this role may be unavoidable. Immersion in a new culture and its accompanying "culture shock" are often associated with feelings of "being more stupid than a child." Ability to communicate effectively is such an integral part of our self-concept that when this is taken away, the disorientation can lead to negative emotions and depression. It is healthier to accept the "childlike" learner role and enter into it fully.

Make a game of language learning. Become fascinated with the new sounds you are producing. Enjoy getting a response to your efforts, even when others get a laugh out of your attempts. You'll find that native speakers will not only be forgiving of your mistakes, but will like and appreciate you the more for your efforts and willingness to become vulnerable.

Getting Started

Children seem to learn language randomly. As adults, we can greatly aid our language learning efforts by using a methodology which allows systematic skill building. The system described in LAMP consists of four daily parts:

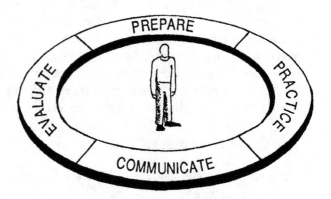

Figure 12-3. The Learning Cycle

- Prepare what you need for the day.

- Practice what you prepare.

- Communicate what you know.

- Evaluate your needs and your progress so you will know what to prepare for the next day.

These four parts function in an integrated, cyclical fashion. By following these steps in sequence, the learner begins to acquire language competency, little by little. The manual recommends that the language learner should initially budget about six hours a day to go through the cycle, gradually tapering this time commitment down to two or three hours daily.

The heart of the learning cycle is the third part. It is also the most difficult component for many language learners. From the first day, learners should be using what they learn, practicing and interacting with people. Without this vital element, language learning will be reduced to an exercise in memorization. Effective communication is the goal. The first tentative steps toward achieving that goal are taken the first day of learning a language.

At the beginning, the learner depends heavily on memorized texts to communicate. To learn these texts, a native speaker of the target language (who has some understanding of the learner's language) is needed. This person becomes the learner's language "helper" or "coach." He or she shows the learner how to say what is needed to communicate and how to pronounce the phrases correctly. The language helper should not be a professional teacher, because such a person is more likely to try to teach about the language than to help the learner practice it. In fact, it is a good idea to avoid using the term "teacher" altogether. The language assistant is the learner's helper. Even when the LAMP approach is used to supplement a more formal language study program, it is wise to develop a relationship with a helper who can coach the learner.

17. *What are the main philosophical and practical points which distinguish the LAMP approach from more conventional language study?*

_____

_____

_____

_____

_____

III. Occupational Identity and Lifestyle

Meeting role expectations is not simply a matter of philosophical orientation. For those targeting unreached people groups, occupational identity is an increasingly important issue. Most of the world's unreached are in countries which do not allow foreign missionaries. Cross-cultural workers must assume occupational roles to obtain residence. Stated roles must match lifestyle, or suspicion and mistrust are created. In the following excerpt, Jonathan Cortes addresses these issues.

❑ *Exploring the Whos and Hows of Tentmaking* *

Jonathan Cortes **

"What's your *real* work here?" the customs official said with a scowl. Bill glanced quickly at what the official was examining. With horror he saw what some well-meaning person from his church had written on his baggage: "For missionary use only."

Bill is a tentmaker. After going through a short course in Teaching English to Speakers of Other Languages (TESOL), he had obtained a job in a "creative access" country in Asia. What was the official to believe? Was Bill an English teacher or a missionary? In fact, he was both.

The uncomfortable situation in which Bill found himself illustrates the difficulty experienced by churches as they make the transition to sending tentmakers—missionaries who use lay credentials as a means of serving in countries which restrict access to regular career missionaries. The situation also reflects the dilemma in which these church-sent tentmakers find themselves as they grapple with their own identity under prevailing security measures in restricted situations.

Bivocational dilemmas

The story of Bill does not end here. Although he eventually got his visa to stay and teach in the country, the questions kept coming. Bill only teaches a couple of hours a week, and outside of his classes he is asked how and why he is living in the country. He is often pressed further with repeated questions of increasing intensity. Although he is on a teaching visa, he knows that he would never have come to this country only to teach English. He is really in the country to be a missionary. He can't say this, however. His evasive answers bother his conscience and create an atmosphere of mistrust, which is hindering his ministry opportunities.

Without much prefield orientation to help him avoid or resolve some of these conflicts beforehand, Bill feels tremendous pressures. These pressures produce stress on his conscience, on his body, on his family (who face the same questions in their everyday lives), on his host organization, on his sending agency, and on the nationals he wants to relate with and serve.

---

* Cortes, J. (1993). Exploring the whos and hows of tentmaking. In J. Lewis (Ed.), *Working your way to the nations: A guide to effective tentmaking* (pp. 5-1 – 5-5). Pasadena: William Carey Library.

** Jonathan Cortes is a frontier missions facilitator for The Navigators. Based in Singapore, he is responsible for preparing the way for tentmakers from developed Christian ministries throughout the world to go to the least evangelized and discipled countries of Asia.

18. What are the possible consequences of such a stressful situation?

_____

_____

_____

Facing the Pressures

The author identifies both external and internal pressures that Bill is facing. There is pressure from external sources as the local people try to figure Bill out. Internally, Bill is experiencing pressure from his conscience, which is beginning to accuse him. Like many tentmakers, Bill didn't have to deal with these issues before he left his own country. Now the pressures seem ready to overwhelm him.

The issue of true identity is one of the most critical to a tentmaker's success. Many tentmakers have failed because they have not dealt with this issue before going to the field. When a tentmaker adopts an occupation simply as a cover, there is a lot of pressure from external sources in trying to reconcile what others see as a contradiction. When a tentmaker's position is untenable, suspicion is a natural reaction. A case in point might be a 35-year-old man with a family, who has been enrolled in the local university for years without making much progress towards a degree. Other examples are a businessman who never seems to do business and a teacher who only teaches a few hours a week.

Most of the unreached areas of the world are poor, and many have repressive governments. It doesn't make sense to the people of such a host country for someone to leave a more developed country—leave family, leave freedom, and leave opportunity—to take up residence in their land. This lack of understanding creates a feeling of distrust. When tentmakers can't be completely open and declare their Christian mission, the situation can wear them down psychologically, no matter how dedicated they may be.

Questions come relentlessly. "Why did you come here to work? This is a poor country with few opportunities. Why would you want to live here instead of in your own country, where there is more freedom and it's easier to earn a living? What about your parents and relatives? Don't you miss them? How much do you make? How can you live as well as you do when you only teach a few hours each week? What is your real reason for being here? Are you a spy, a drug dealer, a subversive, a missionary…?"

The second kind of pressure Bill is facing is internal. Like many tentmakers, he didn't take time back home to deal with what, once on the field, he began to feel was a dishonest lifestyle. Prompted by his evasive answers to people in the host culture, his conscience accused him of being a fake, a fraud, and un-Christian. How could he live a lie? These accusations involved some real ethical questions. In the following sections, our tentmaker author discusses how to face some of these issues.

The obligation to witness

The Christian's ultimate authority to be a witness to and of the gospel is derived from Jesus Christ, to whom all authority has been given in heaven and on earth. Because all authority belongs to Him, we cannot accept the concept of a "closed land." Every land is open to Him who holds the key of David, who opens and no one can shut, who shuts and no one can open (Rev. 3:7).

Satan's power, on the other hand, is both limited and derived, and it is subject to Christ's supreme authority. Though Satan uses others to "close" countries, this prohibition is in direct contradiction to and is invalidated by Jesus Christ's commands to "go into all the world" (Mark 16:15) and to "make disciples of all nations" (Matt. 28:18-20). We must obey God's commands above all others (Acts 4:1-20).

We have an obligation, therefore, to be witnesses for our Lord, even when "proselytizing" is forbidden. This is neither easy nor simple. There are some general principles, however, for thought and prayer. These should be considered in the light of the need for discretion, tact, and care, and they should be balanced with Gideon's warning to those who fear: "Whoever is fearful and afraid, let him return and depart early" (Judg. 7:3).

> *Most cultures have a deep respect for an attitude that says, "I am not ashamed of this message." The "silent witness" is often despised and at best is misunderstood.*

The spoken word of witness was normative in New Testament times. Jesus commissioned His disciples to "herald" the gospel to every creature. This implies spreading the good news by word of mouth. This emphasis links the message with the messenger. God is delighted and honors a witness who says, "I am not ashamed of this message." In fact, most cultures have a deep respect for such an attitude. It is one with which they can identify. The "silent witness" is often despised and at best is misunderstood. As tentmakers invest their lives in the Great Commission, they need to have wisdom and discretion about what they are communicating both verbally and nonverbally.

Witnessing without proselytizing

There is no human law that says you cannot be open in your personal belief in Jesus Christ. Jesus Himself said, "I spoke openly to the world" (John 18:20). Paul said, "I kept back nothing that was profitable to you" (Acts 20:20). We are to walk in the light and never lie or deceive. Yet it is also clear in Scripture that not everything needs to be revealed.

The main reason governments officially ban proselytism is that, in the past, proselytism has involved attacking or insulting the country's main religion, leading men astray from their social and religious groupings, polluting their high moral standards, weaning people away from nationalism, or subverting the state by producing a Western subculture. All of these activities can produce social disorder and problems for the government.

It is possible, by God's grace and wisdom, to be a child of God, a worshiper of Christ, and still be a contributing member to the socio-economic welfare of even an atheistic nation. It is possible to be a servant of Christ and not be a blasphemer of other gods or a traitor to the best interests of another country's government. Indeed, if biblical Christians let the Word become flesh in their lives (John 1:14), if they are able to teach gently as humble servants of Christ (2 Tim. 2:24-26), and if they have a message of *agape* love (John 3:16), they do not come to disrupt the established order. They come to bring Christ, to introduce fellow sinners to a Savior and Redeemer who loves them and who cared enough to die for them.

19. What is the best solution to the external and internal pressures of the bivocational dilemma?

_____

_____

_____

One obvious way to alleviate external pressures is to make certain that the tentmaking occupation isn't simply fabricated as a cover. A relatively well-paying or prestigious position helps affirm this sense of authenticity, as does affiliation with a government or with an international development agency or company. The internal pressures can only be mitigated when a deep conviction of calling and a clear understanding of spiritual authority and spiritual warfare are present. Missionaries are God's agents in enemy-held territory. In these situations, they truly need the cunning of serpents and the innocence of doves (Matt. 10:16).

Lifestyle Implications

Missionaries' lifestyles will be conditioned by a variety of factors, including financial resources, target group, and, for tentmakers, secular employment. Again, what counts in determining lifestyle issues are the attitudes which condition decisions, rather than the affluence or poverty demonstrated. In the following article, Phil Parshall presents his views on the lifestyle issues from his ample background and experience.

❏ *God's Communicator in the '90s* *

Phil Parshall **

It is a great calling and privilege to be a missionary. It is my joy to have rubbed shoulders with hundreds of foreign missionaries over the past three decades. By and large, they impress me very positively.

The missionary calling has unique features. The missionary must be reasonably well-educated, cross geographical boundaries, leave loved ones behind, sacrifice financially (though not always), adjust to another language and culture, and work on a closely knit team. At the same time, missionaries must open themselves to criticism, from both friend and foe. They must be willing to reevaluate sacrosanct methodology. "Change" must not be a dreaded word, as we consider the qualifications and methods of missionaries for the coming decade. I speak from a heart of love and concern—from within the camp.

Dr. Saeed Khan Kurdistani was an outstanding Iranian Christian who died in 1942. In 1960, a man went to the area where Dr. Saeed had lived and ministered. An aged man of the community was asked by the visitor if he had known Dr. Saeed. The elderly man caught his breath and whispered: "Dr. Saeed was Christ Himself!" Reverently, it can be said that this is our goal. But as we head into the 1990s we need to take a hard look at such practical matters as missionary finances, housing, intellectual life, and ministry with churches.

Finances

There is an overwhelming difference of opinion on this subject. Some feel it is imperative to "go native" and to denounce all who do not meet their standard. Others feel strongly that they must live on a Western standard for the sake of their family's mental and physical health. They defend their position by saying the nationals will understand their needs. Between these two extremes will be found every conceivable view.

Many Third World countries are economically depressed. This fact sets the stage for the conflict between the living standard of the Western mission-

* Parshall, P. (1992). God's communicator in the '90s. In R. D. Winter & S. C. Hawthorne (Eds.), *Perspectives on the world Christian movement: A reader* (rev. ed.) (pp. C131-C136). Pasadena: William Carey Library.

** Phil Parshall is a missionary in the Philippines serving as Director of SIM's Asian Research Center. He has authored five books, the latest of which is *The Cross and the Crescent*.

ary and the national. Chaeok Chun, a Korean missionary in Pakistan, comments on this tension.

> I think it is significant that today's image of the Christian missionary endeavor from the Asian receptor's point of view is an image of comfort and privilege. Hence, Asians tended to reject the missionary and misunderstand his message.*

The Irish monks of the seventh and eighth centuries were well-known for their asceticism. Their entire outfit consisted of a pilgrim's staff, a wallet, a leather water bottle, and some relics. When they received money from the wealthy, they quickly gave it away to the needy.** Is this a proper model for the contemporary missionary? In this vein, Dr. Donald McGavran suggested that "the missionary from affluent countries lives on a standard far higher than he needs to. What is called for—if we are to meet this problem head on—is an order of missionaries, celibate or married without children, who live in Bangladesh on 300 rupees a month (i.e., $10.00). But any such move is at present unthinkable, alas."***

I would, at the risk of being controversial, like to pull some thoughts together on this very important issue.

1. It does matter what nationals think about the financial profile of the missionary community. Generally, they are appalled at the gap between the living standard of themselves and the Western missionary. If we turn away from this concern with indifference, we are in danger of being insensitive to Paul's clear teaching about being a stumbling block to others.

2. Singles and couples without children can more easily make the adjustment to a simple lifestyle. This should be encouraged but not legislated.

3. Experimentation should be allowed. One couple with a newborn infant is living in a bamboo hut with a mud floor in a Muslim rural village. They should be supported, but at the same time, not made to feel embarrassment when at any time they feel withdrawal advisable.

4. Each family should be open before the Lord on this subject. They should prayerfully evaluate their own physical and emotional needs. The goal is to live as closely as possible to the style of life of their target people without adverse results to anyone in the family. Balance is a key word.

The goal is to live as closely as possible to the style of life of their target people without adverse results to anyone in the family. Balance is a key word.

---

5. Often the missionary can reside in stark simplicity in a rural area and then take an occasional weekend trip to a nearby city for relaxation and necessary shopping. This accommodation to our cultural backgrounds is not, in my view, an act of hypocrisy. We must be realistic concerning our needs and various levels of capacity to endure deprivation within foreign culture.

6. It is permissible to consider this a moot issue with missionaries, but idle criticism, a judgmental attitude, and self-righteousness must be studiously avoided. Often, missionaries living in extreme poverty or those living in great affluence are the most opinionated and self-defensive. For the sake of unity in the body, it may be wise to avoid entering into heavy discussions with these particular missionaries on this subject.

---

* Chun, C. (1977). *An exploration of the community model for Muslim missionary outreach by Asian women.* Unpublished doctoral dissertation, Fuller Theological Seminary, Pasadena.

** Just, M. (1957). *Digest of Catholic mission history* (p. 22). Maryknoll, NY: Maryknoll Publications.

*** McGavran, D. (1979, March). Letter to author.

20. How do decisions relating to one's financial "profile" on the mission field affect ministry potential?

_____

_____

_____

Housing

The day of the "mission compound" is by no means over. These Western enclaves are still found throughout the developing world. They are often misunderstood and, in some cases, despised by the nationals. A convert questioned their existence by asking, "Am I wrong if I say that mission bungalows are often a partition wall between the hearts of the people and the missionaries?"*

It is my personal conviction that remaining mission compounds should be dismantled. This would free the missionary to move into the community and share his incarnational testimony among them, rather than being shut off in a large plot of land that has a very negative appraisal in the minds of the people. It is preferable also for the Christians to scatter out among their non-Christian townspeople rather than live in a sealed-off community. Light must be diffused to be of any benefit.

Our first five-year term living in a small town in Bangladesh was a great learning and sharing experience. Just outside the bedroom window of our rented home lived a Muslim lady who was separated from her husband. Her two young daughters lived with her. Quickly we became very intimate friends. The girls were always coming over to borrow a spice or an egg. We felt free to do the same. When the youngest daughter had a raging fever, we brought her over and nursed her. From our bedroom window, we learned more about Muslim culture than scores of books could ever have taught us. A mission compound experience would not have made such a lifestyle and involvement in the community possible.

There needs to be some latitude as regards city, town, or village life. The main concern is to relate to the group with whom one is working. Student work in a university area would demand facilities quite different from a rural village setting.

Intellectual life

Missionary work has undergone a radical transformation since the end of the colonial era. New approaches and attitudes have been demanded. Pioneers like Dr. Donald McGavran have popularized the science of missiology. Hundreds of case studies and textbooks are now on the market that can be utilized as resource material. Outstanding graduate schools with mission studies include Fuller, Trinity, Columbia, Dallas, Wheaton, and Asbury. Extension study for the missionary on the field is offered through Fuller, Columbia, and Wheaton. Journals like *Evangelical Missions Quarterly* and *Missiology* keep the missionary abreast of fast-breaking concepts and practical outreaches around the world.

One relevant bit of advice to missionaries is that they should "keep an open mind, realizing that times change and one must make adjustments. Tactics of 10 years ago will not work and even those of five years ago are outdated."** It is always sad to see older missionaries become rutted and inflexible. Their orientation and allegiance to traditional methodology make it seem to them to be almost a denial of truth to move carefully into new areas of sensitive experimentation. Younger missionaries arriving on the field become frustrated. Their ideas and zeal are often lost in a patronizing, "Keep it under your hat for a few years. Experience will mellow you and

---

* Chowdhury, D. A. (1939). The Bengal church and the convert. *The Moslem World, 29,* 347.

** McCoy, J. A. (1962). *Advice from the field* (p. 144). Baltimore: Helicon Press.

mature your input." There must develop a fresh and non-threatening relationship between the senior and junior missionary. One adds experience, and the other brings the latest in theory and enthusiasm. United, they are almost unbeatable. Divided, they are a catastrophe, not only to the inner team of missionaries, but also to the perceptive onlooking national community.

Our commitment to Jesus Christ means that we want to be the best servants possible for His glory. It means stretching, not only in spirit, but also in intellect. True academic excellence leads to greater effectiveness, not to pride or snobbery. We must beware of vegetating on the mission field. Both our hearts and our minds must stay alive and alert.

21. *What should be the predominant guiding principle in selection of housing? What guiding principle applies to intellectual life?*

_____

_____

_____

Attitudes

Still fresh in my mind are the words that Harold Cook, Professor of Missions at Moody Bible Institute, told his missions class in 1959:

> Students, the single most important area of your life and ministry will be in the realm of attitudes. It is here you will either succeed or fail as a missionary. Attitudes touch every nerve end of life. Your relationship to Christ, fellow missionary, national believer, and non-Christian will be deeply affected by proper or improper attitudes.

> *Attitudes touch every nerve end of life. Your relationship to Christ, fellow missionary, national believer, and non-Christian will be deeply affected by proper or improper attitudes.*

There are a number of ingredients to a positive attitude toward nationals. One is empathy. Let me illustrate. Each morning at sunrise, a Hindu neighbor in our village would rise up, wash, and go out and stand near his cow. He would then look up at the sun, fold his hands, and go through a ceremony which involved worship of both the sun and the cow.

I watched our Hindu friend perform this ritual scores of times. One day the cow became ill and died suddenly. Grief struck the Hindu household. It was indeed a tragic loss to them. I personally disagreed with worshiping a cow, but I had somehow entered into the worldview of that Hindu. He hurt and I hurt. Quickly I learned a few appropriate phrases (as we were new in the country) and went along to his shop. I stuttered out a few incorrectly pronounced words about being sorry that his cow had died. My Hindu friend was deeply touched. Though we were worlds apart in culture and religion, yet I cared. I had for a brief moment stepped into his life.

There is an old adage that contains a great deal of truth. "The gift without the giver is bare." Missionaries are giving people. Their job demands that role. They may be engaged in relief, teaching, medical work, or some other ministry that necessitates the act of sharing. But the act of giving is inadequate in itself. What is the force behind the action? Is there love? Is there a deep concern for the other person? Has giving become a professional obligation? Have the poor or the heathen become a product to sell? These are heavy questions.

Ministry

It is time now to consider the ministerial focus of the missionary. When we turn to New Testament missions, we find that Paul's involvement was exceedingly temporary. He came, stayed a few weeks or months, or at most a few years, and left to go into new areas. The churches he planted did not remain in his control. Even if a heretical influence came into the churches, Paul could only exhort the Christians to walk in truth. He had no funds to cut off. The believers were totally free. Certainly the contemporary picture of missions is different from Paul's day.

> ***The missionary must move on as soon as possible after worshiping groups have been established.***

Leslie Newbegin writes of Paul totally entrusting leadership into local hands. He pungently comments that Paul didn't do what modern missionaries have done, "He does not build a bungalow."* George Peters maintains Paul could have rightfully said, "Here is enough work for me to do. This is where I am." Paul resisted the temptation and kept on the move.** Roland Allen points out that Paul didn't neglect the churches. He continued to visit and correspond with them. But the basic leadership responsibility was all put in local hands.***

Now, Western missionaries have a very difficult time completely turning over control to the younger churches. At times, missionaries may be withdrawn as denominational budgets flounder. Even in these cases, funds continue to go directly to the churches, thus perpetuating dependence. And worst of all, the missionaries are not deployed in a virgin area in the task of church planting. Rather, they are brought home under the camouflage that now the emerging church can take care of its own evangelistic responsibility.

In other situations, missionaries have been content to be resident in one mission station working among a small cluster of churches for a full missionary career of 35 years. In many ways, the ministry is fulfilling. One experiences joy in seeing children born, later becoming Christians, getting married, and on to settling into good professions. There is a continuity and routine about such a life. National Christians, too, feel good about having a foreign missionary around to assist them in their times of need. However, this is inadequate strategy for the '90s.

The missionary must move on as soon as possible after worshiping groups have been established. Converts must not transfer their dependence onto the missionary and away from the Lord.

> Having travailed, given birth, and cared for young churches, the missionaries (whether Tamilian or Naga or American or Australian) should turn over authority to indigenous leaders. Travail must not go on too long. It must be followed by weaning and pushing out of the nest. Then the missionary goes on and repeats the process.****

The missionary must keep before him constantly the imperative of pressing out to new frontiers.

Conclusion

I am an optimist concerning the decade of challenge that lies just before us. There will surely be opening doors, closing doors, and revolving doors within the great challenge of reaching the nations for Christ in the '90s. A beautiful picture of a ship on an ocean in the midst of a storm graces my bedroom door. The inscription reads, "A ship in a harbor is safe, but that is not what ships are built for." The front line of a battle is risky, but no victory has ever been registered in the annals of history as having been won solely by those supportive people who linger far behind the range of enemy gunfire. Our task calls for reflection, decision, and engagement.

---

* Newbegin, L. (1978). *The open secret* (p. 144). London: SPCK.

** Peters, G. W. (1977). *Evangelical missions tomorrow* (p. 162). Pasadena: William Carey Library.

*** Allen, R. (1962). *Missionary methods: St. Paul's or ours?* (p. 151). Grand Rapids: Eerdmans.

**** McGavran, D. (1979). *Ethnic realities and the church* (p. 130). Pasadena: William Carey Library.

22. How do attitudes affect ministry focus?

_____

_____

_____

Summary

"Bonding" achieves true identification with people in another culture. Much depends on this time of initiation. The attachments made during the first few days will have a critical influence on the whole process of acculturation. The unconscious attitudes formed in this early stage could well determine the effectiveness of missionaries during their entire career.

As a missionary enters a new culture, there are several roles which may be assumed. These conform to expectations created by the missionary, the sending agency, the missionary community, and the local residents. Three encounter models—the schoolhouse, the marketplace, and the courtroom—provide the response environment for new missionaries as they assume the roles of student/teacher, buyer/seller, and accused/accuser. Any of the roles taken may disappoint the expectations of one or more of the primary groups involved. The initial roles of student, buyer, and accused may provide the best environment for cross-cultural adaptation. Also affecting this process is the approach to language learning. The most effective way to learn language is to use it. The LAMP approach suggests a field method by which any language can be acquired.

The phenomenon of "closed" countries dictates that missionaries increasingly are called on to equip themselves with secular occupations to enter these areas. These vocations must be legitimate in order for missionaries to avoid external pressures, which are created when the stated reasons for being in the country do not make sense to the host population. Internal pressures are produced by ethical questions which may arise in "closed" countries. A legitimate role, a firm calling, and a clear understanding of spiritual authority are necessary to minimize these pressures. As missionaries settle into appropriate roles, issues must be resolved regarding approaches to finances, housing, intellectual life, attitudes, and ministry. A balanced approach which meets family and ministry needs, along with acceptance by the culture, must be achieved.

Integrative Assignment

This is the last assignment in the series related to the unreached people you have targeted. Imagine you have been asked to present a proposal to the leadership of your church or mission agency for launching a mission to your targeted group. In the proposal you will want to present the people and their need, suggest a process for reaching them, present a plan to implement the project, and appeal to your audience for the resources to carry out the plan. If you have completed the previous assignments, you have already done most of this work.

Your proposal should be as succinct as possible. In written form, it should be no more than three to five pages long. If you are presenting your proposal orally, limit yourself to 15 to 20 minutes. Presenting your ideas concisely, whether in written or oral form, will require considerable refinement, but such polishing is essential for an effective presentation.

WORKSHEET #6: PEOPLE GROUP PROPOSAL

Goal Statement

Write your goal succinctly and in measurable terms. Let your audience know what your proposal intends to do.

State the Need

Describe the group briefly and present their need in terms of the reached/unreached paradigm. Also state their specific felt needs which you will be using as a bridge for reaching the people. For this section, you will use the information from Worksheet # 1 (Chapter 7) and *Worksheet # 2* (Chapter 8).

Describe the Mission Process

List and describe the specific steps needed to reach the people. This is similar to what you did in *Worksheet # 3* (Chapter 9) and *Worksheet # 4* (Chapter 10). You may want to use the following outline or create one which better suits your own purposes.

1. Mobilizing the force for evangelization.

2. Establishing a presence among the people (entry strategy).

3. The identification phase (pre-evangelistic).

4. Evangelism and church planting phase.

5. Leadership development phase.

6. Maintaining a spontaneous church planting movement.

7. Closure (finishing the task and moving on).

In describing these process steps, state specific objectives which must be reached.

Present a Plan

In this section, you will want to demonstrate how you intend to implement your plan. Project what needs to happen in the next three to five years to initiate the process. This section should focus primarily on the first part of the process: mobilizing the force for evangelism. You may want to outline your plan in table form as in the example on the next page:

Three-Year Plan to Mobilize Our Church for Reaching the Tbuli

Date	Objectives
June 1994	– Contact mission agencies which may be interested in this proposal. – Ask for addresses of missionaries in the target area.
August	– Evaluate missions by their responses. – Solicit application materials. – Initiate correspondence with missionaries in the area and the established national church. – Evaluation of project by missions committee.
September	– Present project at the church's annual missions conference and begin recruiting a tentmaker team. – Write first prayer letter to friends and prospective supporters of the project.
October	– Begin weekly prayer and orientation meeting with prospective team members.
etc.	

Appeal for Resources

In this section, you will want to appeal to your audience for the resources (prayer, personnel, funds, etc.) they can provide in reaching the target group. List what you expect to receive from your audience, as well as resources which may already exist or which you are expecting from other sources such as other churches or missions, employment, friends, investors, etc. It should be clear that the resources are needed to implement the plan you have just presented.

Conclusion

Conclude your proposal with a faith statement about what you hope for if your proposal is accepted. Describe the church which will emerge (by faith), using the information from *Worksheet #5* (Chapter 11).

Questions for Reflection

1. *"Let this attitude be in you which was also in Christ Jesus" (Phil. 2:5).*

   Much of what we've spoken about in this chapter has to do with our attitude towards others. Meditate on Philippians 2:1-12. What kind of attitude have you been developing towards others? Have you learned to regard others as more important than yourself? Humility of mind is not an easy quality to develop. Yet it is the only way to greatness in the kingdom of God. Are your attitudes keeping you from becoming "great"? If so, consider asking God to change you. To reach a lost world, God needs "great" kingdom citizens. Write your thoughts below.

   _____

   _____

   _____

   _____

   _____

   _____

   _____

   _____

   _____

2. Look up Romans 1:14-16. What was Paul's basic attitude towards the gospel? Why? How should this attitude be expressed in the missionary's life?

   _____

   _____

   _____

   _____

   _____

   _____

   _____

   _____

CHAPTER 13

Keys to Communication

Our examination of cultural considerations in mission has shown us that to be effective communicators, missionaries must not only become students of the culture, but also belongers in that culture. When missionaries fail to achieve genuine identification, their ministries are often limited to areas which don't require an insider's performance. It is all too easy for missionaries to perform technical skills in missionary institutions without giving much effort to becoming belongers. Their services are useful, but as the old adage puts it, "The gift without the giver is bare."

In this chapter, we will consider the challenge that belongers face, once they have found their place in the culture. Remember, the goal of identification is to be an effective communicator. An essential part of this process is learning the language and culture, but there is more to communication than simply relating the message in understandable terms. There are keys within each culture which, if discovered, can greatly aid in the acceptance of the gospel message.

How do missionaries who have their own cultural orientation discover what makes the people of a different culture "tick"? How do they come to understand the people's "worldview," and how do they go about "contextualizing" the message? How do they discover "keys" which will make the gospel more easily accepted by the people?

I. Intercultural Communication

In the following article, David Hesselgrave presents a basic model for intercultural communication. He reviews some points already made in earlier chapters, but such review is helpful in getting a good grasp of the process involved in communicating biblical truth from culture to culture. Read this article carefully.

❑ *The Role of Culture in Communication* *

David J. Hesselgrave

There was a time in the history of man (and it was not long ago!) when the barriers between the earth's peoples seemed to be mainly physical. The problem was one of transporting men, messages, and material goods across treacherous seas, towering mountains, and trackless deserts. Missionaries knew all too well how formidable those challenges were. Today, thanks to jumbo jets, giant ocean vessels, and towering antennae, those earlier problems have been largely resolved. We can deliver a man or a Bible or a sewing machine anywhere on the face of the earth within a matter of hours, and we can transmit a sound or a picture within seconds. This does not end the matter, however. To quote Robert Park:

> One can transport words across cultural boundaries (like bricks), but interpretation will depend on the context which their differ-

ent interpreters bring to them. And that context will depend more on past experience and present temper of the people to whom the words are addressed than on the good will of the persons who report them.**

Park goes on to assert that the traits of material culture are more easily diffused than those of non-material culture. He illustrates his point by citing the example of the African chief whose immediate response upon seeing a plow in operation was, "It's worth as much as 10 wives!" One wonders how much prayer and how many hours of study and patient instruction would have been necessary to convince that chief that Christ is infinitely more valuable than plows or wives or fetishes and false gods! Yes, the barriers are, after all, very real and challenging. But they are no longer essentially physical—if, indeed, they ever were.

---

1. Why has mission emphasis changed from crossing physical barriers to crossing cultural barriers?

_____

_____

_____

The cultural barrier to missionary communication

There is a very real danger that, as our technology advances and enables us to cross geographical and national boundaries with singular ease and increasing frequency, we may forget that *it is the cultural barriers which are the most formidable*. The gap between our technological advances and our communication skills is perhaps one of the most chal-

lenging aspects of modern civilization. Western diplomats are beginning to realize that they need much more than a knowledge of their message and a good interpreter or English-speaking national. Many educators have come to the position that cross-cultural communication is a *sine qua non* (absolute prerequisite) for citizenship in this new world. Missionar-

---

* Hesselgrave, D. J. (1978). *Communicating Christ cross-culturally* (pp. 67-78). Grand Rapids: Zondervan.

** Park, R. (1966). Reflections on communication and culture. In B. Berelson & M. Janowitz (Eds.), *Reader in public opinion and communication* (2nd ed.) (p. 167). New York: Free Press.

ies now understand that much more than a microphone and increased volume is involved in penetrating cultural barriers.

Unfortunately, intercultural communication is as complex as the sum total of human differences. The word "culture" is a very inclusive term. It takes into account linguistic, political, economic, social, psychological, religious, national, racial, and other differences. Communication reflects all these differences, for, as Clyde Kluckhohn says, "Culture is a way of thinking, feeling, believing. It is the group's knowledge stored up for future use."*

Or, as Louis Luzbetak writes:

> Culture is a design for living. It is a plan according to which society adapts itself to its physical, social, and ideational environment. A plan for coping with the physical environment would include such matters as food production and all technological knowledge and skill. Political systems, kinships and family organization, and law are examples of social adaptation, a plan according to which one is to interact with his fellows. Man copes with his ideational environment through knowledge, art, magic, science, philosophy, and religion. Cultures are but different answers to essentially the same human problems.**

Missionaries must come to an even greater realization of the importance of culture in communicating Christ. In the final analysis, they can effectively communicate to the people of any given culture to the extent that they understand that culture (language being but one aspect of culture). Before missionaries go to a foreign country the first time, they tend to think primarily of the great distance they must travel to get to their field of labor. Often it means traveling thousands of miles from their homes. But once they arrive on the field, they begin to realize that in this modern age it is nothing to travel great distances. The great problem to be faced is the last 18 inches! What a shock! The missionary has studied for many years. He has traveled 10,000 miles to communicate the gospel of Christ. He now stands face to face with the people of his respondent culture, and he is unable to communicate the most simple message! Ask experienced missionaries about their frustrating experiences on the field, and most of them will respond by telling of their problems in communication.

In the final analysis, missionaries can effectively communicate to the people of any given culture to the extent that they understand that culture.

Missionaries should prepare for this frustration. They have been preoccupied with their message! By believing it, they were saved. By studying it, they have been strengthened. Now they want to preach it to those who have not heard it, for that is a great part of what it means to be a missionary! But before they can do so effectively, they must study again—not just the language, but also the audience. They must learn before they can teach and listen before they can speak. They need to know the message for the world, but also the world in which the message must be communicated.

---

* Kluckhohn, C. (1949). *Mirror for man* (p. 23). New York: Whittlesev.

** Luzbetak, L. J. (1963). *The church and cultures* (pp. 60-61). Techny, IL: Divine Word.

2. *Missionaries have a message to deliver, but what must happen before they can deliver it effectively?*

_____

_____

_____

A three-culture model of missionary communication

Eugene Nida of the American Bible Society has made important contributions toward an understanding of the communication problems of the missionary. The discussion and diagram in his chapter on "Structure of Communication" furnish the basis for our consideration of a "three-culture model" of missionary communication.*

As a communicator, the missionary stands on middle ground and looks in two directions (see Figure 13-1). In the first place, he looks to the Scriptures. The message is not really his. He did not originate it. He was not there when it was first given. His own words are not "inspired" in the biblical sense. He cannot say as could the apostle:

> What was from the beginning, what we have heard, what we have seen with our eyes, what we beheld and our hands handled, concerning the Word of life—and the life was manifested

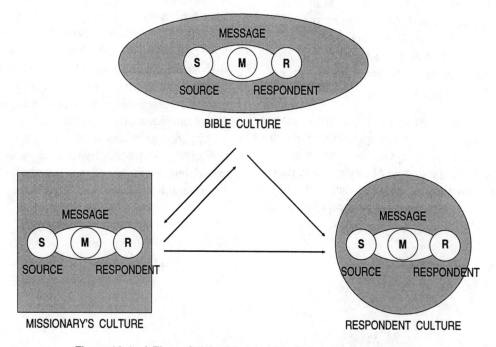

Figure 13-1. A Three-Culture Model of Missionary Communication

---

* Nida, E. A. (1960). *Message and mission: The communication of the Christian faith* (pp. 33-58). New York: Harper & Row.

and we have seen and bear witness and proclaim to you the eternal life, which was with the Father and was manifested to us (1 John 1:1-2).

He knows that he must be diligent to present himself "approved to God as a workman who does not need to be ashamed, handling accurately the word of truth" (2 Tim. 2:15). He knows that he must study and obey the Word of God. He is aware that there are some very solemn warnings to be absolutely faithful to that original message:

> I testify to everyone who hears the words of the prophecy of this book: if anyone adds to them, God shall add to him the plagues which are written in this book; and if anyone takes away from the words of the book of this prophecy, God shall take away his part from the tree of life and from the holy city, which are written in this book (Rev. 22:18-19).

In summary, in relationship to the biblical message, the missionary is simply a messenger, an ambassador—a secondary, never a primary source.

In the second place, when the missionary lifts up his eyes and looks to the fields, he sees people—millions of them—who need the message. If only they could understand their real need! If only their worship were directed to the true God! If only their faith were to be placed in the one Savior and Lord. If only they could be reached, instructed, and persuaded to repent. It is these of whom his Lord spoke when He said, "All authority has been given to Me in heaven and in earth. Go, therefore, and make disciples of all the nations, baptizing them in the name of the Father and the Son and the Holy Spirit, teaching them to observe all that I commanded you" (Matt. 28:18-20). But looking at his respondent culture, he realizes that he will never be an indigenous source. The language of that culture will always have an element of strangeness. That culture will always be his adopted culture, never his native culture.

It is this intermediate position, this looking in two directions, that constitutes the special challenge and unusual opportunity of the missionary as an ambassador of Christ. It is a special challenge because of the comprehensive and demanding nature of the task. It is an unusual opportunity because it means

giving the one needful message to those who have not understood or believed it.

Let's take another look at what is involved from the perspective of communication. At the primary level, the missionary message is the message of the Bible. It was given by God through the apostles and prophets in the languages and cultural contexts of the Bible. For the sake of simplification we will say that "Bible culture" includes all cultural contexts in which the message of the Bible was originally given, whether Judah at the time of Ezra, Jerusalem at the time of Christ, or Athens at the time of Paul. In those cultural contexts there were sources (Ezra, our Lord Christ, or Paul), messages, and respondents. The sources of the messages were identified with the cultures we have labeled "Bible culture." They encoded the messages in forms that were understandable in those cultures to respondents who were members of those cultures.

In relationship to the biblical message, the missionary is simply a messenger, an ambassador—a secondary, never a primary source.

At the secondary level, the missionary is a citizen of a quite different culture, whether his home address is in London, Chicago, or even Tokyo. He has been brought up in his own culture and has been schooled in its language, worldview, and value system. He has received the Christian message in the context of culture as it was communicated by a source who most likely was a citizen of the culture. We will label that culture the "missionary's culture."

At the tertiary level, there are people in still another culture with its own sources, messages, and respondents. We will label this third culture the "respondent culture" (and, occasionally, the "target culture"). In relationship to this respondent culture, the missionary has immediate and ultimate objectives. First, he desires to communicate Christ in such a way that the people will understand, repent, and believe the gospel. Second, he wants to commit the message to "faithful men who will be able to teach others" (2 Tim. 2:2) in culturally relevant terms that only they, in the final analysis, can command.

3. How are three cultures involved in communicating the gospel cross-culturally?

_____

_____

_____

4. What must the missionary be able to do in order to transfer the message successfully from the source culture to the respondent culture?

_____

_____

_____

The missionary task can now be seen in clearer perspective. Starting from the missionary's culture, cultural boundaries must be traversed in two directions. The missionary's first responsibility is to study the Scriptures, in the original languages if possible, but always in terms of the "Bible culture" context. Any sound system of hermeneutics must take into account the cultural context in which the message was originally communicated, the background and syntax and style, the characteristics of the audience, and the special circumstances in which the message was given. This process is essential to Bible exegesis. The important thing, after all, is not what the Bible reader or interpreter feels the meaning to be; the important thing is what the source intended that his respondents should understand by his message! The Bible interpreter is constantly tempted to project the meanings of his own cultural background into the exegetical process with the result that the original meaning is missed or perverted. This temptation is heightened by the fact that, for the most part, all of us learn our own culture quite unconsciously and uncritically. Therefore, there is the ever-present tendency to generalize from our own experience.

Most Bible readers and interpreters will find sufficient reason for confessing to their weakness in this area. For example, a friend of mine recently joined a tour group in Palestine. While walking under a tree in the Jordan Valley, the guide reached up, picked some fruit, peeled away the husk, and ate the fruit. As he did so, he turned to the group and said,

"According to the Bible, John the Baptist's diet consisted of this fruit and wild honey. This is the locust." Almost to a person the members of the group expressed astonishment. They had always supposed that the locusts mentioned in Matthew and Mark were grasshoppers! As a matter of fact, they probably were correct. The point is that they had not thought of this second possibility because in their own culture "grasshopper locusts" are prevalent while "locust fruit" is not!

Another example of this tendency to interpret the Word of God through cultural glasses related to the Authorized Version's translation of our Lord's instructions to His disciples at the Passover meal, "Drink ye all of it" (Matt. 26:27, KJV). Perhaps most Protestant congregations in America (and not a few ministers) understand this to mean that all the wine is to be consumed, though little significance is attached to the phrase in view of the fact that the elements usually come in such miniscule proportions that consuming all is not a very challenging task! How much more significant is the original meaning which, properly translated, would be: "Drink from it, all of you" (NASB) or, "All of you drink some of it" (Williams). Two facts of American culture militate against this original meaning, however. First, most of us do not drink from a common cup in the manner to which the disciples were accustomed. And second, the syntax of the English language as spoken by most Americans makes it unlikely that they will decode the message in accordance with the original meaning.

5. Describe the problem one's own cultural background produces in trying to understand the original meaning of Bible texts. How is this problem overcome?

_____

_____

_____

_____

Proper exegesis, however, is but the beginning of missionary responsibility. The missionary must now look in another direction—the direction of the respondent culture with its own worldview, value system, and codes of communication. He must remember that respondents in that culture have imbibed as deeply of its particular ideas and values as he has of his. It is likely that they will be more ignorant of the "Bible culture" than non-Christian members of the "missionary's culture" are. Further, they will exhibit the same tendency to generalize and project their own cultural understandings into the message of the Bible culture. The missionary task, therefore, is to properly exegete (decode) the biblical message. With minimal intrusion of his own cultural understanding, he must encode the message in a culturally relevant form in the target culture so that the respondents will understand as much as possible of the original message. This is not the simple task that many have supposed. Consider what is involved in translating Revelation 3:20 in terms which are meaningful to the Zanaki people.

One cannot say to the Zanaki people along the winding shores of sprawling Lake Victoria, "Behold, I stand at the door and knock" (Rev. 3:20). This would mean that Christ was declaring Himself to be a thief, for in Zanaki land thieves generally make it a practice to knock on the door of a hut which they hope to burglarize; and if they hear any movement of noise inside, they dash off into the dark. An honest man will come to a house and call the name of the person inside, and this way identify himself by his voice. Accordingly, in the Zanaki translation it is necessary to say,

"Behold, I stand at the door and call." This wording may be slightly strange to us, but the meaning is the same. In each case Christ is asking people to open the door. He is no thief, and He will not force an entrance; He knocks and in Zanaki "He calls." If anything, the Zanaki expression is a little more personal than our own.*

The missionary task is to properly decode the biblical message. He must encode the message in a culturally relevant form in the target culture so that the respondents will understand as much as possible of the original message.

Or, consider the strangeness of the phrase "devours widows' houses" in a still different respondent culture:

To understand a strange culture one must enter as much as possible into the very life and viewpoint of the native people. Otherwise, a person will not realize how ridiculous it is to talk to Indians of southern Mexico about scribes who "devour widows' houses" (Mark 12:40). Their houses are often made with cornstalk walls and grass roofs, and farm animals do eat them when fodder gets scarce, so that people guard against hungry cows breaking in to eat down a house. "Devouring widows' houses" is no bold metaphor in some places but a real danger. Hence the native

---

* Nida, E. A. (1952). *God's Word in man's language* (pp. 45-46). New York: Harper & Row.

reader wonders, "What were these 'scribes' anyway? Was this just a name for starved, ravenous cattle?" In such cases one must translate "destroy widows' houses."*

There remains still another important aspect of missionary communication. The ultimate goal of the missionary is to raise up effective sources of the Christian message from within the target culture. Missionary communication that does not keep this goal in mind is myopic. The world mission of the

> *For the most part, missionaries have not communicated Christ's concern for the people of still other respondent cultures.*

church has been greatly weakened by lack of vision at this point. It is not so much that missionaries have been remiss in encouraging the emergence of Christian leadership in the Third World. But it has been all too easy to encourage (perhaps unconsciously) those leaders to become Western in their thinking and approach. After a course in cross-cultural communication, a national pastor of five years of experience confessed that throughout his ministry he had preached "Western sermons" to Asian audiences. After all, he had learned the gospel from American missionaries: he had studied his theology, homiletics, and evangelism from English and German textbooks; and the great percentage of his Christian training had been in the language and other patterns of Western culture. No wonder his Christian communication lacked "respondent cultural relevance" even though the respondent culture in this case was his own culture!

Furthermore, for the most part, missionaries have not communicated Christ's concern for the people of still other respondent cultures. As a result, many Christians in Hong Kong have little vision for Indonesia, and many Christians in Venezuela exhibit little concern for unbelievers in Peru. When missionary vision is born (and it has been born in many churches in the Third World), it seldom occurs as a result of the ministry of the North American or European missionary. Though the state of affairs is ironic and deplorable, it is understandable. The missionary's own missionary concern has been expressed in terms of *his* target culture. Unless he keeps his eyes on the fields, unless he sees the whole world as the object of God's love, and unless he communicates this to national Christians, *their vision will tend to be limited by his own!*

6. What is the ultimate goal of missionary communication, and how is this goal most often frustrated?

_____

_____

_____

7. The author points out that for the most part missionaries have neglected to communicate Christ's concern for the people of still other respondent cultures. What is the negative result?

_____

_____

_____

---

* Nida, E. A. (1952). *God's Word in man's language* (p. 45). New York: Harper & Row.

Decoding and encoding the gospel message are complex tasks and require a great deal of technical skill. In the following excerpt, Hesselgrave outlines seven dimensions of the holistic process of cross-cultural communication.

❑ *Seven Dimensions of Cross-Cultural Communication* *

David J. Hesselgrave

1. Worldviews: Ways of perceiving the world

No one sees the world exactly as it is. Each one sees it through the tinted glasses of his own worldview. Most people neither carefully evaluate their own particular worldview, nor meticulously interpret messages that come to them from sources with other worldviews. In other words, few people take off the glasses of their own worldview to examine them. And perhaps still fewer people decode "cross-worldview" messages in the light of—or by "putting on the glasses of"—the message source. If *respondents* are not disposed to exchange glasses in order to decode cross-cultural messages correctly, *sources* must assume the responsibility of encoding messages with the worldview of the respondents in mind.

2. Cognitive processes: Ways of thinking

Studies show that the ability to think clearly is a function of social or educational opportunity rather than of ethnic origin. All normal people of all cultures have the ability to think. But they think differently. People in different cultures tend to arrive at conclusions through differing thought processes.

For example, most missionaries will agree with the Hindu notion that the mystery of divine reality eludes the mystery of speech and symbol. But the fundamental question is not whether there is a sense in which that notion is true. Rather, the question is this: Does true knowledge of God come primarily through subjective experience or objective revelation?

Here again, the missionary must *help* the Hindu understand. But, humanly speaking, that is possible only as he himself takes the Hindu way of thinking into account when communicating Christ.

3. Linguistic forms: Ways of expressing ideas

Of all the seven dimensions of cross-cultural communication, language is the one that is the most obvious and the one with which the missionary is best prepared (in terms of awareness) to cope. But language is more important than many missionaries realize.

Languages tend to reflect that which is important in a given culture. For example, European languages reflect the primary importance of time in Euro-American culture. A man was, is, or will be sick. Languages that by virtue of their grammatical structures do not require this distinction between past, present, and future may seem strange to Westerners. But they are instructive at the very point of their strangeness. "Learning the language," then, means more than learning enough of the receptor language to transliterate English sentences into it. Languages constitute veritable gold mines of information about the people and cultures that employ them.

4. Behavioral patterns: Ways of acting

William S. Howell has asserted that "the Ugly American award is won more often by failing to meet expectations of appropriate behavior than by misusing the local language." Whether the newcomer to a neighborhood visits others or waits for them to visit him, the ways in which one receives

---

* Hesselgrave, D. J. (1978). *Communicating Christ cross-culturally* (pp. 164-168). Grand Rapids: Zondervan.

guests and gifts, public behavior vis-à-vis members of the opposite sex—thousands of such items are matters of cultural definition. Since they are learned informally for the most part, they are seldom pondered and justified. They simply constitute ways in which people "ought" to act.

To be sure, as a Christian the missionary cannot accept all the behavior patterns of any given culture. But there is nothing inherently wrong with the great majority of cultural ways of doing things. "Christian" or "un-Christian," correct or incorrect—an inventory of cultural behavior, therefore, is essential for the missionary who would communicate Christ.

5. Social structures: Ways of interacting

Men and women not only have ways of *acting* according to accepted codes of conduct, they also have ways of *interacting* on the basis of where they fit in the social structure. The conventions of social structure dictate which channels of communication are open and which are closed; who talks to whom, in what way, and with what effect; and when one communicates which type of message.

By way of example, consider the familiar story of Jesus and the Samaritan woman in John 4. Given some knowledge of the societal arrangements and relationships in that time and place, we can understand why they met at a well, why the woman

> *Missionaries should no more think of communicating Christ in a society without a societal map than they would think of motoring through a country without a road map!*

expressed surprise when Jesus spoke to her, and why it was particularly unusual that he would ask a favor of her (cf. v. 9). Moreover, we can make some educated guesses as to why the woman went to the men in the city and invited them to investigate the claims of Christ (cf. v. 29).

A "map" of societal arrangements is also a guide to communication. Missionaries should no more think of communicating Christ in a society without a societal map than they would think of motoring through a country without a road map!

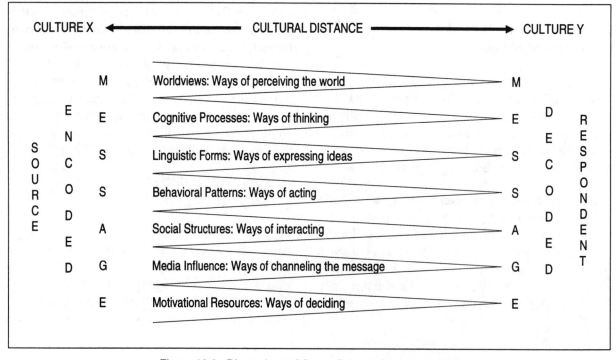

Figure 13-2. Dimensions of Cross-Cultural Communication

6. Media influence: Ways of channeling the message

In times past, the emphases in communication have been on sources and respondents, the contexts in which messages are sent and received, and the messages themselves—their content, organization, and style. Recently we have become increasingly aware of the fact that the media that are used to transmit messages are by no means neutral. First, they affect the message in the transmission of it. Second, in one sense, they themselves constitute messages.

Take, as an obvious example, the case of a missionary who enters an illiterate society with the objective of reducing the language to writing, teaching literacy, translating the Bible, and establishing a Christian church. Very little imagination is required to realize that the difference between the spoken and the written word will be a major factor in communicating Christ in that culture. But beyond that, think of the tremendous changes that will be set in motion with the introduction of written messages!

Missionaries tend to think of media in simplistic terms such as message availability, audience size, and interest factors. But far more is involved.

7. Motivational resources: Ways of deciding

The missionary who communicates Christ presses for a verdict as did his first-century counterparts, the apostles. Of course, people of all cultures have to make many decisions. But again, the ways in which people of various cultures think of decision making and the ways in which they arrive at decisions are very diverse.

Think, for example, of the case of the American missionary who presents a Chinese with the opportunity to receive Christ. If the decision is *for* Christ, the missionary will be elated and grateful. But imagine his disappointment when sometime later, the Chinese convert does an about-face and evidences a lapse of faith. The response of the missionary is predictable. But it never occurs to him that his Chinese "disciple in the rough" may be simply reflecting the philosophy of Confucius (not because he is Confucian but because he is Chinese) who said, "The superior man goes through his life without any one preconceived course of action or any taboo. He merely decides for the moment what is the right thing to do." To point out the problem is not to argue for the correctness of Confucian, or Chinese, or American approaches to decision making. Rather, it is a plea for understanding and preparedness.

8. What must a missionary do and/or be in order to demonstrate "understanding and preparedness" as a cross-cultural communicator?

II. Putting on Worldview Glasses

In this section, we return to Hesselgrave's writings, this time to deepen our understanding of worldview and its critical importance to the missionary endeavour.

❑ *Fitting Two Thirds World Believers With Christian Worldview Glasses* *

David J. Hesselgrave

Every day it becomes more apparent that millions of Christians worldwide still see the world through glasses that distort and discolor it. They profess Christianity but do not possess a Christian worldview. At the same time there is mounting evidence

---

Millions of Christians worldwide still see the world through glasses that distort and discolor it.

---

that some Christian leaders at least are becoming aware of the problem and are trying to do something about it—trying to fit Two Thirds World Christians with Christian worldview glasses, so to speak.

That sounds a bit cryptic. What do we mean?

Worldview glasses

The metaphor is that of Christian philosopher Norman Geisler.** He says that in the process of learning one's culture (the technical term is "enculturation"), one obtains worldview glasses. In other words, one comes to perceive the world—God, man, nature, history, values, and so forth—in a way prescribed by one's own culture and/or subculture. Thus the majority of Asian Indians will grow up to think of the world as inhabited by many gods, of birth and rebirth as being the destiny of man as determined by his *karma*, and of history as an almost interminable cyclical series progressing toward reabsorption into the *Brahman* or ultimate reality. As Indians study and mature, the nuances, values, and obligations of this Hindu worldview will be elaborated and clarified.

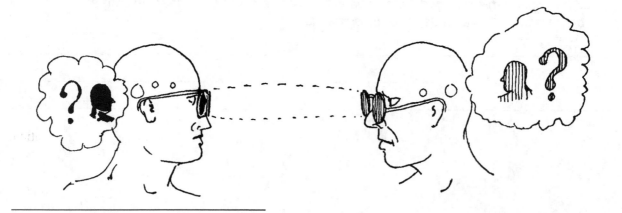

---

* Hesselgrave, D. J. (1987, June). Fitting Two Thirds World believers with Christian worldview glasses. *Journal of the Evangelical Theological Society*, 215-222.

** Geisler, N. L. (1978). Some philosophical perspectives on missionary dialogue. In D. J. Hesselgrave (Ed.), *Theology and missions: Papers given at Trinity Consultation No. 1* (pp. 241-258). Grand Rapids: Baker Book House.

The same process of worldview acquisition occurs in all cultures. Everyone everywhere receives worldview glasses. The problem is that, for the most part, their worldview glasses do not reflect the world as it actually is but nevertheless determine how the wearer will actually perceive it.

There is something else that we must understand about culturally prescribed worldview glasses: They are exceedingly difficult to remove and re-place. Once put on, it is as though they were secured by super glue. An attempt to remove one's original worldview glasses and try to put on the glasses of a different worldview will necessarily involve considerable effort and even pain. From a Christian perspective, the tragic result of this fact is that without replacing old glasses it is impossible to see in a Christian way, no matter how sincere one may be in his or her determination to be a Christian.

9. *What is meant by the term "worldview glasses"?*

_____

_____

_____

Worldview and contextualization

Traditionally we missionaries have carried on our mission by introducing the gospel in a rather piece-meal fashion: translating this or that New Testament Gospel, preaching on this or that Bible passage, teaching from one or another Bible book as we see fit. Even when we have attempted to be more systematic, we have usually divided up Christian teaching in a topical fashion dealing with God, sin, salvation, the Christian life, and so forth. This approach is endemic in Western instruction, but it is not well-suited to the rest of the world. (And perhaps it is not nearly so effective in the West as we have thought previous.) As a matter of fact, our Western approaches are so ingrained in us that the reader may wonder what alternative would be superior.

In a tremendously insightful little book, H. R. Weber provides us with an illustration of how Christian communicators can go about the business of teaching the Bible in a way that better equips believers to adopt a truly Christian worldview.*

Weber's account takes us to Luwuk-Banggai, Indonesia. Very remote, the area was almost untouched until this century. Then in 1912, Muslim traders tried to convert to Islam some of its 100,000 scattered natives. Partly in response to the pleas of the Dutch government, the Reformed State Church sent a minister to the area. Over a few years he baptized thousands without giving them proper instruction or follow-up.

Converts were of three types: (1) Some were sincere, (2) some felt under obligation to adopt the religion of the rulers, and (3) some became Christians in order to remain pagan. (Explanation: They thought that they had to accept either Christianity or Islam, and only the former would allow them to keep the pigs and dogs that were so important to their animistic sacrifices.)

After World War II there were 30,000 nominal Christians in numerous churches in Luwuk-Banggai. They were Christians and congregations without the Word of God, and most of them were nonliterates. In 1952, Weber, who was an experienced missionary with a knowledge of the local language, was asked to go and teach the basics of the Bible. He was given no money and no helpers except indigenous personnel.

---

* Weber, H. R. (1957). *The communication of the gospel to illiterates: Based on a missionary experience in Indonesia.* London: BCM.

The church was already divided into seven districts. It was decided to hold short Bible courses in each district. A team of district evangelists and ministers was chosen, and each congregation was invited to send some leaders to a five-day Bible course in a central village. They were to pay for this course in money or in kind. Those who attended had, on the average, three years of elementary education. The format was simple but profound. By way of introduction, Weber stressed the importance of the Bible in the life of the individual Christian and local congregation. The first evening, the travel route to be taken through the Bible was sketched: from creation in Genesis to the kingdom of God in Revelation with Christ at the center of the whole, and including the fall, the covenants with Israel, the church, and the second coming. The four succeeding days highlighted Genesis 3:1, Exodus 19:1-6, Luke 2:18-48, and Acts 1:6-11.

---

10.   How did the format of Weber's Bible "course" differ from the typical Western approach?

_____

_____

_____

Each day began with worship, the reading of the Scripture passage for the day, and prayer for guidance. Then the passage for the day was studied in small groups (making sure it was linked with preceding studies). Each group reported its findings, and a summary was drawn up. (Later this was to be given to each student to aid him as a catechist.) Afternoons were spent in discussing community life, the meaning of baptism and communion, evangelism, and so forth. The evenings were devoted to a discussion of Christians in a tribal community, modern Islam, and the world.

> **Weber began to look upon the nonliterates as artists. He began to see himself as a stunted intellectual with but one method of communication—pallid, abstract ideas.**

On the last evening the witnessing theme was exemplified by inviting the whole village to a special gathering. The temple in Jerusalem was "created," and Psalms 24 and 100 were recited antiphonally by a "priest" and "Levite" on one side and a chorus of men and women on the other. Parables such as Luke 10:30-37 were mimed, and people were asked to guess the meaning. Then the parable was read from Scripture and explained, and a challenge was given. This was followed by hymns and tea-time. Finally, the Genesis 1 lesson of the first evening was balanced with Revelation 21 with its vision of a recreated world of peace and righteousness.

Weber himself made a great discovery as time progressed. He kept hearing about tremendous Christians who would like to attend the studies but could not do so because they were *buta kuruf* ("blind with regard to letters"—that is, nonliterate). Realizing that the great majority came in that category, Weber started talking to some nonliterates and discovered that, though he spoke their language, communication was very difficult. When he asked the meaning of a word, they would not respond with a synonym or an abstract description. Instead they would use words to paint a picture that gave the exact meaning. When describing a person, they would not talk about his character but rather would tell a few experiences that pointed up the kind of person he was. Weber began to look upon the nonliterates as artists. He began to see himself as a stunted intellectual with but one method of communication—pallid, abstract ideas. He became a pupil in order to learn how to communicate picturesquely and dramatically rather than intellectually and verbally.

Weber then tried out his discovery in the nonliterate village of Taulan. There the whole village assembled. Weber asked the heathen priest to tell the story of creation as the tribe knew it. Then he used simple drawings on a blackboard to illustrate the Genesis story. He did the same with the fall and other biblical events. Finally Weber instituted Bible study courses for nonliterates on the model above but modified by his discovery. Later in Java and Bali he added the use of symbols—contrasting the Buddhist *zoetrope*, the Taoist sign, and the hammer and sickle with various Christian symbols such as the cross and the crown.

11. *What can we learn from Weber's "discovery" regarding his own communication style and his response to it?*

_____

_____

_____

Principles to be observed

If we can bring ourselves to the difficult admission that we have contributed to the problem of tainted glasses (and that Weber's approach certainly has much to commend it), we are in a position to review some essential principles. In a unique way, Weber takes us back to the way God Himself communicated His truth to us when He gave us the Holy Scriptures. The Bible, after all, is not primarily a book of systematic theology. Neither is it a series of disconnected episodes without meaningful arrangement or continuity. It is a divine record that (even

---

The Bible is the revelation of all that is necessary—and nothing that is superfluous—for the manufacture and fitting of new, Christian worldview glasses.

---

allowing for human instrumentality in the arrangement of its books) progresses from essential beginnings through all-important events and divine disclosures to a prophetic ending and new beginning. In short, it is the revelation of all that is necessary—and nothing that is superfluous—for the manufacture and fitting of new, Christian worldview glasses.

With that in mind, what should we avoid and what should we incorporate into our discipling approaches? Missionary experiences, criticisms coming from Two Thirds World theologians, the pattern of biblical theology that follows the unfolding of God's will and way to mankind, the low level of Bible literacy in many of our churches—all of these factors conspire to teach us the following principles.

1. *It is a mistake to concentrate on only one book of the Bible in translating the Bible into new languages.* It is better to select certain specially important passages—passages that can be used to tell the larger story of God's dealings with people over the course of time—and translate them. I am aware of the fact that some translators are now adopting this approach. It is to be hoped that still more of them will do so in the future, for in so doing translators lay the groundwork for the kind of instruction being advocated here.

2. *Instead of choosing disconnected Bible stories or even logically connected Bible topics in order to reach the Christian faith, the continuity and progressive nature of biblical revelation should be preserved in initiating Christian instruction.*

In giving us the Bible that He gave us and in the way He gave it to us, God accomplished some very important objectives that we tend to forget. First, He kept doctrine in the context of life situations and in the context of history. Second, He provided us with the big picture into which the small scenes fit. Third, He provided us with a progression in which more complex and advanced teachings are built upon those that are more elementary.

We forget all this at our peril. People in the Two Thirds World are capable of mastering large quantities of material when it is presented in narrative and pictorial forms. They identify with the Old Testament readily because it speaks to their situation. The sacrificial system of Genesis and Leviticus has special relevance. The idolatry of heathen tribes—and even Israel's tendency to take and make false gods—do not require lengthy explanation and careful redefinition. Ancestors, ancestral spirits, witchcraft, and the like are aspects of daily life. Polygamy is seen as a biblical problem as well as a contemporary one. Abraham's resort to cohabitation with Hagar in order to secure a son and realize God's promise is seen in a new light. So are God's prohibitions against intermarriage with heathen tribes and the evil consequences of, for example, Solomon's disregard of that prohibition. The refusal of Daniel and his friends to bow to Nebuchadnezzar's image speaks to a fundamental issue in the Two Thirds World. And the distinction between true and false prophets is of the essence.

3. *As one teaches, it is important to compare and contrast biblical history and truth with cultural myths and errors.* Of course this must be done accurately and sensitively. But the old mythological framework must be shattered (even though it likely contains some important elements of truth) if the biblical worldview is to

---

The old mythological framework must be shattered (even though it likely contains some important elements of truth) if the biblical worldview is to predominate.

---

predominate. Once the biblical worldview is in the ascendancy, the commitment of Two Thirds World Christians will take on an entirely new configuration. A person's ability to cope with the common trials of life, to say nothing of life's unexpected catastrophes, is in large part determined by his or her ability to integrate those trials and tragedies into an all-encompassing worldview and thereby find some meaning for them.

The importance of worldview can hardly be overstated. Hindus are able to live with monstrous inequalities and inequities because they can be meaningfully related to *karma* and *samsara* (the wheel of birth and rebirth). Tribalists counter "bad medicine" with "good medicine" and cope with tragedy and death by ascertaining and avenging their cause. Similarly, Christians can confront evil and overcome temptation, not only because of the indwelling Spirit, but also because they understand how God deals with evil in history and how He will deal with it in the future.

At one time or another most of us have had the experience of putting a jigsaw puzzle together—not just the simple one designed for children but the complex one designed to challenge adult ingenuity for seemingly endless hours. If so, we have probably discovered that the saving factor in the situation was the small reproduction of the completed picture on the cover of the box. By observing the subject, outline, and shadings of the completed picture, we were aided in discovering how to fit miniscule pieces into the whole. Ultimately we were able to put them in just the right place and experience a significant degree of satisfaction in doing so.

In like manner, Christians quite naturally relate new experiences—particularly those experiences that cry out for an understandable explanation and an appropriate response—to whatever worldview they know best. In terms of the jigsaw analogy, they fit their experiences into the picture that is most familiar to them. To return to our earlier metaphor, they perceive their experiences in a way dictated by the worldview glasses they happen to be wearing at the time, and they respond accordingly.

In the light of our present knowledge of our Two Thirds World churches, missionary and national teachers who are serious about discipling the nations by baptizing and "teaching them to observe all that I commanded you" (Matt. 28:20) will want to give careful attention to ways of fitting Two Thirds World believers with Christian worldview glasses.

12. *Why does the author suggest that the sequence and essential nature of biblical revelation be preserved in teaching new Christians?*

_____

_____

_____

_____

13. *Why is it so critical that new believers understand the Christian worldview? What can happen if they continue to function with their previous worldview?*

_____

_____

_____

Hesselgrave has eloquently argued for the need to contextualize the gospel message and, in so doing, to establish a firm basis for the developing Christian worldview in the new believer. In the following section, he outlines four fundamental elements in the process of contextualizing the message.

❑ *Worldview and the Substance of the Missionary Message* *

David J. Hesselgrave

The Christian message is universal. It is for all men irrespective of race, language, culture, or circumstance. Some have therefore naively assumed that this ends the matter. If one knows what the gospel is, all that remains is the motivation to deliver it. There is, of course, "one Lord, one faith, one baptism, one God and Father of all" (Eph. 4:5-6). But without betraying that unique message in any way, the gospel writers and preachers of the New Testament demonstrated a remarkable variegation in their communication of it, not only in style but in substance.

It would seem that in the New Testament, missionary communication involved either making a case for Christian claims from the Old Testament, in the case of those who held to the Judeo-Christian worldview, or filling in the information concerning God, His world, man, and history which the Old Testament affords, in the case of those who had non-Judeo-Christian worldviews. Notice that in the partially recorded discourses of Paul at Lystra (Acts 14:15-17) and on Mars Hill (17:22-31), Paul begins with the Creator God who was unknown to those Gentile polytheists. Paul's approach is elaborated in the first chapters of Romans.

We conclude, therefore, that while certain general statements can be made concerning the substance of the gospel (e.g., 1 Cor. 15:1-9) and the spiritual need of man as a sinner (e.g., Rom. 3:9-18), the communication of these truths in specific situations involves a contextualization process which includes *definition*, *selection*, *adaptation*, and *application*.

* Hesselgrave, D. J. (1978). *Communicating Christ cross-culturally* (pp. 134-140). Grand Rapids: Zondervan.

Definition

One of the disastrous aspects of man's sin was that he did not retain God in his knowledge. As a result, man's understanding has been perverted in precisely those areas where divine revelation is crystal clear. The true God is excluded, but false gods abound. Men distinguish between good and evil in some way but not in accordance with the biblical view. A majority of men believe themselves to be immortal in some sense of the term, but the forms of immortality vary greatly with worldviews. Geoffrey Bull's reflections on presenting Christ to Tibetan Buddhists illustrates the point well:

> The expansion of the Tibetan language came with the growth of Buddhist philosophy; thus, words used often represent two distinct concepts. We take up and use a word in Tibetan, unconsciously giving it a Christian content. For them, however, it has a Buddhist content. We speak of God. In our minds this word conveys to us the concept of the Supreme and Eternal Spirit, Creator and Sustainer of all things, whose essence is love, whose presence is all holy, and whose ways are all righteous. For them, the Tibetan word god means nothing of the kind. We speak of prayer, the spiritual communion between God our Father and His children. For them prayer is a repetition of abstruse formulae and mystic phrases handed down from time immemorial. We speak of sin. For them the main emphasis is in the condemnation of killing animals.

> When I was at Batang I saw an open-air performance of a Buddhist play. One of the chief sins depicted there was the catching of fish. When I asked the special significance of the "transgression," I was told, "Oh, fishes mustn't be killed, they can't speak," meaning, I presume, that they utter no sound. It is a common sight to see a man, when killing a yak, at the same time muttering his "prayers" furiously. Gross immorality is also condemned by the most thoughtful lamas, but

> rarely publicly. We speak of the Savior. They think of Buddha or the Dalai Lama. We speak of God being a Trinity. They will say: "Yes, god the Buddha, god the whole canon of Buddhist scripture, and god the whole body of the Buddhist priesthood." We speak of man's spirit being dead in sin and his thus being cut off from God. They cannot understand. A person, they say, is only soul and body. What do you mean by the third concept, a man's spirit? When a man dies, they believe his soul escapes by one of the nine holes in his body; we know nothing of his spirit, they say. We speak of a revelation from God, His own Word which we are commanded to believe, and they know no word but the vast collection of Buddhist sayings, which only one in a thousand even vaguely understands. Those who have studied them believe that only in the exercise of the human intellect, in meditation and contemplation over a very long period, can one begin to enter into the deep things of the "spirit." What "spirit" though, perhaps few of them realize.

> We, of course, speak of the Holy Spirit as a gift of God to the believer in Christ. They say, "What nonsense! As if a man could obtain the Holy Spirit as easily as that." Of course, I would point out the other aspect; that it is not so much our possessing the Spirit as the Spirit possessing us. On acceptance of Christ, the believer is born of the Spirit, yet it may be but slowly that He will obtain full sovereignty of the heart and will. This is dismissed as being contrary to the concept of God being a Spirit. We speak of the Almighty power of God and yet of man being responsible to Him, particularly in his acceptance or rejection of His way of salvation. I was told this was a "lower doctrine," cause and effect as a fatalistic law being widely propounded by the lamas.*

The missionary who takes the fall seriously, then, must stop to define his terms, as we have seen.

---

* Bull, G. T. (1967). *When iron gates yield* (pp. 97-99). London: Hodder & Stoughton.

Which terms? He must define those terms dictated by the distance between divine truth and cultural error. The definitional process must proceed by comparison and contrast. If this process seems too painstaking for the Western missionary who is used to instant everything—from instant cake to instant coffee to instant conversion—so be it. But he should know that to build Christian conversion on non-Christian worldviews is like building skyscrapers on sand. The mission fields are well populated with men and women who have been ushered into the heavenlies without knowing why they got on the elevator. Once back on earth they have no intention of being taken for another ride.

14. Why are definitions so important to effective contextualization?

_____

_____

_____

Selection

The previous point may become more understandable if we realize that the missionary must always give a partial message in the particular situation. Christ commanded us to teach men to observe all things which He commanded (Matt. 28:20), but certainly He did not intend that we deliver everything in one sitting! As a matter of fact, Christ never did that Himself, nor did the apostles. The world could not contain all the books that could be written about Christ and truth of God (John 21:25). Selection has always been necessary! Thus, while the missionary communicates nothing but the truth, he communicates the whole truth only over a period of time. Priorities are essential. Understanding comes with precept taught upon precept and line upon line.

> **The missionary must always give a partial message in the particular situation.**

It was an awareness of the need for selection that prompted many early missionaries to avoid Old Testament passages concerning the wars of the Israelites. Their rationale was that the people were already too warlike. Of course, it would be both fallacious and faithless to think that the exploits of Israel could be forever neglected. But in every case care should be exercised in selecting culturally appropriate expressions of God's message to man. Let the polytheist be told of the power of Christ, not just to save souls, but to subdue all things to Himself. Let him hear that the "unknown God" has revealed Himself to men. Let the Confucianist know that the only superior Man is the Son of God and Savior of men who recreates men and makes them into better husbands, wives, children, friends, and citizens. Let the Muslim see that God is love and hear why God can be just and the Justifier of the one who believes in Jesus. Let our Jewish friends hear once again that Christians believe that God still has a great future for them as a people and that a new day will dawn for any Jew who will look long enough at Jesus of Nazareth to see who He really is. All of this is, of course, oversimplified and somewhat redundant. But if it is also suggestive, it serves a purpose.

Adaptation

The sensitive missionary as a source of gospel communication defines his terms and makes a careful selection of content from the larger revelation of God. He also carries on a closely related and continual process of adaptation. He notes the special concerns occasioned by the particular worldview and adjusts to those concerns.

For example, in the Hindu-Buddhistic or Taoist contexts, there is little point in attempting to demonstrate the sinfulness of man initially by showing that men are liars. Where all propositional statements (and especially those of a religious nature) are mere approximations, lying becomes in one sense a necessary concomitant of communication itself!

But selfishness and covetousness are already matters of great concern. Is there any *biblical* ground for labeling these fundamental human weaknesses as sin? There most assuredly is such a basis. Then we can *all* agree that selfishness and covetousness are indeed evil. And we can point out how God looks upon these evils and deals with them.

The missionary does well to answer problems posed but not answered in the false systems.

The missionary does well to answer problems posed but not answered in the false systems. When problems of an other-worldly nature were put to Confucius, he answered very matter-of-factly that he hardly understood this world and should not be expected to know about another world. On the basis of their own worldview, Communists are hard pressed to give a satisfactory answer as to why extreme sacrifices should be made by the present generation of men for the generations yet unborn. Many Hindus must recoil in utter despair when faced with the seemingly numberless existences required to effect their final emancipation from the wheel of existence. Christ has real answers for these problems if only His ambassadors will deliver them.

Adaptation also requires that we answer objections that respondents can be expected to raise vis-à-vis the Christian message. The literature of Nichiren Buddhism, for example, makes much of the point that a man who knows the truth will die peacefully and with happiness apparent in his very facial expression. That Christ died on a cross while raising the anguished cry, "My God, my God, why hast thou forsaken me?" (Matt. 27:46, KJV) raises for these Buddhists a serious question as to whether Christ Himself knew the truth. A brief apologetic *before* the problem is articulated will go far to disarm the objector.

Finally, the missionary should also be alert to watch for special entries to these non-Christian systems. Confucius said:

> A holy man I shall not live to see; enough could I find a gentleman! A good man I shall not live to see; enough could I find a steadfast one! But when nothing poses as something, cloud as substance, want as riches, steadfastness must be rare.*

Lao-tze said, "He who bears the sins of the world is fit to rule the world."** These quotations furnish the Christian communicator with communication opportunities that should not be overlooked.

15. *What kinds of opportunities should a missionary look for in adapting the message to the culture?*

_____

_____

_____

_____

---

* Selections from the Analects. (1963). In O. M. Frazier (Ed.), *Readings in Eastern religious thought: Vol. 3. Chinese and Japanese religions* (p. 74). Philadelphia: Westminster.

** McHovec, F. J. (Trans.). (1962). *The book of Tao* (Sutra 78, p. 17). Mt. Vernon, NY: Peter Pauper.

Application

As is the case in all communication, the missionary message becomes most compelling when it ceases to be general and becomes personal. We are not, in the final analysis, speaking to worldviews but to the minds and hearts of men of flesh and blood who live out these worldviews in their decisions and actions. Can we make the message of Christ compelling to them? We can and we must. It is in application that we say, "Thou art the man" (2 Sam. 12:7, KJV).

The missionary message becomes most compelling when it ceases to be general and becomes personal.

Of course, ultimately the Holy Spirit must apply the Word. Geoffrey Bull illustrates that truth in his illustration of a Tibetan Buddhist military governor who refused to be moved by the most obvious refutation of his own faith.

> I was surprised how even a man like the Dege Sey believed in reincarnation. There was rather an amusing incident. He was saying to me how they had to be very careful, for even one of the domestic animals might be his grandmother. I was about to make some mildly humorous comment as to the general treatment of dogs in Tibet, when the words were taken out of my mouth and far more eloquent sounds fell on our ears. From the courtyard came the piercing squeals of some pitiful canine, which had just been either kicked or battered with a brick bat. The Dege Sey, generally quick to see a joke, sat quite unmoved. Incarnation as a doctrine itself is readily accepted by the Tibetans, but when we assert there is but one incarnation of the Living and True God, "The Word made flesh," it is totally unacceptable to them.*

If application is a function of knowledge, it is also a function of faith. It is not according to the usual bent of human nature to admit that one is wrong or to agree with God that we are sinners—especially helpless sinners whose only hope is in divine grace. When God's truth is faithfully and lovingly applied, however, there will be a response throughout Adam's race if that truth is presented intelligently and in dependence upon the Spirit.

16. *What is the objective in application of the message?*

_____

_____

_____

Worldview and the style of the missionary message

A "contextualized content" requires the accompaniment of a "contextualized style." Style can best be thought of as the personal imprint of the source upon his message. Its ingredients vary with the communication code, whether linguistic or nonlinguistic, and therefore we can speak of style as it relates to sermons, lectures, magazine articles, books, drawings, or films, and even to the way in which one lives out his Christian faith before other people. It can be studied in relation to the source, message, code, and respondents. It should be evaluated as to correctness, clarity, and appropriateness. Style is that part

---

* Bull, G. T. (1967). *When iron gates yield* (p. 63). London: Hodder & Stoughton.

of missionary communication in which the source's understanding of his respondent culture, his powers of imagination, and his skill in the manipulation of symbols are given most reign and can be put to great service for the kingdom. At the same time, a style that is out of keeping with the respondent culture does the kingdom a disservice.

A style that is out of keeping with the respondent culture does the kingdom a disservice.

Think for a moment in terms of the respondent culture the author knows best—Japan. To contemporary Japanese, much missionary communication (as reflected not only by missionaries but by national pastors and workers who often simply duplicate Western patterns) must seem to exhibit a great lack of style, though it is not so much a lack of style as a foreignness of style that is at the root of the problem. There are numerous aspects of the Judeo-Christian worldview as it has come through the Western mold that must stamp missionary communication as un-Japanese. Some of these would be directness, brusqueness, matter-of-factness, lack of awe and a sense of mystery, oversimplification, narrow scope of interest, aloofness from everyday concerns, and insensitivity to the feelings of the audience.

On the other hand, the missionary who by his demeanor and speech communicates the greatness and holiness of God, a deep appreciation for the beauty of God's world, and the mystery of Christian teachings such as the Trinity, the incarnation, and the atonement will find that his audience will be much more "at home" with his message.

17. Of what importance is "style" to the missionary message?

_____

_____

_____

In summary

The Christian message is, indeed, abiding and universal. It is for all men of every time in history and of every culture on earth. But the cultural contexts in which God revealed it and the missionary delivers it are distinct and different. They cannot be superimposed upon one another. If Christian meaning is not to be lost in the communication process, contextualization is required. There are many facets of contextualization, but at the very least it involves appropriate responses to cultural differences in local perceptions of the missionary source and in the substance and style of the missionary's message.

Hesselgrave's articles set before us the challenge and magnitude of the task of communicating the gospel message in the context of those whose worldview is much different from our own. His insights are especially valuable to those making the transition from "outsider" to "insider" or from "trader" to "story teller." Missionaries would do well to review these elements of contextualization often as they face the challenge of communicating the gospel.

III. Finding the Keys

Don Richardson successfully applied the principles of contextualization in communicating the gospel to the Sawi tribe of Irian Jaya. The thrilling story of his discovery of the key to the Sawi's assimilation of the gospel message is told in his book Peace Child and has been made into a film viewed worldwide. In the following article, Richardson graphically illustrates how the missionary can be aided tremendously in his communication of the gospel through insights into the respondent's worldview.

❑ *Concept Fulfillment* *

Don Richardson

When a missionary enters another culture, he is conspicuously foreign, and that is to be expected. But often the gospel he preaches is labeled foreign. How can he explain the gospel so it seems culturally right?

The New Testament way seems to be through concept fulfillment. Consider:

- The Jewish people practiced lamb sacrifice. John the Baptist proclaimed Jesus as the perfect, personal fulfillment of that sacrifice by saying, "Behold the Lamb of God, who takes away the sin of the world!"

This is concept fulfillment.

- Nicodemus, a Jewish teacher, knew that Moses had lifted up a serpent of brass upon a pole, so that Jews when dying of snakebite could look at it and be healed. Jesus promised: "As Moses lifted up the serpent in the wilderness, even so must the Son of Man be lifted up, that whoever believes in Him should not perish, but have everlasting life."

This, too, is concept fulfillment.

- A Jewish multitude, recalling that Moses had provided miraculous manna on a six-day-a-week basis, hinted that Jesus ought to repeat His miracle of the loaves and fishes on a similar schedule. Jesus replied, "Moses gave you not the true bread from heaven. The true bread from heaven is He who comes down from heaven and gives life to the world.... I am that Bread of Life!"

Once again, concept fulfillment.

When some charged that Christianity was destroying the Jewish culture, the writer to the Hebrews showed how Christ actually fulfilled all the central elements of Jewish culture—the priesthood, tabernacle, sacrifices, and even the Sabbath rest. Let's call these redemptive analogies—looking for their fulfillment in Christ. Their God-ordained purpose was to pre-condition the Jewish mind to recognize Jesus as Messiah.

18. *Identify and briefly describe the principle illustrated by Richardson's biblical examples.*

_____

_____

_____

_____

* Richardson, D. (1992). Concept fulfillment. In R. D. Winter & S. C. Hawthorne (Eds.), *Perspectives on the world Christian movement: A reader* (rev. ed.) (pp. C59-C63). Pasadena: William Carey Library.

Application today

The strategy of concept fulfillment can be applied by missionaries today—if only we learn to discern the particular redemptive analogies of each culture.

Consider the advantage: When conversion is accompanied by concept fulfillment, the individuals redeemed become aware of the spiritual meaning dormant within their own culture. Conversion does not deny their cultural background, leaving them disoriented. Rather they experience heightened insight into both the Scriptures and their own human setting and are thus better prepared to share Christ meaningfully with other members of their own societies. See how concept fulfillment has worked in other cultures:

Examples in other cultures

The Damal and "hai"

Less than one generation ago, the Damal people of Irian Jaya were living in the Stone Age. A subservient tribe, they lived under the shadow of a politically more powerful people called the Dani.

What hope could there be, you may ask, of finding a redemptive analogy in such a Stone Age setting?

And yet the Damal talked of a concept called *hai*. *Hai* was a Damal term for a long-anticipated golden age, a Stone Age utopia in which wars would cease, men would no longer oppress one another, and sickness would be rare.

Mugumenday, a Damal leader, had yearned to see the advent of *hai*. At the end of his life, Mugumenday called his son Dem to his side and said, "My son, *hai* has not come during my lifetime: now you must watch for *hai*. Perhaps it will come before you die."

Years later, Gordon Larson, John Ellenburger, and Don Gibbons and their wives entered the Damal valley where Dem lived. After tackling the Damal language they began to teach the gospel.

The people, including Dem, listened politely. Then one day....

"O my people!" Dem, now a mature adult, had risen to his feet. "How long our forefathers searched for *hai*. How sadly my father died without seeing it. But now, don't you understand, these strangers have brought *hai* to us! We must believe their words, or we will miss the fulfillment of our ancient expectation."

A breakthrough began. Virtually the entire population welcomed the gospel. Within a few years congregations sprang up in nearly every Damal village.

But that was not the end.

The Dani and "nabelan-kabelan"

The Dani, haughty overlords of the Damal, were intrigued by all the excitement. Curious, they sent Damal-speaking representatives to inquire. Learning that the Damal were rejoicing in the fulfillment of their ancient hope, the Dani were stunned. They too had been waiting for the fulfillment of something they called *nabelan-kabelan*—the belief that one day immortality would return to mankind.

Was it possible that the message which was *hai* to the Damal could also be *nabelan-kabelan* to the Dani?

By then Gordon and Peggy Larson had been assigned to work among the Dani. Dani warriors now recalled that they often mentioned "words of life" and a man named Jesus who not only could raise the dead but also rose again Himself.

Suddenly everything fell into place for the Dani as it had for the Damal. The word spread. In valley after valley the once barbarous Dani listened to the words of life. A church was born.

Concept fulfillment.

The Karen and a black book

The Karen tribe in Burma had a legend that one day a teacher of truth would appear, and he would carry a black object tucked under his arm. The first missionary to come among them always carried a black, leather-covered Bible tucked under his arm. The Karen listened with rapt attention every time he took the Bible out from under his arm and preached.

Triggered by this catalyzing cultural element, a great moving of the Spirit of God soon swept thousands of Karen into the church of Jesus Christ. Yet some studies of the phenomenal growth of the church among the Karen fail to mention this detail.

The Asmat and a new birth

When Jesus told Nicodemus he must be born again, Nicodemus was astounded. Even though he was well educated, he met Jesus' assertion with a naively literal, almost childish objection:

"How can a man be born when he is old? Can he enter into his mother's womb a second time and be born?"

Surely if a theologian like Nicodemus had that hard a time comprehending the meaning of "new birth," then a naked, illiterate, Stone Age cannibal would have a thousand times more difficulty.

On the contrary, one part of Irian Jaya's Asmat tribe have a way of making peace which requires representatives from two warring villages to pass through a symbolic birth canal formed by the bodies of a number of men and women from both villages. Those who pass through the canal are considered reborn into the kinship systems of their respective enemy villages. Rocked, lullabied, cradled, and coddled like new-born infants, they become the focus of a joyful celebration. From then on they may travel freely back and forth between the two formerly warring villages, serving as living peace bonds.

For no one knows how many centuries, this custom has impressed deeply upon the Asmat mind a vital concept: True peace can come only through a new birth experience!

Suppose God called you to communicate the gospel to these Asmat people. What would be your logical starting point? Let us assume you have learned their language and are competent to discuss the things dear to their hearts.

One day you visit a typical Asmat man—let's call him Erypeet—in his longhouse. First you discuss with him a former period of war and the new birth transaction which brought it to an end. Then....

"Erypeet, I too am very interested in new birth. You see, I was at war with an enemy named God. While I was at war with God, life was grim, as it was for you and your enemies.

"But one day my enemy God approached me and said, 'I have prepared a new birth whereby I can be born in you and you can be born again in Me, so that we can be at peace....'"

By this time Erypeet is leaning forward on his mat, asking, "You and your people have a new birth too?" He is amazed to find that you, an alien, are sophisticated enough to even think in terms of a new birth, let alone experience one!

"Yes," you reply.

"Is it like ours?"

"Well, Erypeet, there are some similarities, and there are some differences. Let me tell you about them...."

Erypeet understands.

What makes the difference between Erypeet's and Nicodemus's responses? Erypeet's mind has been pre-conditioned by an Asmat redemptive analogy to acknowledge man's need for a new birth. Our task is simply to convince him that he needs spiritual rebirth.

Do redemptive analogies like these occur by mere coincidence? Because their strategic use is foreshadowed in the New Testament and because they are so widespread, we discern the grace of God working. Our God, after all, is far too sovereign to be merely lucky.

But has anyone found a culture lacking concepts suitable for redemptive analogies?

The Yali and "osuwa"

A formidable candidate for this grim distinction was the cannibal Yali culture of Irian Jaya. If ever a tribe needed some Christ-foreshadowing belief a missionary could appeal to, it was the Yali.

By 1966 missionaries of the Regions Beyond Missionary Union had succeeded in winning about 20 Yali to Christ. Priests of the Yali god Kembu promptly martyred two of the 20. Two years later they killed missionaries Stan Dale and Phillip Masters, driving about 100 arrows into each of their bodies. Then the Indonesian government, also threatened by the Yali, stepped in to quell further uprisings. Awed by the power of the government, the Yali decided they would rather have missionaries than soldiers. But the missionaries could find no analogy in Yali culture to make the gospel clear.

Last year another missionary and I conducted a much belated "culture probe" to learn more about Yali customs and beliefs. One day a young Yali named Erariek shared with us the following story from his past:

"Long ago my brother Sunahan and a friend named Kahalek were ambushed by enemies from across the river. Kahalek was killed, but Sunahan fled to a circular stone wall nearby. Leaping inside it, he turned, bared his chest at his enemies, and laughed at them. The enemies immediately lowered their weapons and hurried away."

I nearly dropped my pen. "Why didn't they kill him?" I asked.

Erariek smiled. "If they had shed one drop of my brother's blood while he stood within that sacred stone wall—we call it an *osuwa*—their own people would have killed them."

Yali pastors and the missionaries working with them now have a new evangelistic tool. Christ is the spiritual Osuwa, the perfect place of refuge. For Yali culture instinctively echoes the Christian teaching that man needs a place of refuge. Ages earlier they had established a network of *osuwa* in areas where most of their battles took place. Missionaries had noticed the stone walls but had never ferreted out their full significance.

Redemption and resistance

Concepts like the Damal's *hai*, the Dani's *nabelan-kabelan*, the Asmat new birth, and the Yali *osuwa* form the very heart of their cultural life. When outsiders obliterate distinctives like these, something dies within the hearts of the people. But the gospel preserves these concepts. Converts among such tribes then find, along with their personal redemption, that they become resistant to apathy, the great destroyer of indigenous peoples overcome by culture shock.

Sensitive culture probes may discover undreamed-of possibilities for spiritual penetration through concept fulfillment.

Hundreds of areas remain where response to the gospel has been unsatisfactory or even non-existent. In many of these areas, sensitive culture probes may discover undreamed-of possibilities for spiritual penetration through concept fulfillment. Discouraged missionaries or national pastors may gain fresh confidence in their ability to make the gospel understood.

19. *How would you attempt to apply the principle of redemptive analogies as you enter a new culture?*

Finding redemptive analogies within a culture has often made the difference between an indifferent or hostile reception to the gospel and its whole-hearted acceptance. In the next article, Richardson demonstrates how this principle works not only cross-culturally, but also in everyday witness.

❏ *Finding the Eye Opener* *

Don Richardson

In Acts 26:17-18, the Apostle Paul articulated before King Agrippa the formula that Jesus Christ—appearing to Paul in a vision on the road to Damascus—gave as a basis for ministering the gospel. Follow carefully to see if I quote it correctly. I might make a mistake.

Jesus said to Paul, "… I am sending you to turn them from darkness to light and from the power of Satan to God, so that they may receive forgiveness of sins and a place among those who are sanctified by faith in me."

Notice that I omitted an entire phrase: "… to open their eyes." At first glance, the formula seems complete without the missing phrase. And indeed many missionaries have set out without ever thinking of the importance of opening people's eyes so that they can see the difference between darkness and light. "Opening their eyes" means establishing a beachhead for the truth in the understanding. It's the equivalent of getting to first base in the game of baseball. Of course, getting to first base doesn't count as a run, but it is a necessary first step if a run is to be scored.

In baseball, it's not enough merely to touch all four bases. You have to touch them in the right order, first base first, second base second, third base third. I know of some missionaries who have gone out full of zeal into cross-cultural situations and have started in right away rebuking people for their sins. They were intent upon turning people from darkness to light but without first having opened their eyes to see the difference between darkness and light.

Often, when eyes are not opened first, people get their back up; they take offense and they start trying to avoid this obnoxious foreigner with his ministry of rebuke. The missionary soon finds he is not getting anywhere. Years pass and no church is established. There will be some who will take it and respond, but usually the majority will not. And then he will say, "Lord, what am I doing wrong? You want me to preach against sin, don't you? They need to be turned from darkness to light, don't they? I've preached faithfully against sin. I've rebuked evil. I upheld that which was good, and the people don't respond."

But there is a missing element. He has not found the eye opener that clears the way for that sort of ministry. What, then, do we need to "open their eyes"? You don't know? What do you need to open a tin can? A can opener! What do you need to open someone's eyes? An eye opener! And don't you think that the God who commands us to open people's eyes is responsible to provide the eye openers we need to fulfill His command?

---

20. *What point does Richardson make with his baseball illustration?*

_____

_____

_____

---

* Richardson, D. (1992). Finding the eye opener. In R. D. Winter & S. C. Hawthorne (Eds.), *Perspectives on the world Christian movement: A reader* (rev. ed.) (pp. C64-C70). Pasadena: William Carey Library.

The example of Jesus

In chapter 4 of John's Gospel, the Lord Jesus Himself "touched first base first." In John 4 He's experienced what you might call a "close encounter of a cross-cultural kind." Jesus came to a town in Samaria called Sychar, near the plot of ground that Jacob gave to his son Joseph. Jacob's well was there.

That well was to Sychar what Valley Forge is to Philadelphia. If you had gone to visit someone in that town back in those days, you wouldn't have been in the home of your host and hostess very long before they would take you around to show you Jacob's Well. And they would give you the "tour guide's pitch" concerning how their forefather Jacob had dug it himself. So Jesus sat down by that very significant well, the thing that put Sychar on the map more than probably anything else.

His disciples had gone into the town to buy food. A Samaritan woman came to draw water. Jesus said to her, "Will you give me a drink?" The Samaritan woman said to Him, "You are a Jew and I am a Samaritan." There's that cultural chasm. She was ever so much aware of the cultural barrier between Him and her. "How can you ask me for a drink?" And here is the parenthesis—"for Jews do not associate with Samaritans." Jesus answered her, "If you knew the gift of God and who it is who asked you for a drink, you would have asked Him and He would have given you living water."

"Sir," the woman said, "you have nothing to draw with and the well is deep. Where can you get this living water? Are you greater than our father, Jacob, who gave us this well and drank from it himself, as did also his sons, flocks, and herds?" That's the tour guide's pitch. Hear her civic pride coming through! She was determined that this strange Jew should be duly impressed with the fact that that was actually Jacob's Well and that it was given to her forefathers. But notice that Jesus made her civic pride in the well to be His ally.

Jesus answered, "Everyone who drinks this water will get thirsty again. Even though your forefather Jacob dug it himself and drank from it, as did his children and his herds and his cattle, it is still ordinary water. You drink it and you get thirsty again. But whoever drinks the water that I give him will

never thirst. Indeed, the water I give him will become inside him a well of water springing up into everlasting life!"

Now, how many wells are in the picture? Two. The external, physical, historically significant well and the internal, eternal, spiritually satisfying well of living water! He used this object of her civic pride as an analogy to talk about a well that can be inside a person. That was His eye opener! And it worked!

"Sir," the woman said, "give me this water so I won't get thirsty and have to keep coming here to draw water." He told her, "Go, call your husband and come back." "I have no husband," she said. Jesus said to her, "You are right when you say you have no husband. The fact is, you have had five husbands, and the man you now have is not your husband. What you have just said is quite true."

The conversation has turned in a new direction! He used the eye opener to reach first base by awakening spiritual thirst. But what stood in the way of her receiving that living water? The sin in her life; thus, He had proceeded now towards "second base," turning her from darkness to light! The problem of her loose morals had to be dealt with early. He was following the same formula He would outline later for the Apostle Paul in that remarkable vision on the road to Damascus.

And notice how positive the Lord is! When she said, "I have no husband," some of us, if we had the insight into her history that Jesus had, would have pounced at once, saying, "You liar! You are hiding your sin behind a half-truth! The fact is, you are living with a man out of wedlock." But Jesus said— so positively, gently, and delicately—"What you have just said is quite true. You have had five husbands. The man you have now is not your husband. So you are quite right when you say you have no husband." He could have crushed her, but He didn't.

I think that's the kind of spirit He wants us to have. And I've seen many missionaries fail for lack of that kind of a spirit of love. At the same time, you must be careful not to become sentimental. The sentiments of human nature can easily revert to the sediments of fallen human nature. You may have been through a secular university or college course where you have been told that there is no such thing as guilt or real evil. If someone goes out and shoots somebody else or rapes somebody's wife or burns down somebody's house, he does it because society hasn't treated him right; you have to correct society and then the behavior of the individual will be corrected.

That philosophy is humanistic, not theistic. There is real evil out there, and it lies within human nature. And you have to be against it, and if you are not against it, the Spirit of God will not be for you. You will lose His blessing. The Son of Man has come to destroy the works of the devil and to deliver people from sin in whatever form it occurs.

You need to maintain this crucial balance of loving the sinner while hating the sin. And it's not always going to be easy to come into confrontation with evil without becoming obnoxious, unloving, or unwise in your approach to people. On the other hand, there is a danger of finding the eye opener and securing a beachhead of understanding in the minds of the people who need Christ and then be so delighted when they tell you that they understand that you stop right there and think that your job is done. It isn't! You've still got to "round first" and "head for second." They've got to be turned from darkness to light and from the power of Satan to God, etc.

Yes, even then, when the person begins to see that he needs to make certain changes in his lifestyle in order to live consistent with the will of God, he's going to find that there is a power trying to keep him from making those changes. This is the power of the evil one himself and of his hosts of demons. Winning the victory against the unseen forces who are "behind the sins" in a person's life will bring you around to "third base." But a run is not scored until he himself "touches home plate." And that occurs only when that person receives from God the forgiveness of sins and a place among those who are sanctified by faith in Him. What a beautiful formula—if only we can remember it! Touch all four bases!

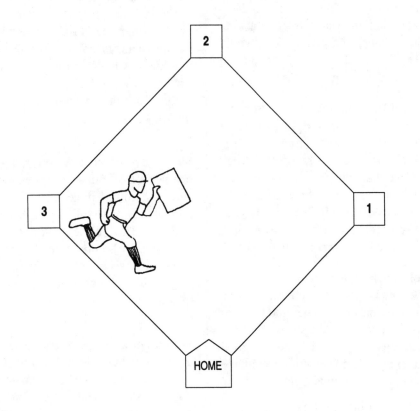

21. *What was the "eye opener" that Jesus used with the Samaritan woman? Why was it effective?*

_____

_____

_____

22. *What can we learn from Christ's example about rebuking those who are living in sin?*

_____

_____

_____

The example of Paul

I want to look at yet another example of an eye opener, found in Acts 17. First, here is some historical background to this story of Paul at Mars Hill:

Three ancient Greek writers, Diogenes Laertius, Philostratus, and Pausanias, referred to a plague that struck the city of Athens and began to decimate the population around 600 B.C. The people of Athens offered sacrifices to their thousands of gods, asking them to intervene and halt the plague. You would think that 30,000 gods could do something, but the sacrifices were futile. The plague persisted.

In desperation, the elders of the city sent messengers to summon a Greek hero known as Epimenedes. He came in response, and they said to him, "There is terror in our city. No one knows who will be struck down next. We have done all that we know to do. We have offered thousands of sacrifices to our gods, and the plague persists. Will you please apply your wisdom to our desperate situation and save our city? We have heard that you have rapport with the gods."

Epimenedes took stock of the situation and then took a course of action based on two premises. First, he reasoned that there must be another god who did not consider himself represented by any of the thousands of idols in the city but who was hopefully good enough and great enough to do something about the plague. They had to contact him and enlist his help.

For those who replied, "What if we don't know his name? How can we contact him?" Epimenedes was ready with premise number two: Any god who is great enough and good enough to do something about the plague is probably also great enough and good enough to smile upon us in our ignorance if we openly acknowledge our ignorance of him.

Epimenedes called for the people to bring a flock of sheep to Mars Hill, a plot of sacred ground in the city of Athens. He specified that the sheep had to be of more than one color, reasoning that since they did not know which color of sheep that god might prefer, they would give him a choice. Then he commanded that this multicolored flock be released on Mars Hill.

Sheep so released on a grassy knoll will normally begin to graze. But as the sheep meandered, grazing across the hill, Epimenedes, first commanding the men of the city to follow the sheep, called upon any god concerned in the matter of the plague to cause the sheep to lie down on the spot where that god wanted that sheep offered as a sacrifice to him. This they would take as a sign of the god's willingness to help.

We do not know how many sheep lay down upon the ground, but at least one and perhaps several did so. Wherever a sheep lay down upon the ground, the Athenians built an altar there and inscribed upon its side, "To an Unknown God." And then those sheep were offered as sacrifices to the unknown god.

All three writers confirm the plague was lifted immediately. The city was delivered. The people of Athens quickly returned to the worship of those thousands of futile gods, but they left at least one of those altars standing on Mars Hill.

Six centuries later, while the Apostle Paul was waiting for his friends in Athens, he was greatly distressed to see that the city was full of idols. If I can read between the lines a little bit, I can imagine what had happened. If six centuries earlier they had 30,000 gods, probably by Paul's time they had 40,000, still equally as futile, but still drawing the attention of the people away from the true God.

This glut of gods in the city of Athens is confirmed by another writer named Patronius, who visited Athens in ancient times, came away shaking his head, and wrote sarcastically in one of his books that in Athens it was easier to find a god than it was a man! Athens was a byword in the ancient world for this surfeit of gods.

We cannot go forth on a mission energized by the Holy Spirit without feeling anguish over evil and sin.

And what is Paul's emotional reaction at the sight of thousands of Athenians prostituting the image of God that is in them by bowing down to false gods? He was greatly distressed and obviously determined to do something about it.

I fear for anyone who can go out to the mission field and confront such things as widows flinging themselves on the funeral pyres of their husbands, or little children being forced into prostitution in temples, or ritualized wife trading as we find in some cultures in the southern part of Irian Jaya, or whatever else and not feel something of the distress, the anguish that Paul felt over the idols in Athens. We cannot go forth on a mission energized by the Holy Spirit without feeling anguish over evil and sin. We must be able to look upon sin with something of the perspective that God has.

Paul was in anguish. So he reasoned day by day with those who happened to be there. A group of Epicurean and Stoic philosophers began to dispute with him. Some of them asked, "What is this babbler trying to say?" and you can hear the scorn behind the words. Others remarked, "He seems to be advocating foreign gods." In other words, Paul, whoever you are, we already have 30,000 gods here in Athens, and you are bringing us the message of still another god? We need another god like we need a hole in our heads! We've got so many gods here in Athens we can't keep track of them all!

Who would have the audacity to proclaim another god in that context? Paul, of course. And how does he respond to the charge that he's advocating some superfluous or nuisance god in the city already afflicted with 30,000 or more of them? He stood up in the meeting of the Areopagus, another name for Mars Hill, and said, "Men of Athens, I see that in every way you are very religious. (Doesn't that remind you of Jesus at the well, saying to the woman, "You're quite right when you say you have no husband"?) For as I walked around and observed your objects of worship, I even found an altar with this inscription, 'To the Unknown God.' Now what you worship as someone unknown, I am going to proclaim to you." Paul, in effect, was saying: "Foreign God? No! The God I proclaim is that God who did not consider Himself represented by any of the idols in the city so many hundreds of years ago, but who delivered your city from the plague when you simply acknowledged your ignorance of Him. But why be ignorant of Him any longer, if you can know Him?"

In this way Paul used that familiar Athenian altar as an eye opener to get to first base. Then he went on to try to turn his listeners from the darkness of idolatry to the light of God's truth. He reminded the people of their gross ingratitude to that delivering, prayer-answering God. He found a residual testimony, didn't he, in this unexpected form? And he appropriated it. That was part, at least, of the testimony that God had reserved to Himself in that pagan context. And this unknown God has left a witness to Himself in hundreds of other cultures around the world.

23. What did Paul use as an "eye opener" in Athens?

_____

_____

_____

24. How did he demonstrate that he understood the importance of finding a positive launching point for witness?

_____

_____

_____

The principle defined

The principle that I have been talking about comes down to this: The reason that an analogy based upon a "peace child" ideal in the Sawi culture works for the Sawi, or a reference to a place of refuge has special appeal to a Yali mind, or new birth attracts an Asmat mind is because the people of each of these respective cultures cherish that particular idea or concept or ceremony. They see these things as the best in their world. When you start talking about something new in reference to this cherished, familiar thing, you have an automatic interest.

> **When you start talking about something new in reference to this cherished, familiar thing, you have an automatic interest.**

So we need to ask ourselves, what is it that my neighbor, my fellow student on campus, my professor, my associate in business, or my friend of another culture cherishes in this world? You may know someone who has no time for God at all. But he loves his wife. There are some unsaved men who really do love their wives. They find meaning in the marriage relationship. Doesn't the Bible have a lot to say about the parallels between marriage and redemption?

You may find someone else who doesn't love his wife and who may be on the edge of divorce, but see if he loves his children. The parent/child relationship has often been paralleled with redemption. Or he may neglect his kids or be a child abuser, but perhaps he really cherishes his job.

You just never know what sort of a spiritual chain reaction you are going to be a part of, maybe today or tomorrow or the next day, maybe in your own culture or in another culture, as you ask God to make you a communicator of good news. God can give us an instinct, an ability to sniff out, to sense in the hearts and minds of people that which they are committed to, and which may yield an analogy which will give us a handle on their hearts. And if you try it and get rebuffed, don't give up; try again. It takes time to learn, doesn't it?

You're like a law student: the more case histories you can absorb and meditate on, the more your imagination will be stretched to anticipate what God may be waiting to do. And sometimes it will not so much be what you say, it will be the timing. And God will arrange the timing.

So don't ever allow yourself to say, "This is an absolutely impossible situation; there is no way." God is the God who makes ways where there are no ways. And he is the One, after all, who is sending you out there and going ahead of you.

25. How does the principle of redemptive analogies apply to our daily walk and witness?

_____

_____

_____

Summary

In any mission venture, the gospel moves through at least three cultures—the "Bible culture," the missionary's culture, and the respondent's culture. Missionaries play a key role in this process, and for this reason it is not sufficient for them merely to know the message; they must also communicate and proclaim it. In doing so, they must be sensitive to the cultural context of the original message, to its assimilation into their own culture, and to the context of those who are recipients of the message.

In order to touch the heart of a people, missionaries must gain insight into the people's worldview. They must accept that worldview as valid in the context of the people's world. They must then use their knowledge not as a basis for ridicule, but as a cultural bridge for the gospel. The good aspects of the culture can be used as a launching point for contextualization of the gospel. The process of contextualization is then undertaken through definition, selection, adaptation, and application of the message. In addition to contextualizing the message, missionaries, through their sensitivity to the culture, also learn to deliver that message in the appropriate "style."

From the evidence of Scripture and mission history, it is apparent that God does not leave cultures without their own witness of Him. By carefully examining the traditions of a culture, missionaries may find redemptive analogies which serve as vessels for the gospel message. The gospel's fulfillment of a cultural concept not only serves as a vehicle of communication, but also provides an immediate and profound context for the gospel. It serves as an "eye opener" in terms of the people's understanding, permitting missionaries to move forward in the process of turning the people from darkness to light. Not only does this principle have a wide cross-cultural application, it is critical to effective witness in our daily lives.

Integrative Assignment

1. Select a passage of Scripture such as I Corinthians 7:17-19 or Matthew 22:17-21, whose context has obvious cultural features. Then, using the "Three-Culture Model of Missionary Communication" as a basis, describe the contextualization process in each of three cultures as follows:

   a. First, define the principle being illustrated, commanded, or taught.

   b. Second, show how the principle has been "contextualized" in the particular "Bible culture" in which it is found.

   c. Third, show how the principle is or could be contextualized in your own cultural situation.

   d. Fourth, show how the principle is or could be contextualized within a recipient culture such as the one you described for your Unreached Peoples Project (Chapters 7-12).

2. *Every religious tradition has commendable features. Select a belief system with which you are somewhat familiar (besides evangelical Christianity) and analyze it for good points. Then, using this background as a launching point, create a bridge for the gospel message. Write a short paper describing the religion's strong points, the bridge you would use for the gospel, and the response you might expect from a devotee when using this approach.*

Questions for Reflection

An excellent way to learn how to understand another culture is to observe our own. Much in our lives is regulated by cultural norms of which we are largely unaware. Such things as what, how, and when we eat, how we dress, and how we greet each other are obvious behaviors based on cultural assumptions. Even more subtle are things such as eye contact, posture, and how we walk. On the deepest level, the concepts we use to define reality and even our rational processes are shaped by our cultural background. If we expect to understand other cultures, we need to begin by understanding our own. These same principles have a personal application. A healthy amount of introspection is a vital part of understanding ourselves. By understanding ourselves as God sees us, we begin to understand others. And only by understanding other people can we discover the "eye openers" by which we can share Christ with them. The meditative application of scriptural principles to our own walk is a method God has chosen for His children to lead them in an understanding of themselves and of others. It is the insights God gives us through this process which provide a basis for exhortation and mutual encouragement. If we are sensitive to the Holy Spirit, He will show us points of empathy with believers and unbelievers whereby we can minister Christ to them.

Have you learned to apply God's Word to your life through meditation? What has God shown you? Have you learned to empathize with others in order to encourage them through word or deed? Read Psalm 1:1-3. Write your thoughts below.

CHAPTER 14

Church Growth and Social Structures

In the preceding chapters, some of our cultural nearsightedness was stripped away, and we began to catch a glimpse of "other worlds." We saw how important it is for the missionary to gain an appreciation and understanding of the host culture.

When a worldview permeates a people group and is generally accepted by all, we refer to the group as *homogeneous*. Many tribal societies function in this manner. All the members of the society participate in a common way of life. The society is essentially an integrated whole and not an aggregate of subcultures.

Most societies, however, are too complex to describe as homogeneous. We label them *heterogeneous*, indicating that within them exist several levels, classes, or ethnic groupings, each with its own distinctive. Large cities are heterogeneous in their social composition. A comprehensive analysis of any large city will reveal upper class, lower class, and middle class neighborhoods. In addition to this stratification by economic level, we are likely to find ethnic enclaves, where members of a minority group live in proximity to each other. These groups often maintain the customs and language of their national origin. Most cities are therefore a complex mosaic of homogeneous people groups.

Without a doubt, people gravitate towards groups which express their own cultural and social norms. When the church is homogeneous, the potential for growth increases because more consistent and socially appropriate expressions of the church can emerge to meet the standards and needs of each group. Where significant social and/or cultural barriers have to be crossed for individuals to be incorporated into the group, growth will be inhibited.

In this chapter, we will explore roles and social structures as they affect communication. Special attention will be given to reaching the cities—a monumental challenge for the church. We will also look at the difficult question of church contextualization and its implication for missionary work.

I. Status, Roles, and Communication

Successfully crossing cultural barriers and effectively communicating the gospel are not ends in themselves. There are limits to a missionary's witness, and the true objective is to see a cluster of reproducing churches established within the target group. The missionary's link to this goal is the innovator—the national who will initiate change. From this beginning, the message must flow throughout the people group. Social structures and the flow of communication through those structures are of key significance at this stage of mission work. In the following article, Paul G. Hiebert discusses the concepts of status and roles as they affect missionaries in their relationships to the national workers and others.

❏ *Social Structure and Church Growth* *

Paul G. Hiebert

People are social beings, born, raised, married, and usually buried in the company of their fellow humans. They form groups, institutions, and societies. Social structure is the ways in which they organize their relationships with one another and build societies.

Societies can be studied on two levels: that of interpersonal relation and of the society as a whole. A study of missions at each of these levels can help us a great deal to understand how churches grow.

Interpersonal relationships: The bicultural bridge

When a missionary goes overseas and settles down, what does he do? Whatever his specific task, he is involved in interpersonal relationships with a great many people. Many of these are not Christians, but, most likely, he will spend much of his time with Christian converts. He will go to the market or preach in the village square, but his closest relationships will be with national pastors, evangelists, teachers, and other Christians. What are the characteristics of these various relationships?

It is clear that in most cases communication across cultures is multi-stepped. The missionary received the message in his family, church, and school. He communicates it to national Christian leaders who in turn pass it on to local Christians and non-Christians in the cities and villages. With few exceptions, the greatest share of the mission work in a country is done by these unheralded nationals.

Here, in order to see how a structural analysis is used, we will look at one link in this chain of communication—the relationship between the missionary and his national counterpart. This has sometimes been called the bicultural bridge and is the critical step in which much of the translation of the message into a new culture occurs.

The bicultural bridge is the critical step in which much of the translation of the message into a new culture occurs.

The bicultural bridge is a set of relationships between people from two cultures. But it is more. It is itself a new culture. The missionary rarely can "go native." He will set up housing, institutions, and customary ways of doing things that reflect his home culture, in part, and, in part, are adapted from the culture in which he finds himself. His national counterparts do the same. It is true that they have not moved out of their own culture, but their interaction with the missionary exposes them to a great many foreign influences that can potentially alienate them from their home culture.

---

* Hiebert, P. G. (1976). Social structure and church growth. In A. F. Glasser et al. (Eds.), *Crucial dimensions in world evangelization* (pp. 61-67, 70-74). Pasadena: William Carey Library.

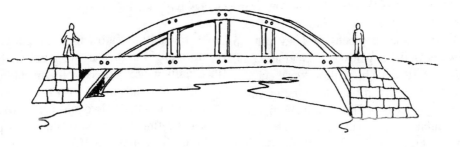

Figure 14-1. The Bicultural Bridge

A great deal of energy in the bicultural setting is spent on defining just how this new culture should operate. Should the missionary have a car in a society where most of the people do not? If so, should his national counterparts have them too? Where should the missionary send his children to school—to the local schools, to a school for missionary children, or to those in North America? What food should the missionary eat, what dress should he wear, and what kind of house should he and the national workers have? These and a thousand more questions arise in the bicultural setting.

Status and role

The term "status" has a number of common meanings, but anthropologists use it in a specific sense, defining it as the "positions in a social system occupied by individuals." At the level of interpersonal relationships, a social organization is made up of a great many such positions: teachers, priests, doctors, fathers, mothers, friends, and so on.

Each status is associated with certain behavioral expectations. For example, we expect a teacher to act in certain ways towards his students. He should show up for class and lead it. He should not sleep in class or come in a dressing gown. A teacher should also act in certain ways vis-à-vis his administrators, the parents of the students, and the public.

All interpersonal relationships can be broken down into complementary role pairs: teacher/student, pastor/parishioner, husband/wife, etc. The nature of the relationship between two individuals is based very much on the status they choose.

The missionary and the nationals

"What are you?" This question is repeatedly asked of a person who goes abroad to settle. The people ask because they want to know how to relate to the newcomer.

Missionaries generally answer, "We are missionaries." In stating this they are naming a status with its associated roles, all of which are perfectly clear to themselves. They know who "missionaries" are and how they should act. But what about the nationals, particularly the non-Christians who have never met a missionary before? What do they think of these foreigners?

> **The nature of the relationship between two individuals is based very much on the status they choose.**

Here we must come back to cultural differences again. Just as languages differ, so also the roles found in one culture differ from those found in another culture. "Missionary" is an English word, representing a status and role found in the West. In most other cultures it does not exist. When a missionary shows up in these cultures, the people must observe him and try to deduce from his behavior which of their roles he fits. They then conclude that he is this type of person and expect him to behave accordingly. We, in fact, do the same thing when a foreigner arrives and announces that he is a *sannyasin*. From his looks we might conclude he is a hippie, when, in fact, he is a Hindu saint.

How have the people perceived the missionaries? In India the missionaries were called *dora*. The word is used for rich farmers and small-time kings. These petty rulers bought large pieces of land, put up compound walls, built bungalows, and had servants. They also erected separate bungalows for their second and third wives. When the missionaries came they bought large pieces of land, put up compound walls, built bungalows, and had servants. They, too, erected separate bungalows, but for the missionary ladies stationed on the same compound.

When the missionary chooses a role, he must remember that the people will judge him according to how well he fulfills their expectations of that role.

Missionary wives were called *dorasani*. The term is used not for the wife of a *dora*, for she should be kept in isolation away from the public eye, but his mistress whom he often took with him in his cart or car.

The problem here is one of cross-cultural misunderstanding. The missionary thought of himself as a "missionary," not realizing that there is no such thing in the traditional Indian society. In order to relate to him, the people had to find him a role within their own set of roles, and they did so. Unfortu-

nately, the missionaries were not aware of how the people perceived them.

A second role into which the people often put the missionary in the past was "colonial ruler." He was usually white, like the colonial rulers, and he sometimes took advantage of this to get the privileges given the rulers. He could get railroad tickets without waiting in line with the local people, and he could influence the officials. To be sure, he often used these privileges to help the poor or oppressed, but by exercising them, he became identified with the colonial rulers.

The problem is that neither of the roles, rich landlord or colonial ruler, permitted the close personal communication or friendship that would have been most effective in sharing the gospel. Their roles often kept the missionaries distant from the people.

But what roles could the missionary have taken? There is no simple answer to this, for the roles must be chosen in each case from the roles in the culture to which he goes. At the outset he can go as a "student" and request that the people teach him their ways. As he learns the roles of their society, he can choose one that allows him to communicate the gospel to them effectively. But when he chooses a role, he must remember that the people will judge him according to how well he fulfills their expectations of that role.

1. What are the possible implications, in terms of status and role expectations, of declaring oneself a missionary?

The missionary and national Christians

The relationship between a missionary and national Christians is different from that between him and non-Christians. The former, after all, are his "spiritual children" and he their "spiritual father."

This parent/child relationship is vertical and authoritarian. The missionary is automatically in charge. He is the example that the people must imitate and their source of knowledge. But people soon become tired of being children, particularly when they are older and in many ways wiser than their parents. If not permitted to be responsible for themselves, they will never mature, or they will rebel and leave home.

The missionary is also imprisoned by this parental role. Not only is it difficult for him to form close relations with the people, with them as his equals, but also he feels he can admit to no wrong. If he were to confess personal sins and weaknesses to the people, he fears that they will lose their faith in Christ. But he is also their model for leadership roles, and they soon come to believe that no leader should admit to sin or failure. Obviously the missionary and the national leaders do sin, and because of their roles, they have ways of confessing sin and experiencing the forgiveness of the Christian community without destroying their ministry.

Another role into which missionaries can slip, often unawares, is that of "empire builders." Each of us needs to feel that we are part of an important task. From this it is only a small step to seeing ourselves as the center of this task and indispensable. We gain personal followers and build large churches, schools, hospitals, and other institutions that prove our worth.

However, this role, like the first, is not the best for effective communication. From a structural perspective, it is a vertical role in which communication proceeds from the top down. There is little feedback from the bottom up. People below comply with the orders from above but often do not internalize the message and make it their own. From a Christian perspective, this role does not fit the example of Christ. On the contrary, it can lead to an exploitation of others for our own personal gain.

What roles can the missionary take? Here, because the missionary and the nationals are Christians, we can turn to a biblical model—that of brotherhood and servanthood. As members of one body we must stress our equality with our national brothers and sisters. There is no separation into two kinds of people, "we" and "they." We trust the nationals just as we trust our fellow missionaries, and we are willing to accept them as colleagues and as administrators over us. Assignments of leadership within the church are not based on culture, race, or even financial power. They are made according to God-given gifts and abilities.

> **The missionary is most dispensable of all, for his task is to plant the church and to move on when his presence begins to hinder its growth.**

There is leadership in the church, just as there must be in any human institution if it is to function. But the biblical concept of leadership is servanthood. The leader is one who seeks the welfare of the others and not himself (Matt. 20:27). He is dispensable, and in this sense the missionary is most dispensable of all, for his task is to plant the church and to move on when his presence begins to hinder its growth.

2. *In relating to national Christians, into what dangerous roles can a missionary unconsciously fall? What is his proper role?*

_____

_____

_____

Identification

Good relationships involve more than choosing suitable roles. Within a role the individual expresses different attitudes that show his deep feelings toward the other person.

If we feel that somehow we are a different kind of people from those with whom we work, this will be communicated to them in a number of subtle ways. We may live apart from them, allow them only into our living rooms which are public space, and not permit our children to play with theirs. Or we may allow no nationals on mission committees.

When we identify with the people, we will do so in formal ways—at an annual feast given to the staff of the school or hospital, in their homes, but only on formal invitation, and on the committees by allowing a few to participate. We may even wear the native dress on certain occasions. But formal identification is identification at arm's length. It stresses the basic difference between people, even as it demonstrates their superficial oneness.

> *The real test of identification is not what we do in formal, structured situations. It is how we handle our informal time and our most precious belongings.*

The real test of identification is not what we do in formal, structured situations. It is how we handle our informal time and our most precious belongings. When the committee meeting is over, do we go aside with fellow Americans to discuss cameras and thereby exclude our national colleagues by our use of space and the topic of discussion? Do we frown on our children playing with the local children?

But is it possible for a missionary ever to "go native"? Obviously not. It takes immigrants from Northern Europe three or four generations to assimilate into American culture, and where the cultural differences are greater, it takes even longer.

The basic issue in identification is not formal equivalence—living in the same houses, eating the same food, and wearing the same dress. We can do so and still communicate to people the mental distinction we make between them and us. The issue is one of mental maps and basic feelings. If we, indeed, see and feel ourselves to be one of them, this message will come through, even if we have different lifestyles. A national gives us his best food, lets us sleep in his guest room and use his oxcart, and we share with him our best food, guest room, and car. The principle is not formal equality but true love and mutual reciprocity.

A sense of oneness with the people creates in us an interest in learning more about them and in sharing in their culture. Our example is Christ who, because of His love, became incarnate among us in order to bring us God's good news.

3. Why isn't it enough to identify just on a physical and material level?

_____

_____

_____

The organization of societies and church growth

Another way of looking at social structures is to see how societies as wholes are put together. What are the various social groups and institutions within a given society, how do these articulate with one another, and how does change occur? Here, again, two or three illustrations can show best the application and usefulness of the concept.

Tribal societies

In many tribes, social groups play an important role in the life of an individual, more so than they do in our own society with its strong emphasis on individualism and freedom. In a tribe a person is born and raised within a large kinship group or lineage made up of all the male descendants of some remote ancestor, plus all the families of these males. To get something of a feel for this type of society, imagine for a moment, living together with all of your relatives who share your last name, on a common farm, and sharing responsibilities for one another. All the men one generation older than you would be your "fathers" responsible for disciplining you when you deviate from the tribal rules and customs. All the women of that generation would be your "mothers" who care for you. All in your lineage of your own age would be "brothers" and "sisters," and all the children of all your "brothers" would be your "sons" and "daughters."

In some tribes, a lineage is made up of all the female descendants of a remote ancestress, together with their families. But, again, the authority of and responsibility to the group remains central in the life of the person.

Strong kinship groups in a tribe provide the individual with a great deal of security. They provide for you when you are sick or without food, support you when you go away to school, contribute to your purchasing a field or acquiring a bride, and fight for you when you are attacked. In turn, the group makes many demands on you. Your lands and your time are not strictly your own. You are expected to share them with those in your lineage who need them.

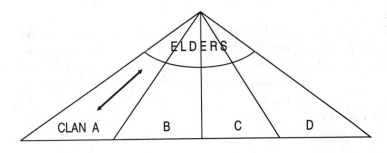

– Stress on kinship as basis for social bonding.

– Strong group orientation with mutual responsibility and group decision-making processes.

– Minimal social hierarchy.

– Vertical communication.

Figure 14-2. Tribal Societies

4. *What is the primary decision making structure in tribal societies?*

_____

_____

_____

Important decisions in these tribes are generally made by the elders—the older men who have had a great deal of experience with life. This is particularly true of one of the most important decisions of life, namely, marriage. Unlike our society, where young people are all too ready to get married when they "fall in love" (analogous to "falling into a mud puddle"?) without carefully testing the other person's social, economic, mental, and spiritual qualifications, in most tribes weddings are arranged by the parents. From long experience they know the dangers and pitfalls of marriage, and they are less swayed by the passing emotional attachments of the present. The parents make the match only after a long and careful examination of all the prospective partners. Love grows in these marriages as in any marriage by each partner learning to live with and to love the other.

Lineage and tribal decisions are also made by the elders. Family heads have their say, but they must comply with the decisions of the leaders if they want to remain a part of the tribe.

This type of social organization raises serious questions for Christian evangelism. Take, for example, Lin Barney's experience. Lin was in Borneo when he was invited to present the gospel to a village tribe high in the mountains. After a difficult trek he arrived at the village and was asked to speak to the men assembled in the longhouse. He shared the

---

> **Group decisions do not mean that all of the members of the group have converted, but it does mean that the group is open to further biblical instruction.**

---

message of the Jesus Way well into the night, and, finally, the elders announced that they would make a decision about this new way. Lineage members gathered in small groups to discuss the matter, and then the lineage leaders gathered to make a final decision. In the end they decided to become Christians, all of them. The decision was by general consensus.

What should the missionary do now? Does he send them all back and make them arrive at the decision individually? We must remember that in these societies no one would think of making so important a decision as marriage apart from the elders. Is it realistic, then, to expect them to make an even more important decision regarding their religion on their own?

Should the missionary accept all of them as born again? But some may not have wanted to become Christian and will continue to worship the gods of their past.

Group decisions do not mean that all of the members of the group have converted, but they do mean that the group is open to further biblical instruction. The task of the missionary is not finished; it has only begun, for he must now teach them the whole of the Scriptures.

Such people movements are not uncommon. In fact, much of the growth of the church in the past has occurred through them, including many of the first Christian ancestors of most of the readers of this book.

5. What is an appropriate response to group decisions for Christ?

_____

_____

_____

Peasant societies

The social organization of peasant societies is quite different from that of tribal societies. Here we often have the weakening of extended kinship ties and the rise of social classes and castes. Power is often concentrated in the hands of an elite that is removed from the commoners.

We can turn to India for an illustration of how peasant social structure influences church growth. Villages are divided into a great many *jatis* or castes. Many of these, such as the Priests, Carpenters, Ironsmiths, Barbers, Washermen, Potters, and Weavers, are associated with certain job monopolies. Not only does a person inherit the right to perform his caste's occupation, he must marry someone from within his own caste. A rough analogy would be for American high school teachers to marry their children to other high school teachers, for preachers to marry their children to other preachers' children, and for each other occupation to do the same. One can see, therefore, the need to begin marriage negotiations early.

Castes are also grouped into the clean castes and the Untouchables. The latter are ritually polluting and their touch, in the past, polluted clean-caste folk

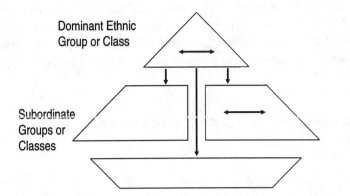

Dominant Ethnic
Group or Class

Subordinate
Groups or
Classes

- Stress on kinship as basis for social bonding.

- Strong group orientation with group decision-making processes.

- Intergroup hierarchs.

- Communication horizontal within groups, vertical between them.

Figure 14-3. Peasant Societies

who had to take a purification bath to restore their purity. Consequently, the Untouchables formerly had to live in hamlets apart from the main villages, and they were forbidden to enter the Hindu temples.

When the gospel came, it tended to move in one of the group of castes or the other, but not in both. Some of the first converts were from the clean castes. But when many of the Untouchables accepted Christ, the clean-caste people objected. They did not want to associate with the folk from the wrong part of town. The missionaries continued to accept all who came and required that they all join the same church. Consequently, many of the clean-caste people reverted back to Hinduism.

6. *What has been an inhibiting factor to the growth of the church in India composed of members from diverse castes?*

_____

_____

_____

The problem here is not a theological one. Many of the high-caste converts sincerely believed the gospel, and even today many are secret believers. It is a social problem. The high-caste folk did not want to associate with the Untouchables. Before we judge them, let us stop and look at the churches and denominations in America. In how many of them do we find a wide mixture of people from different ethnic groups and social classes? How long has it taken them to break down the last remnants of racial segregation? In how many of them have differences in wealth, social class, and political power become unimportant in the fellowship and the operation of the churches?

The dilemma is that theologically the church should be one, but, in fact, people are socially very diverse. Moreover, they find it hard to associate closely and intermarry with people markedly different from themselves. Can we expect people to change their deep-seated social ways at the moment of their conversion—in other words, should we expect them to join the same church? Or is changing our social customs a part of Christian growth—should we allow them to form different churches with the hope that with further teaching they will become one? The question is similar to one many American churches face; is giving up smoking or drinking alcohol or any other behavior defined as sinful essential to salvation, or is it a part of Christian growth?

There have been some in India who have held that the peoples' salvation is not tied to their joining a single church, and they have, therefore, started dif-ferent churches for the clean castes and the Un-touchables. They have had much greater success in winning people from the clean castes, but they have also faced a great deal of criticism from those who argue that this is contrary to the will of God.

7. Why has starting churches for the "clean castes" been a point of controversy?

_____

_____

_____

_____

The urban scene

The recent growth of cities has been phenomenal. In 1800, no city in the world had a population of 1 million, and fewer than 25 had more than 100,000 inhabitants. By 1950, 46 cities had more than 1 million residents. The New York metropolitan area, which had over 15 million people in 1970, may reach 22 million by 1985.

This rapid urbanization of the world raises many questions for those concerned with church growth. What is the social structure of a city, and how does this structure influence communication and deci-sion making? How do changes take place in the highly mobile and varied city society?

The social processes affecting church growth in tribal and peasant societies are less evident in urban societies. Large people movements in which people come to Christ on the basis of group decisions, or in which the message is shared through caste and kin-ship ties, seem almost absent. On the other hand, there are new forces at work. City folk are often caught up in rapid change. Their ideas are molded by mass media, educational institutions, and volun-tary associations. Communication often follows networks of people who are mutually acquainted—in other words, a friend tells a friend, who, in turn, tells another friend.

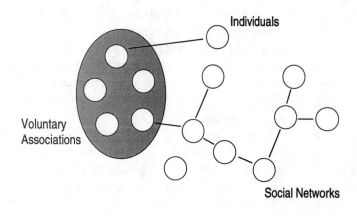

- Stress on individualism and personal decision making.

- Organization on basis of voluntary associations, networks, and geographical groupings.

- Heterogenents and hierarchs.

- Use of mass media in addition to networks.

Figure 14-4. Urban Individualistic Societies

What methods should missions use in the city? So far no clear-cut strategy has emerged. Mass media, friendship, neighborhood and apartment evangelism, large educational and medical institutions, and mass rallies have all been tried, and with mixed success. There is no simple formula that will bring success—there never has been. Building churches is a difficult and long-range task.

Cities also offer tremendous opportunity. They are the centers for world communication, and the source from which ideas spread to the countryside. One reason for the rapid spread of early Christianity was its movement through the cities. We desperately need to look more closely at modern urban dynamics in order to understand how change takes place, and then to apply these insights to today's mission planning.

8. Why do cities defy any simplistic strategy for reaching them?

_____

_____

_____

II. Reaching the City

There is no doubt that the trend towards urbanization of the world's population is one of the most challenging issues facing present-day missions. In the following article, Tim Monsma addresses this question by applying an understanding of sociological principles to this complex consideration.

❏ *The Intersecting Veins of the City* *

Timothy Monsma **

Veins of gold lie buried deep in the earth in places scattered around the globe. The gold is there for the taking, but one must dig for it in order to obtain it!

There is gold for the Lord in the cities of the world. But one must work for it too! Strip mining is not sufficient. One must locate the veins, which are the various kinds of people groups in a city. These veins run in many directions and often intersect. The missionary's challenge is to know enough about each vein to mine it appropriately and extract the priceless ore of human souls to add to the treasury of the King.

Cities are complicated. One or two levels of analysis are not sufficient to understand them. But cities are not incomprehensible. Some guidelines can be given to urban missionaries, along with the promise that their labors will be worth the effort. The gold in the cities of the world is precious in God's sight. And our labors in the city have implications beyond its boundaries. We must remember that as the city goes, so usually goes the nation.

---

* Monsma, T. M. (1990). The intersecting veins of the city. In Greenway & Monsma (Eds.), *Cities: Missions' new frontier* (pp. 112-125). Grand Rapids: Baker Book House.

** Dr. Timothy Monsma is a former professor of missions and noted author on urban ministries. He currently serves as Director of Cities for Christ Worldwide, Escondido, California.

Ethnic groups

Ibu is a young man in his early 20s. He left his home in Ghana to seek work in Abidjan, the capital of the Ivory Coast. Because of his limited knowledge of French, no firm was willing to hire him. But he found work in the home of a wealthy lawyer whose wife works as a part-time teacher. Ibu cares for the yard, mops the floors, and runs errands. He hopes that someday he will become a chauffeur and find a wife to live with him in Abidjan.

Ibu is one of about 200,000 Ghanians who have moved to the Ivory Coast to take advantage of Abidjan's relative prosperity. They are three steps removed from the average resident of Abidjan: their ethnic group is different from any of the ethnic groups of the Ivory Coast, they are not citizens, and they do not speak the national language, French. If they know French at all, it is only conversational French.

People like Ibu have been neglected by the traditional missions in Abidjan. Protestant missionaries and evangelists have had all they can do to reach the French-speaking population. This has left them no time for a concerted outreach to smaller groups, such as the one from Ghana.

Ethnic groups constitute some of the veins of gold awaiting discovery by urban missionary-miners. It is vital to identify which ethnic groups living in a city are being reached with the gospel and which are not. In most major cities today, even those that appear to have many churches, there are pockets of people who are neglected because of their ethnic identity, linguistic problems, or other cultural barriers.

In one predominantly Muslim country, there is a city of 1 million people with 70 churches. On the surface it appears that Christianity is making great strides there. But when one examines the ethnic composition of these churches, one discovers that their members are not indigenous to the area. There is one small denomination for the two indigenous ethnic groups, and that church is shrinking rather than growing. Until a city is analyzed in terms of its ethnic composition, such information does not come to light, and the missionary may be misled by appearances.

Recent missiological thinking has emphasized the need to identify "unreached people groups." Frequently these are ethnic groups. A group is considered unreached if in its midst there is no vigorous church capable of bringing the gospel to the other members of the group. As soon as a vigorous and growing church has been planted in the midst of a group, it is considered reached.

Many have thought that the emphasis on unreached people groups is an emphasis on rural evangelism, for it appears to focus on isolated tribes to whom no missionary has yet been sent. But there are unreached peoples in cities as well. Members of many isolated tribes have already made their way to the cities. And this raises a new question: Is it better to approach a people group in the city first or in the hinterlands? The answer will depend on the circumstances of each individual group. In some cases, groups that are highly resistant to the gospel in their homelands may be very open to the gospel in an urban environment.

> *In some cases, groups that are highly resistant to the gospel in their homelands may be very open to the gospel in an urban environment.*

Most urban immigrants preserve numerous ties with their kin back in the countryside. There is travel back and forth for holidays and other special occasions. Food is sent from the rural area to relatives living in the city, while those in the city send items that cannot be purchased in the village except at a very high price. Public transportation is continually used to convey children, money, animals, food, and manufactured goods back and forth between town and country.

Public transportation between town and country also conveys the news, sometimes very rapidly. After a church service in Lagos, for example, someone said to me, "I hear that a child of one of your missionaries died yesterday in Gboko." Gboko is 800 miles away, but the overnight bus service between Gboko and Lagos had already carried the news.

Because of such relationships, the symbiosis between city and hinterland extends beyond the realm of formal business matters. For the social ties between the members of a particular ethnic group who live in the country and those in the city also help to spread new ideas, including religious ideas. It is not preposterous, therefore, to evangelize the countryside by evangelizing the city or, conversely, to evangelize the city by evangelizing the countryside.

9. *In what ways are urban ethnic populations tied to the traditional homelands?*

_____

_____

_____

_____

In the city there are various social groupings other than ethnic—people of one ethnic group may be separated from one another by class distinctions. Nonetheless, they often have a sense of cohesion and unity that transcends social barriers. This is especially true of relatives. Those within an extended family feel obligations toward one another in spite of social barriers. I have observed illiterate peasants staying with wealthy and cultured relatives in the city, at least temporarily, simply because they were family.

As we seek to measure the progress of the gospel among various groups, the most natural approach to the city is to classify its residents on the basis of their ethnicity. But for the cities of Japan and Korea, where virtually everyone is of the same ethnic stock, such a division is not useful. And in cities where an ethnic group is so small that its members prefer to worship with some other group or groups, the ethnic criterion also loses its value. But in most cases, ethnic divisions are most useful for evaluating the progress of evangelism in the city.

Jakarta, the capital of Indonesia, is a city of churches. Out of a total population of 8 million, about 1 million identify themselves as Protestant Christians. Someone might argue that there are enough Christians in Jakarta to evangelize the rest of the city. And from a strictly numerical point of view, this argument seems valid. But if we think of Jakarta as a gold mine with many intersecting veins, we will realize that there are numerous Christians in some veins, while other veins contain virtually no Christians at all.

We can identify the ethnic groups among whom Christians are few and far between. There are, for example, the Sundanese, a group 20 million strong living on the western end of Java. The Sundanese are committed Muslims and not very willing to give the Christian faith serious consideration.

In most cases, ethnic divisions are most useful for evaluating the progress of evangelism in the city.

The Javanese form another large ethnic group in Jakarta. They make up the bulk of the population of Java, a heavily populated island of almost 100 million people. The Javanese are more willing than the Sundanese to consider various religious options. Some of them in Jakarta profess faith in Christ, but a strong Javanese church has not yet arisen.

Then there are those groups that have migrated to Jakarta from the outlying islands. Some of these islands are predominantly Christian, and it is from there that the majority of the Christian population of Jakarta have come. But other islands, such as Sumatra, are predominantly Muslim, and their people have also moved to Jakarta in large numbers. People from the island of Bali remain Hindu.

One ethnic group in Jakarta that has been reached with the gospel is the Chinese. Although the majority of them are still Buddhists, there is a vigorous and growing Christian church among them. Indonesians of Chinese descent are busy evangelizing their own people, and God is blessing their efforts.

By dividing the population of the city into ethnic groups, we get a better idea of the evangelistic task that remains. It probably will not be possible for foreign missionaries to spread the gospel to the as yet unreached groups in Indonesia, because the government is not granting visas to new missionaries. But Indonesian Christians are able to shoulder this burden. They have already made some efforts in this direction, and they will become more vigorously involved in cross-cultural evangelistic activity as fellow Christians from outside the country remind them of these God-given opportunities.

This writer is convinced that ethnic groups in the cities of the world must be identified by the Christian community. If someday every tribe, tongue, people, and nation are to be gathered before God's throne (Rev. 5:9), then they must hear and believe the good news about Jesus before He returns. Mission scholars have identified many ethnic groups that do not yet have a church in their midst. When these groups have been identified, missionaries and evangelists can prepare to go to them with the gospel.

---

10. Why is it important to analyze cities in terms of ethnic composition?

_____

_____

Increasingly, unreached ethnic groups are represented in cities. In some cases, they have traveled such a distance that they form a totally new group within their chosen city. This happens especially when they cross international borders. But whether they constitute a newly formed group in a foreign country or have remained in their homeland, every urban ethnic group must be reached with the gospel.

Anyone who wishes to investigate a specific city is advised to draw up a list of ethnic groups within that city and to identify those that already have living, growing churches in their midst. In this way one will, by a process of elimination, be able to target those groups still in need of a vital witness. A person who has lived in a city for some time will have contacts who can assist in drawing up the list. But someone who is new to a city will have to prevail upon Christians who are already there to help in this effort. They will probably be willing to do so, provided one does not take up too much of their time.

Once the list has been drawn up, one must determine which of those ethnic groups still in need of a vital witness constitute what missions literature calls "people groups." An urban ethnic group is a people group if one can contemplate planting a church or a worshiping congregation just for them. A given ethnic group may be so similar to other ethnic groups that one church can serve them all in culturally appropriate ways. Or an ethnic group might have so few members in a given city that it would be preferable for them to worship with other Christians in a common language or in the national language of the land.

There is a special advantage in identifying people groups in cities, especially groups that have been resistant to the gospel in rural areas. Sometimes village life is woven so tightly that no one is able to step out of line. No one dares accept a new faith such as Christianity. In extreme cases, those who do may be killed. But in the city there is greater freedom. The social controls of the village are gone. There is less danger of losing one's job when one changes religions in the city. Here there is often a community of Christians who can help new converts make the necessary adjustments.

11. *What advantages are suggested for reaching an ethnic group through a city-based strategy?*

_____

_____

_____

_____

Social groups

At the beginning of this article, the city was called a gold mine with many intersecting veins, some of which are the ethnic groupings we have been discussing. We might picture them as vertical veins running through the city. Just as important in many cases are social distinctions, which we might picture as horizontal veins.

We were in a crowded upper room of a warehouse in Jakarta. The men and women in the room were of all ages and various skin colors. When the chairman asked for a show of hands to determine the islands from which these people had come, it became apparent that there was great ethnic diversity in the room. Yet they all had one thing in common: they were all seamen or the relatives of seamen, and they were all comparatively poor.

Now it is a fact that schooling, occupation, and wealth (or lack of it) tend to determine one's social status. But within the broad categories of upper, middle, and lower class, there are subcategories that group people in terms of how they view themselves or how others view them. The seamen of Jakarta are a case in point. While many others might have an income in the same range as theirs, they would not feel an affinity for each other because their lives revolve around entirely different occupations. That street vendors and seamen have the same level of income does not automatically place them in the same sociological group. In the case of the seamen, the method of earning a living determines the cohesiveness of the group. As a matter of fact, their shared occupation appears more important than their ethnic identity. This, then, is their primary group, the people group among whom we may expect a church to arise.

In the city there are other such occupational groupings that appear to bind their members so closely to one another that they override all ethnic considerations. These occupational groupings tend to cluster both at the top and at the bottom of the socioeconomic scale. Thus, corporation executives, actors, top-level civil servants, and high ranking military officers might feel an affinity for one another that overrides the ethnic pull. Toward the bottom of the socioeconomic scale, pimps and prostitutes, drug dealers, beggars, thieves, and scavengers might feel close to one another and rather distant from their own ethnic groups.

> *In the city there are occupational groupings that appear to bind their members so closely to one another that they override all ethnic considerations.*

We may need a different evangelistic strategy for each one of these groups, for each group may have its own set of needs and interests (although they all need salvation through Christ). For example, what evangelistic strategy would one use with prostitutes? We sense immediately that it will have to differ from that used with women who are wives and mothers, or that used with women who are office workers, nurses, telephone operators, or attorneys.

Simply to tell prostitutes that they are sinners will not make much of an impression, because they know that without being told. Those who have worked with prostitutes in various countries tell us that a holistic approach is needed. Many became prostitutes because they were desperate to find work or because they were duped by someone. Now they cannot get out even if they want to.

Prostitutes must be shown that there is a viable way out. They must be protected from the pimps and brothel owners who may try to reclaim them. Commitment to Jesus Christ must become for them the beginning of a period of cleansing and renewal in body and spirit. It may also involve further education so that they can find their places as useful members of society once again.

Within every people group there are subgroups requiring special evangelistic strategies.

The fact that prostitutes require a special evangelistic strategy, however, does not mean that they are a people group so distinctive that a church can and ought to be planted just for them. If every occupational class were a people group as that term is presently used in missions literature, then there would be virtually no end to the number of people groups in the world, for new occupations are always appearing. Then, too, the people group concept could not be used effectively as a measure to determine the progress of the gospel in the world. It is better to recognize that within every people group there are subgroups requiring special evangelistic strategies. From the point of view of good evangelism, each subgroup, and finally each person, must be taken into account.

The cities of Japan, Korea, and Sweden are, except for foreigners in their midst, made up of people of one ethnic group speaking the same language. In such cities the sociological groupings become very important, for ethnic distinctions are virtually nonexistent. Christian workers will classify such urbanites on the basis of income, education, status in society, and possibly the neighborhoods in which they live. People with similar income levels might be placed in different groups if their occupations and lifestyle so warrant. The number of groups found will reflect the number of different churches needed to minister effectively to all of them.

12. What are two primary influences in social grouping, and in what ways do they affect church planting?

_____

_____

_____

_____

Cities contain areas for the wealthy, the middle class, and the poor—although sometimes middle-class people are mixed in with the wealthy or the poor. While in Western cities, the poor tend to congregate in the inner cities and those with means tend to flock to the suburbs, in the developing world these tendencies are often reversed. Those with means live in the central city not far from the downtown area, while the poor live in shantytowns built on the hills and in the ravines that surround the city. In the West, the poor generally live in slums (formerly good housing that has deteriorated over time). There is slum housing in cities of the Southern World as well, but in addition, there are shantytowns built by people who have recently moved to the city. The residents often experience upward mobility as they find meaningful work and as city governments, recognizing their existence, provide them with electricity, water, schools, and other services.

Many Southern World cities are experiencing chaotic growth, and shantytowns are multiplying. Alongside some upward mobility there is also desperate poverty. Fernando Silva Pontes, who is both a physician and a priest, reports concerning a shantytown of Itapipoca, a city of northeastern Brazil:

All they have is farinha and beans, and some mothers are too sick to supply milk. In one house a baby was crying and crying. The mother was in tears. I told her to give the baby milk, but she didn't want to and I almost forced her. And then I saw the baby suck blood from the mother's breast.*

Viv Grigg describes his similar experiences as a Protestant missionary in a Manila shantytown.**

These examples are mentioned to highlight the fact that in most of the metropolises of Asia, Latin America, and Africa, there are extensive residential areas for the very poor. These areas continue to grow rapidly as the poor are forced out of rural regions and into the cities. We must carefully plan our approach to this large group of people. Will we plant churches among them that cater to their ethnic origins, or is their poverty so pervasive that it is the chief determinant of the type of church which will arise in their midst? On-site research, city by city and area by area, is needed to determine the type of people group most significant to the poor and the shape of the church which will emerge among them.

In compiling a list of the people groups within a city, there is the possibility of including the same individuals twice: first as members of an ethnic group and then as members of some sociological group. For example, a person (P) might be viewed as a member of ethnic group Y and social group X (see

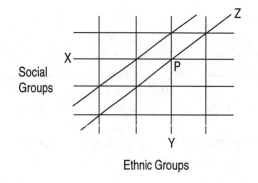

Figure 14-5. People Groups Within a City

Figure 14-5). To complicate matters further, P might also be a member of group Z, which intersects with the others diagonally. Group Z might be a veterans' organization, a mothers' group in a specific neighborhood, or a religion.

For the purpose of measuring the progress of the gospel, P should be regarded primarily as a member of ethnic group Y unless there are very good reasons for identification with a sociological group. In general, we will assign persons to the group whose church we expect them to attend after conversion to Jesus Christ. But evangelistic strategies may differ widely, depending on people's interests and needs when they are first approached.

13. To the church planter, what is the primary concern when attempting to identify a person's "group"?

_____

_____

_____

---

* Vesilind, P. J. (1987). Brazil: Moments of promise and pain. *National Geographic, 171*(3), 258, 360.

** Grigg, V. (1984). *Companion to the poor.* Sutherland, Australia: Albatross.

The city as an organism

The city is a gold mine. It has prominent ethnic (vertical) veins. It has prominent sociological (horizontal) veins. And it has other veins that run at will in all directions. This image is useful in helping us schematize and also simplify in our own thinking a complex evangelistic task. But there is yet another level of complexity to be examined. The city and its suburbs are more than a static entity to be charted in one way or another. The city is also an organism that is constantly on the move. This movement is not random like the movement of atoms within a molecule. It is concerted and interconnected, like that of an animal or a human body. Without losing sight of the intersecting veins, we need also to see the city as a giant organism pulsing with life.

> *Urban life breeds interdependence,*
> *whether urban residents like it or not.*

As the first rays of sunlight stretch across the eastern sky, every city is like a giant arousing from deep slumber. In house after house, the lights go on. Soon the streets are filled with people on their way to work. As the sun rises higher, children make their way to school; trucks, trains, and airplanes ply their routes; and shoppers begin to crowd the markets and stores.

The various occupational groups that live in the city are dependent on one another. This interdependence might be called the essence of urban life. Teachers depend on cobblers to repair their shoes, who call on mechanics to repair their cars, who buy food from women at the market, who need nurses when they are sick, who are licensed by the government, which uses secretaries and computer operators to keep track of all its business. One could go on and on.

The point is this: Urban life is the opposite of life in isolated and self-contained societies where virtually every member does all the tasks traditionally assigned to his or her sex. Urban life breeds interdependence, whether urban residents like it or not.

In 1 Corinthians 12 and Romans 12 the Apostle Paul compares the Christian congregation to the human body. Each member of the body has its own unique function that the other members cannot perform—be it seeing, hearing, talking, or walking. The members depend on one another and cooperate with one another so that the body achieves its goals. It would be ludicrous for the members of the body to fight with one another.

The congregation is an organism because all its members are joined to Christ and find unity in Him. The city is an organism because all its residents depend on one another for their well-being. The city is an organism in spite of all the ethnic and sociological diversity described earlier in this chapter.

While evangelism must take urban diversity into account, spiritual care leading to growth in Christ must work for Christian unity. It can do so by keeping in view biblical passages like Paul's description of the church as a body. In addition, the very structure and interrelationships of the city can be used as a model for Christians of various ethnic groups and social strata to follow in developing spiritual interdependence. If there is interdependence in the workplace, surely there is need for interdependence within the body of Christ.

---

14. *What parallels exist between the composition of the city and the composition of the body of Christ?*

Social networks

When one thinks of the city as an organism, one can't help noticing that most people who live in the city interact with one another through a web of interlocking relationships. This web of relationships is called a network by social scientists. The following account, which is a composite story drawing on my firsthand observation of urbanization in Nigerian cities, will serve to illustrate.

When George Aduku graduated from secondary school and did not pass the university entrance exam, he decided to go to a city in order to find work. He had an uncle living in Kaduna, over 400 miles from his home. So George took a passenger truck to Makurdi and from there traveled by train to Kaduna.

When George arrived in Kaduna, his uncle and aunt welcomed him into their home and provided both food and lodging at no charge, because George was their nephew. The next day George went out looking for work. For an entire week he searched for a job. He could have taken temporary work cleaning up the market at the close of the day, but felt that such a job was too low-paying and demeaning for a high school graduate. In any case, he was looking for permanent employment.

After one week, George's Uncle Samuel came home with good news. A fellow worker at the textile mill had told him that the ordnance factory in Kaduna would be hiring clerks and supervisors the following day. A cousin who worked in the personnel office would put in a good word for George if Uncle Samuel recommended him without reservation.

As a result, George Aduku found meaningful work in Kaduna before many others with the same qualifications. By the time he received his first paycheck, he had sensed that his aunt was growing weary of having him around the house and that it would be good for him to move into an apartment. A workmate from his own ethnic group invited George to move into the apartment he shared with another young man. Although this workmate was Catholic and George was Protestant, he felt that their shared tribal identity would prevent any problems.

George and his new friend were now both workmates and roommates. They sometimes played together as well, although George slowly developed other friends whose tastes in recreation were more similar to his. He began saving money for the time several years away when he would be able to pay the price for a bride from his ethnic homeland and bring her to live with him in Kaduna.

To accomplish his goals, George and his uncle made use of several networks. George started with the network already in place when he arrived in the city, his relatives. His Uncle Samuel in turn activated another network, that of his workmates. Once George had work, he also could use this network to find a place to live. And when he had a place to live, a third network emerged, that of his neighbors. From his workmates, his neighbors, and possibly other relatives in the city, he could develop his playmates, those with whom he pursued recreation.

Notice that we have already mentioned four networks: relatives, workmates, neighbors, and playmates. The members of George's church or his fellow believers might constitute a fifth network. The term fellow believer is used because if George were a Muslim, he might find help at the mosque rather than at church.

I was in the city of Zaria in Nigeria when a Christian man was hit by a triple tragedy. First he lost his job, and then his 10-year-old daughter died while his wife was in the hospital with a terminal illness. His wife was so sick that no one dared tell her about the death of the daughter. Fellow Christians rallied around the man; many attended the daughter's burial, at which I was asked to officiate.

When the wife also died, the Christian community put forth more strenuous efforts to help. One church member arranged for the wife's body to be kept refrigerated in the hospital morgue, while another, who was with the police force, used the police radio to notify relatives back home. This made it possible for them to arrive in Zaria in time for the burial. Generous gifts were also donated to the widower to tide him over until new work could be found. He had a network that sustained him in time of tragedy—the members of his church.

15. What are networks, and what social function do they perform?

_____

_____

_____

Such networks could be called homogeneous networks because the people involved in them have something in common. They are joined to one another by (usually) several webs of common interests and mutual benefits.* Donald McGavran wrote and spoke about "homogeneous units" and "webs of relationships" long before the term "network" became common among social scientists. Such relationships do not disappear in the city. In some cases they are strengthened there. The fact that they are informal and are often invoked in an ad hoc manner to deal with specific problems does not detract from their helpfulness.

===

When people recommend Jesus Christ to other members of their networks, it is a potent endorsement.

===

Both flexible and productive, these networks can be used as an avenue for the spread of the gospel. People tend to trust those who are members of their networks, not only for information about where to find work, medical help, or good housing at a reasonable price. They also lean on network members for advice on deeper needs, such as whom to marry, how to deal with marital problems, and how to handle depression. Among these deeper needs is one's religious allegiance. When people recommend Jesus Christ to other members of their networks, it is a potent endorsement.

Networks can facilitate the spread of the gospel within a people group. For example, Tiv people living in the cities of Nigeria have used their networks to spread the Christian faith. During the Nigerian civil war (1967-1970), many Tiv young men who had been involved in Christian work as laymen went off to join the army. In the army they continued to witness to their fellow Tiv about Jesus Christ, even though they now received no payment for this witness and no church was supervising them. Workmates (in this case soldiers) witnessed to their fellows and thus spread the gospel. The wives and children of married soldiers also became involved. And so the network of workmates was extended by adding a network of relatives. The result was the spread of the gospel among Tiv soldiers and their families both during and, most notably, after the war.

In addition, a network of workmates often becomes a bridge for the gospel to pass from one people group to another. When the Nigerian civil war was over, I spoke to Tiv soldiers and their families at the Rainbow Army Camp at Port Harcourt. Hausa-speaking soldiers were also present, and whatever I said in Tiv was translated into Hausa. Tiv soldiers who were Christians had told their fellow Hausa soldiers that a missionary was speaking in the army chapel that evening. They too came to participate. Joint service in the Nigerian army created a bridge from one group to another.

But the same networks that serve as a bridge for the gospel can also present obstacles to its spread. Some people may hesitate to declare faith in Christ because they fear ridicule from others in their networks. Others may fear the loss of the support of their networks if they make a firm Christian commitment. Or one might feel free to talk with fellow workers about Jesus Christ, but be reluctant to approach relatives, who may disparage anything having to do with Christianity. Playmates might not disparage Christianity, but they might present so

---

* For a fuller discussion of homogeneous networks, see the June 1987 issue of the *International Journal of Frontier Missions*, pp. 45-52.

many tempting alternatives to the Christian life that the growing seeds of faith are choked.

Christian workers who recognize and understand these networks will wish to utilize them for the spread of the gospel, and will try to minimize any detrimental effects. They may also assist new Christians in finding new networks if this is necessary.

In addition to networks, there are what Kenneth Little describes as "voluntary associations." Voluntary associations differ from networks in that they are more formalized. They are organizations that one can join. By joining, one comes to participate in both the benefits and the obligations of membership. Little mentions tribal associations, mutual aid societies, recreation societies, Christian clubs, syncretis-

tic cults, and cultural societies, all of which seek to benefit both their members and others in various ways. Scholarships, funeral expenses, and civic improvement in the home area are among the common benefits provided by such associations. Although Little wrote about West Africa, evidence suggests that helpful voluntary associations are a worldwide urban phenomenon. Together with networks, they help to ease the stress of urban life and even to make such life enjoyable.

The church as an institution (formalized and organized under officers) is like a voluntary association; the church as the people of God out in the world is more like a helpful network of fellow believers. It is often difficult, however, to tell where the voluntary association stops and the network starts.

16. *Why is an understanding of networks so important to the discussion of urban church planting?*

_____

_____

_____

_____

III. The Church in Culture

It is not enough that the gospel be communicated in strategic ways. What emerges once the church is conceived is of fundamental importance also. As the *Willowbank Report* states, "If the gospel must be contextualized, so must the church." In January, 1978, a group of 33 anthropologists, linguists, missionaries, and pastors met in Willowbank, Somerset Bridge, Bermuda, for a consultation on "Gospel and Culture." Seventeen written papers were circulated among the participants before the consultation, and a comprehensive report was produced, part of which follows. The report's provocative message challenges all missions to integrity in allowing the church to be "real" to its own culture.

❑ *Church and Culture* *

In the process of church formation, as in the communication and reception of the gospel, the question of culture is vital. If the gospel must be contextualized, so must the church. Indeed, the subtitle of our Consultation has been, "The Contextualization of Word and Church in a Missionary Situation."

Older, traditional approaches

During the missionary expansion of the early part of the 19th century, it was generally assumed that churches "on the mission field" would be modeled on churches "at home." The tendency was to produce almost exact replicas. Gothic architecture, prayer book liturgies, clerical dress, musical instruments, hymns and tunes, decision-making processes, synods and committees, superintendents and archdeacons—all were exported and unimaginatively introduced into the new mission-founded churches. It should be added that these patterns were also eagerly adopted by the new Christians, determined not to be at any point behind their Western friends, whose habits and ways of worship they had been attentively watching. But all this was based on the false assumptions that the Bible gave specific instructions about such matters and that the home churches' pattern of government, worship, ministry, and life were themselves exemplary.

In reaction to this monocultural export system, pioneer missionary thinkers like Henry Venn and Rufus Anderson in the middle of the last century and Roland Allen earlier in this century popularized the concept of "indigenous" churches, which would be "self-governing, self-supporting, and self-propagating." They argued their case well. They pointed out that the policy of the Apostle Paul was to plant churches, not to found mission stations. They also added pragmatic arguments to biblical ones, namely, that indigeneity was indispensable to the church's growth in maturity and mission. Henry Venn confidently looked forward to the day when missions would hand over all responsibility to national churches, and then what he called "the euthanasia of the mission" would take place. These views gained wide acceptance and were immensely influential.

A more radical concept of indigenous church life needs to be developed, by which each church may discover and express its selfhood as the body of Christ within its own culture.

In our day, however, they are being criticized, not because of the ideal itself, but because of the way it has often been applied. Some missions, for example, have accepted the need for indigenous leadership and have then gone on to recruit and train local leaders, indoctrinating them (the word is harsh but not unfair) in Western ways of thought and procedure. These Westernized local leaders have then preserved a very Western-looking church, and the foreign orientation has persisted, only lightly cloaked by the appearance of indigeneity.

Now, therefore, a more radical concept of indigenous church life needs to be developed, by which each church may discover and express its selfhood as the body of Christ within its own culture.

---

* Lausanne Committee for World Evangelization (1978). *The Willowbank report: Gospel and culture* (Lausanne Occasional Papers No. 2, Sec. 8). Wheaton, IL: Author.

17. *Why have the three "self" criteria for church planting failed to produce truly contextualized churches?*

The dynamic equivalence model

Using the distinctions between "form" and "meaning" and between "formal correspondence" and "dynamic equivalence," which have been developed in translation theory and on which we have commented, it is being suggested that an analogy may be drawn between Bible translation and church formation. "Formal correspondence" speaks of a slavish imitation, whether in translating a word into another language or exporting a church model to another culture. Just as a "dynamic equivalence" translation, however, seeks to convey to contemporary readers meanings equivalent to those conveyed to the original readers, by using appropriate cultural forms, so would a "dynamic equivalence" church. It would look in its culture as a good Bible translation looks in its language. It would preserve the essential meanings and functions which the New Testament predicated of the church, but would seek to express these in forms equivalent to the originals but appropriate to the local culture.

We have all found this model helpful and suggestive, and we strongly affirm the ideals it seeks to express. It rightly rejects foreign imports and imitation and rigid structures. It rightly looks to the New Testament for the principles of church formation, rather than to either tradition or culture, and it equally rightly looks to the local culture for the appropriate forms in which these principles should be expressed. All of us (even those who see limitations in the model) share the vision which it is trying to describe.

Thus, the New Testament indicates that the church is always a worshiping community, "a holy priesthood to offer spiritual sacrifices to God through Jesus Christ" (1 Pet. 2:5), but forms of worship (including the presence or absence of different kinds of liturgy, ceremony, music, color, drama, etc.) will be developed by the church in keeping with indigenous culture. Similarly, the church is always a witnessing and a serving community, but its methods of evangelism and its program of social involvement will vary. Again, God desires all churches to have pastoral oversight, but forms of government and ministry may differ widely, and the selection, training, ordination, service, dress, payment, and accountability of pastors will be determined by the church to accord with biblical principles and to suit the local culture.

A "dynamic equivalence" church would preserve the essential meanings and functions which the New Testament predicated of the church, but would seek to express these in forms equivalent to the originals but appropriate to the local culture.

The questions which are being asked about the "dynamic equivalence" model are whether by itself it is large enough and dynamic enough to provide all the guidance which is needed. The analogy between Bible translation and church formation is not exact. In the former the translator controls the work, and when the task is complete it is possible to make a comparison of the two texts. In the latter, however, the original to which an equivalent is being sought is not a detailed text but a series of glimpses of the early church in operation, making the comparison more difficult, and instead of a controlling translator the whole community of faith must be involved. Further, a translator aims at personal objectivity, but when the local church is seeking to relate itself appropriately to the local culture, it finds objectivity almost impossible. In many situations it is caught in "an encounter between two civilizations" (that of its own society and that of the missionaries'). Furthermore, it may have great difficulty in responding to the conflicting voices of the local community. Some clamor for change (in terms of literacy, education, technology, modern medicine, industrialization, etc.), while others insist on the conservation of the old culture and resist the arrival of a new day. It is asked whether the "dynamic equivalence" model is dynamic enough to face this kind of challenge.

The test of this or any other model for helping churches develop appropriately is whether it can enable God's people to capture in their hearts and minds the grand design of which their church is to be the local expression. Every model presents only a partial picture. Local churches need to rely ultimately on the dynamic pressure of the living Lord of history. For it is He who will guide His people in every age to develop their church life in such a way as both to obey the instructions He has given in Scripture and to reflect the good elements of their local culture.

18. *What is the application of a dynamic equivalence model supposed to achieve?*

_____

_____

_____

The freedom of the church

If each church is to develop creatively in such a way as to find and express itself, it must be free to do so. This is its inalienable right. For each church is God's church. United to Christ, it is a dwelling place of God through His Spirit (Eph. 2:22). Some missions and missionaries have been slow to recognize this and to accept its implications in the direction of indigenous forms and an every-member ministry. This is one of the many causes which have led to the formation of independent churches, notably in Africa, which are seeking new ways of self-expression in terms of local culture.

Although local church leaders have also sometimes impeded indigenous development, the chief blame lies elsewhere. It would not be fair to generalize. The situation has always been diverse. In earlier generations there were missions which never manifested a spirit of domination. In this century some churches have sprung up which have never been under missionary control, having enjoyed self-government from the start. In other cases missions have entirely surrendered their former power, so that some mission-founded churches are now fully autonomous, and many missions now work in genuine partnership with churches.

Yet this is not the whole picture. Other churches are still almost completely inhibited from developing their own identity and program by policies laid down from afar, by the introduction and continuation of foreign traditions, by the use of expatriate leadership, by alien decision-making processes, and especially by the manipulative use of money. Those

> *Although local church leaders have also sometimes impeded indigenous development, the chief blame lies elsewhere.*

who maintain such control may be genuinely unaware of the way in which their actions are regarded and experienced at the other end. They may be felt by the churches concerned to be a tyranny. The fact that this is neither intended nor realized illustrates perfectly how all of us (whether we know it or not) are involved in the culture which has made us what we are. We strongly oppose such "foreignness," wherever it exists, as a serious obstacle to maturity and mission and a quenching of the Holy Spirit of God.

It was in protest against the continuance of foreign control that a few years ago the call was made to withdraw all missionaries. In this debate some of us want to avoid the word "moratorium" because it has become an emotive term and sometimes betrays a resentment against the very concept of "missionar-ies." Others of us wish to retain the word in order to emphasize the truth it expresses. To us it means not a rejection of missionary personnel and money in themselves, but only of their misuse in such a way as to suffocate local initiative. We all agree with the statement of the Lausanne Covenant that "a reduc-tion of foreign missionaries and money... may sometimes be necessary to facilitate the national church's growth in self-reliance...." (para. 9).

---

19. How can missionaries and their money interfere with church freedom?

_____

_____

_____

Power structures and mission

What we have just written is part of a much wider problem, which we have not felt able to ignore. The contemporary world does not consist of isolated atomic societies, but is an interrelated global system of economic, political, technological, and ideologi-cal macro-structures, which undoubtedly results in much exploitation and oppression.

What has this got to do with mission? And why do we raise it here? Partly because it is the context within which the gospel must be preached to all nations today. Partly also because nearly all of us either belong to the Third World, or live and work there, or have done so, or have visited some coun-tries in it. So we have seen with our own eyes the poverty of the masses, we feel for them and with them, and we have some understanding that their plight is due in part to an economic system which is controlled mostly by the North Atlantic countries (although others are now also involved). Those of us who are citizens of North American or European countries cannot avoid some feeling of embarrass-ment and shame, by reason of the oppression in which our countries in various degrees have been involved. Of course, we know that there is oppres-sion in many countries today, and we oppose it everywhere. But now we are talking about our-selves, our own countries, and our responsibility as Christians. Most of the world's missionaries and missionary money come from these countries, often at great personal sacrifice. Yet we have to confess that some missionaries themselves reflect a neo-colonial attitude and even defend it, together with outposts of Western power and exploitation.

So what should we do? The only honest response is to say that we do not know. Armchair criticism smacks of hypocrisy. We have no ready-made solu-tions to offer to this worldwide problem. Indeed, we feel victims of the system ourselves. And yet we are also part of it. So we feel able to make only these comments:

First, Jesus Himself constantly identified with the poor and weak. We accept the obligation to follow in His footsteps in this matter as in all others. At least by the love which prays and gives, we mean to strengthen our solidarity with them.

Jesus did more than identify, however. In His teach-ing and that of the apostles, the corollary of good news to the oppressed was a word of judgment to the oppressor (e.g., Luke 6:24-26; James 5:1-6). We confess that in complex economic situations it is not easy to identify oppressors in order to denounce them, without resorting to a shrill rhetoric which neither costs nor accomplishes anything. Neverthe-less, we accept that there will be occasions when it is our Christian duty to speak out against injustice in the name of the Lord who is the God of justice as well as of justification. We shall seek from Him the courage and wisdom to do so.

Thirdly, this Consultation has expressed its concern about syncretism in Third World churches. But we have not forgotten that Western churches fall prey to the same sin. Indeed, perhaps the most insidious form of syncretism in the world today is the attempt to mix a privatized gospel of personal forgiveness with a worldly (even demonic) attitude of wealth and power. We are not guiltless in this matter ourselves. Yet we desire to be integrated Christians for whom Jesus is truly Lord of all. So we who belong to or come from the West will examine ourselves and seek to purge ourselves of Western-style syncretism. We agree that "the salvation we claim should be transforming us in the totality of our personal and social responsibilities. Faith without works is dead" (Lausanne Covenant, para. 5).

---

20. Why can't the controversial issue of power structures be ignored by Christian mission?

_____

_____

_____

The danger of provincialism

We have emphasized that the church must be allowed to indigenize itself and to "celebrate, sing, and dance" the gospel in its own cultural medium. At the same time, we wish to be alert to the dangers of this process. Some churches in all six continents go beyond a joyful and thankful discovery of their local cultural heritage and either become boastful and assertive about it (a form of chauvinism) or even absolutize it (a form of idolatry). More common than either of these extremes, however, is "provincialism," that is, such a retreat into their own culture as cuts them adrift from the rest of the church and from the wider world. This is a frequent stance in Western churches as well as in the Third World. It denies the God of creation and redemption. It is to proclaim one's freedom, only to enter another bondage. We draw attention to the three major reasons why we think this attitude should be avoided:

First, each church is part of the universal church. The people of God are by His grace a unique multi-racial, multinational, multicultural community. This community is God's new creation, His new humanity, in which Christ has abolished all barriers (see Ephesians 2 and 3). There is therefore no room for racism in the Christian society or for tribalism—whether in its African form or in the form of European social classes or of the Indian caste system.

Despite the church's failures, this vision of a supra-ethnic community of love is not a romantic ideal but a command of the Lord. Therefore, while rejoicing in our cultural inheritance and developing our own indigenous forms, we must always remember that our primary identity as Christians is not in our particular cultures but in the one Lord and His one body (Eph. 4:3-6).

Our church should never become so culture-bound that visitors from another culture do not feel welcome.

Secondly, each church worships the living God of cultural diversity. If we thank Him for our cultural heritage, we should thank Him for others' also. Our church should never become so culture-bound that visitors from another culture do not feel welcome. Indeed, we believe it is enriching for Christians, if they have the opportunity, to develop a bicultural and even a multicultural existence, like the Apostle Paul, who was both a Hebrew of the Hebrews, a master of the Greek language, and a Roman citizen.

Thirdly, each church should enter into a "partnership... in giving and receiving" (Phil. 4:15). No church is, or should try to become, self-sufficient. So churches should develop with each other relationships of prayer, fellowship, interchange of ministry, and cooperation. Provided that we share the same central truths (including the supreme Lordship of Christ, the authority of Scripture, the necessity of conversion, confidence in the power of the Holy Spirit, and the obligations of holiness and witness), we should be outgoing and not timid in seeking fellowship; and we should share our spiritual gifts and ministries, knowledge, skills, experience, and financial resources. The same principle applies to cultures. A church must be free to reject alien cultural forms and develop its own; it should also feel free to borrow from others. This way lies maturity.

One example of this concerns theology. Cross-cultural witnesses must not attempt to impose a ready-made theological tradition on the church in which they serve, either by personal teaching or by literature or by controlling seminary and Bible college curricula. For every theological tradition both contains elements which are biblically questionable and have been ecclesiastically divisive and omits elements which, while they might be of no great consequence in the country where they originated, may be of immense importance in other contexts. At the same time, although missionaries ought not to impose their own tradition on others, they also ought not to deny them access to it (in the form of books, confessions, catechism, liturgies, and hymns), since it doubtless represents a rich heritage of faith. Moreover, although the theological controversies of the

---

> *A church must be free to reject alien cultural forms and develop its own; it should also feel free to borrow from others.*

---

older churches should not be exported to the younger churches, yet an understanding of the issues and of the work of the Holy Spirit in the unfolding history of Christian doctrine should help to protect them from unprofitable repetition of the same battles.

Thus we should seek with equal care to avoid theological imperialism or theological provincialism. A church's theology should be developed by the community of faith out of the Scripture in interaction with other theologies of the past and present and with the local culture and its needs.

21. *In what way do theological imperialism and theological provincialism provoke the same kind of error?*

The danger of syncretism

As the church seeks to express its life in local cultural forms, it soon has to face the problem of cultural elements which either are evil or have evil associations. How should the church react to these? Elements which are intrinsically false or evil clearly cannot be assimilated into Christianity without a lapse into syncretism. This is a danger for all churches in all cultures. If the evil is in the association only, however, we believe it is right to seek to "baptize" it into Christ. It is the principle on which William Booth operated when he set Christian words to popular music, asking why the devil should have all the best tunes. Thus many African churches now use drums to summon people to worship, although previously they were unacceptable, as being associated with war dances and mediumistic rites.

Yet this principle raises problems. In a proper reaction against foreigners, an improper flirtation with the demonic element of local culture sometimes takes place. So the church, being first and foremost a servant of Jesus Christ, must learn to scrutinize all culture, both foreign and local, in the light of His Lordship and God's revelation. By what guidelines, therefore, does a church accept or reject culture traits in the process of contextualization? How does it prevent or detect and eliminate heresy (wrong teaching) and syncretism (harmful carry-overs from the old way of life)? How does it protect itself from becoming a "folk church" in which church and society are virtually synonymous?

The church, being first and foremost a servant of Jesus Christ, must learn to scrutinize all culture, both foreign and local, in the light of His Lordship and God's revelation.

One particular model we have studied is that of the church in Bali, Indonesia, which is now about 40 years old. Its experience has provided the following guidelines:

The believing community first searched the Scriptures and learned from them many important biblical truths. They then observed that other churches (e.g., around the Mediterranean) used architecture to symbolize Christian truth. This was important because the Balinese are very "visual" people and value visible signs. So it was decided, for example, to express their affirmation of faith in the Trinity in a Balinese-style three-tiered roof for their church buildings. The symbol was first considered by the council of elders who, after studying both biblical

and cultural factors, recommended it to local congregations.

The detection and elimination of heresy followed a similar pattern. When believers suspected an error in life or teaching, they would report it to an elder, who would take it to the council of elders. Having considered the matter, they in their turn passed their recommendations to the local churches who had the final word.

What was the most important safeguard of the church? To this question the answer was, "We believe that Jesus Christ is Lord and Master of all powers." By preaching His power, "the same yesterday and today and forever," by insisting at all times on the normative nature of the Scriptures, by entrusting elders with the obligation to reflect on Scripture and culture, by breaking down all barriers to fellowship, and by building into structures, catechism, art forms, drama, etc., constant reminders of the exalted position of Jesus Christ, His church has been preserved in truth and holiness.

Sometimes, in different parts of the world, a cultural element may be adopted which deeply disturbs oversensitive consciences, especially those of new converts. This is the problem of the "weaker brother" of whom Paul writes in connection with idol-meats. Since idols were nothing, Paul himself had liberty of conscience to eat these meats. But for the sake of "weaker" Christians with a less well-educated conscience, who would be offended to see him eat, he refrained, at least in specific situations in which such offense might be caused. The principle still applies today. Scripture takes conscience seriously and tells us not to violate it. It needs to be educated in order to become "strong," but while it remains "weak" it must be respected. A strong conscience will give us freedom, but love limits liberty.

22. *What is the most effective safeguard against syncretism?*

_____

_____

_____

The church's influence on culture

We deplore the pessimism which leads some Christians to disapprove of active cultural engagement in the world, and the defeatism which persuades others that they could do no good there anyway and should therefore wait in inactivity for Christ to put things right when He comes. Many historical examples could be given, drawn from different ages and countries, of the powerful influence which—under God—the church has exerted on a prevailing culture, purging, claiming, and beautifying it for Christ. Though all such attempts have had defects, they do not prove the enterprise mistaken.

We prefer, however, to base the church's cultural responsibility on Scripture rather than on history. We have reminded ourselves that our fellow men and women are made in God's image and that we are commanded to honor, love, and serve them in every sphere of life. To this argument from God's creation we add another from His kingdom, which broke into the world through Jesus Christ. All authority belongs to Christ. He is Lord of both universe and church. And He has sent us into the world to be its salt and light. As His new community, He expects us to permeate society.

Thus we are to challenge what is evil and affirm what is good; to welcome and seek to promote all that is wholesome and enriching in art, science, technology, agriculture, industry, education, community development, and social welfare; to denounce injustice and support the powerless and the oppressed; to spread the good news of Jesus Christ, which is the most liberating and humanizing force in the world; and to actively engage in good works of love. Although in social and cultural activity, as in evangelism, we must leave the results to God, we are confident that He will bless our endeavors and use them to develop in our community a new consciousness of what is "true, noble, right, pure, lovely, and honorable" (Phil. 4:8, TEV). Of course, the church cannot impose Christian standards on an unwilling society, but it can commend them by both argument and example. All this will bring glory to God and greater opportunities of humanness to our fellow human being whom He made and loves. As the Lausanne Covenant put it, "Churches must seek to transform and enrich culture, all for the glory of God" (para. 10).

Nevertheless, naive optimism is as foolish as dark pessimism. In place of both, we seek a sober Christian realism. On the one hand, Jesus Christ reigns. On the other, He has not yet destroyed the forces of evil; they still rampage. So in every culture Christians find themselves in a situation of conflict and often of suffering. We are called to fight against the "cosmic powers of this dark age" (Eph. 6:12, TEV). So we need each other. We must put on all God's armor, especially the mighty weapon of believing

---

> **The church cannot impose Christian standards on an unwilling society, but it can commend them by both argument and example.**

---

prayer. We also remember the warnings of Christ and His apostles that before the end there will be an unprecedented outbreak of wickedness and violence. Some events and developments in our contemporary world indicate that the spirit of the coming Antichrist is already at work not only in the non-Christian world, but both in our own partially Christianized societies and even in the churches themselves. "We therefore reject as a proud, self-confident dream the notion that man can ever build a utopia on earth" (Lausanne Covenant, para. 15) and as a groundless fantasy that society is going to evolve into perfection.

Instead, while energetically laboring on earth, we look forward with joyful anticipation to the return of Christ and to the new heavens and new earth in which righteousness will dwell. For then not only will culture be transformed, as the nations bring their glory into the New Jerusalem (Rev. 21:24-26), but the whole creation will be liberated from its present bondage of futility, decay, and pain, so as to share the glorious freedom of God's children (Rom. 8:18-25, TEV). Then at last every knee will bow to Christ and every tongue openly proclaim that He is Lord, to the glory of God the Father (Phil. 2:9-11).

23. Contrast "Christian realism" with "naive optimism" and "dark pessimism."

Having considered some of the cultural factors in Christian conversion, we come finally to the relations between culture and Christian ethical behavior. For the new life Christ gives His people is bound to issue a new lifestyle.

Christ centeredness and Christlikeness

One of the themes running right through our Consultation has been the supreme Lordship of Jesus Christ. He is Lord of the universe and the church; He is Lord of the individual believer also. We find ourselves gripped by the love of Christ. It hems us in and leaves us no escape. Because we enjoy newness of life through His death for us, we have no alternative (and desire none) but to live for Him who died for us and rose again (2 Cor. 5:14-15). Our first loyalty is to Him, to seek to please Him, to live a life worthy of Him, and to obey Him. This necessitates the renunciation of all lesser loyalties. So we are forbidden to conform ourselves to this world's standards, that is, to any prevailing culture which

fails to honor God, and are commanded instead to be transformed in our conduct by renewed minds which perceive the will of God.

God's will was perfectly obeyed by Jesus. Therefore, "the most outstanding thing about a Christian should not be his culture, but his Christlikeness." As the mid-second century Letter to Diognetus puts it: "Christians are not distinguished from the rest of

---

The most outstanding thing about a Christian should not be his culture, but his Christlikeness.

---

mankind by country or by speech or by customs… they follow the customs of the land in clothing and food and other matters of daily life, yet the condition of citizenship which they exhibit is wonderful… in a word, what the soul is in the body, that Christians are in the world."

Summary

Societies can be analyzed from the standpoint of interpersonal relationships and from communication patterns between social groupings in the overall structure. On a personal level, the bicultural bridge is a set of relationships between people from two cultures. As this "bridge" is created, many personal and lifestyle decisions are made. These decisions affect missionaries' relationships with nationals, as well as the role and status with which the missionaries are perceived. Communication patterns are also affected. An appropriate role involves effective identification with the people. How different societies function in terms of decision making is also crucial to effective communication of the gospel. Group decisions present a challenge to individualistic Westerners. The "homogeneous unit principle" applied to church planting may stimulate church growth, but it is controversial.

Social links within cities can be described as "veins" with multiple intersecting points. Most cities contain ethnic groupings which should be identified and targeted for church planting if the Great Commission is to be fulfilled. These strategies may be a link to reaching groups in the hinterland. Social groupings can be identified by economic level as well as occupation. Ethnicity is a primary consideration in identification of social groupings, but these other social factors are also critical. City dwellers develop complex webs of relationships which link them to others in "networks." Communication travels along these lines, and an awareness of this fact can be of great help to church planters.

The objective of mission work should be "indigenous" churches, which are "self-governing, self-supporting, and self-propagating." Even when the three "selfs" are espoused, however, Western missions have inhibited the development of contextualized churches through indoctrination of the national leadership and other controls. Dynamic equivalence models are called for, which will allow the church to develop along culturally sensitive lines. Each church should be free to seek this indigenous expression. Complicating these issues are the sensitive areas of power structures and the missionary's role in denouncing corruption and injustice. A call to balance in unity is needed to combat the errors of provincialism and theological imperialism. Adaptation of cultural forms must be analyzed in terms of the potential for syncretism. The church is a proactive agent in bringing about positive cultural change through submission to the Lordship of Christ.

Integrative Assignment

1. Describe the steps you would take in building a bicultural bridge. What criteria would you establish for making decisions regarding lifestyle choices? Project yourself into a cross-cultural situation, and from your imagination, write a descriptive narrative of your experience in building a bicultural bridge.

2. How many different networks are you a part of? How do you respond to each one in terms of your faith in Christ? How can each of these be "mined" for the Lord? Write a paper entitled, "Insights on Reaching Others Within My Own Networks."

3. Is the church of which you are a part contextualized? Analyze its forms and structures (i.e., worship, government, building, programs, etc.) and explain why you think each element is contextualized or not.

Questions for Reflection

Being a cross-cultural missionary is not an easy task. It requires a great deal of self-denial and loving sensitivity to others. These are qualities which have always characterized the most effective missionaries. Apart from Christ, the Apostle Paul was perhaps the most effective missionary of all time. The evidence from the book of Acts and the Epistles indicates that he had cross-cultural awareness. He was also willing to pay the price of self-denial to be effective. His cross-cultural philosophy is reflected in I Corinthians 9:19-23. Read this passage and reflect on the ways Paul's statements were exemplified in his ministry. What philosophy are you willing to follow? Write your thoughts below.

_____

_____

_____

_____

_____

_____

_____

_____

_____

_____

_____

_____

CHAPTER 15

World Christian Teamwork

All Christians have a responsibility towards fulfillment of the Great Commission. Not all can or should go as missionaries, but for everyone who does go, many must stay behind in coordinated, active support roles. There are no "solo" performers. Where war is being waged, the success of the front lines depends largely upon the support received from the rear. The teamwork needed calls for a clear understanding of the mission by those who are sent *and those who send them.*

World Christian teamwork, however, is more than the interaction between goers and senders. If the war is to be won, we must know our allies and enter into strategic partnership with them. During World War II, the Normandy invasion for the liberation of France required the Allied forces to combine and coordinate their efforts. The armies of several autonomous nations were involved, but each one worked in a coordinated fashion towards the common objective. Reaching the nations, particularly in "restricted access" countries, will require a level of interaction which has been uncommon in missions. Recognizing our one Commander-in-Chief and His objectives, we must coordinate our efforts across national, denominational, and mission boundaries.

In this final chapter of our study, we will explore the different components of world Christian teamwork. We begin with an individual's personal covenant with God to be involved in fulfilling His world mission. This basic commitment is expressed outwardly in joining forces with other "World Christians." Teamwork begins to happen at the local church level through prayer groups and missions committee work. It enlarges and gathers force with enabling structures such as foreign mission agencies and ministries with international students. It reaches its maximum potential through interagency cooperation and strategic alliances targeting specific nations. With world Christian teamwork, the task can be completed.

I. Teaming Up With God

Most people who claim to be Christians recognize Christ as Savior; relatively few recognize His authority as Lord of their lives. Christ's sovereignty is usually a vague and generalized notion. Christ is a benign ruler whose laws should be obeyed in gratitude for salvation and other blessings. Commitment to God means going to church and maintaining a reasonably decent code of behavior.

We know differently. God's purpose is our purpose. He calls His people to engage in spiritual warfare to the ends of the earth. If the scriptural mandate is so clear, why is mission so unheralded in the church today? In the following article, Bill and Amy Stearns share their thoughts on this troubling question.

❑ *The Catch* *

Bill and Amy Stearns **

Through our study, you might have wondered: If the biblical mandate is so clear, if the big picture of what God is doing in our world today is so exciting, if the 12,000 remaining people groups could be reached within a few years' time, if millions are dying without God and without hope, if we can push back the powers of darkness over whole nations near to the heart of God, why isn't all Christendom buzzing with the news that we can finish the task?

The cost for Christian organizations is to give up small ambitions, to selflessly cooperate, not needlessly duplicate efforts and compete for funds.

What's the catch?

Here's the easy answer: There is a cost involved.

That's the catch. Obedience costs. Real discipleship costs. The price? Giving up our small, personal agendas that detract from God's global cause. Forsaking our comfortable lives, giving up claims of ownership to affluence, to security.

The challenge today is exactly that of Francis Xavier, who 500 years ago dreamed of returning to Paris from his mission work in India, China, and Japan. Why? So he could "go shouting up and down the streets to tell the students to give up their small ambitions and come eastward to preach the gospel of Christ!"

The cost for Christian organizations is to give up small ambitions, to selflessly cooperate, not needlessly duplicate efforts and compete for funds. Paul McKaughan of the Evangelical Fellowship of Mission Agencies says to these organizations:

It is important that we as leaders begin to interact together and find out what God's will is for us collectively.... We may be talking about surrendering some of our prerogatives. We may be talking about applying some of our computer skills. We may be talking about some of our unreached peoples ground forces.

We are all accumulating a body of knowledge, and we're all trying to do everything. We can't do everything in the world in which we live. And we're going to have to begin to

---

* Stearns, W., & Stearns, A. (1991). *Catch the vision 2000* (pp. 157-160). Minneapolis: Bethany House.

** Bill and Amy Stearns are on the staff of Adopt-A-People Clearinghouse on the campus of the U.S. Center for World Mission, where they work in the publications and personnel departments. Bill has written 10 books as well as numerous magazine articles. He is the editor of *Paraclete Mission Perspectives* magazine and has written Bible study curricula for a number of publishers. Bill and Amy offer *Catch the Vision* seminars for churches, conferences, and student fellowships.

trust one another enough to use the tools and the abilities and the giftedness of the various members of our community in order that the body of Christ can move with an expeditious and a decided tread toward this goal of world evangelization.*

1. What is the "price" of obedience to the mandate in both personal and organizational terms?

Obedience means giving up our small, personal ambitions. Obedience means shifting our expectations to becoming a blessing instead of merely being blessed. The price of being a part of God's historic, global purpose is losing your life for His sake. Denying your old self. Taking up your cross—which in Jesus' day meant you wouldn't need to

> *Obedience means shifting our expectations to becoming a blessing instead of merely being blessed.*

worry much about things that most people worry about. Taking up your cross is a picture of your standing with a noose around your neck; you've put yourself at God's disposal so thoroughly that you have nothing left to lose.

An old parable often told among believers across Africa pictures just how tough it is to give up our own ambitions:

One day Jesus asked each of His disciples to pick up a stone to carry for Him. John took the biggest one he could find, while Peter picked a small one. Jesus took them up to the top of a mountain and commanded the stones to be bread. Each was allowed to eat the bread he found in his hands, but of course Peter did not have much to eat at all. John then shared some of his with Peter.

On another occasion Jesus again asked the disciples to carry stones for Him. This time, instead of leading them to a mountaintop, He took them to the River Jordan. "Cast the stones into the river," was His command this time. The disciples looked at one another in bewilderment. What could be the point? They had lugged those stones all this way. (And you know who picked the big one this time, don't you?) Throw them into the river? Why? But they obeyed.

Jesus turned to them and said, "For whom did you carry the stone?"

2. What does this old African parable teach us about our natural tendencies even when we want to obey Christ?

---

* McKaughan, P. (1990, May-August). A.D. 2000 and beyond. *A.D. 2000,* 5-9.

Sometimes the Christian disciplines of denial of self, of facing afflictions, of solid prayer and study in the Word seem pointless. What's the purpose of denying self and taking up your cross daily? A nicer life? Success? Or is discipleship a discipline with purpose: To become a closer follower of Christ, to live in obedience, to "make disciples of all *ethne*."

Jesus didn't pander to our lazy, self-seeking instincts:

> "He who loves father or mother more than Me is not worthy of Me; and he who loves son or daughter more than Me is not worthy of Me. And he who does not take his cross and follow after Me is not worthy of Me. He who has found his life shall lose it, and he who has lost his life for My sake shall find it" (Matt. 10:37-39).

> And looking at him, Jesus felt a love for him, and said to him, "One thing you lack: Go and sell all you possess, and give to the poor, and you shall have treasure in heaven; and come, follow Me" (Mark 10:21).

> And another also said, "I will follow You, Lord; but first permit me to say good-bye to those at home." But Jesus said to him, "No one, after putting his hand to the plow and looking back, is fit for the kingdom of God" (Luke 9:61-62).

> "So therefore, no one of you can be My disciple who does not give up all his own possessions" (Luke 14:33).

There are many fine expositions and Bible studies published on these and other "hard" passages concerning the disciplines of true discipleship. But even the most earnest attempts to soften these stringencies of following Jesus must conclude that the price of selling yourself as a bondslave for the Master's use can be high. In the Bible, a life sold out to His purpose is compared to the rigors of the lifestyle of an athlete in training, a hard-working farmer, a combat soldier (2 Tim. 2:3-10).

Can we visualize—can we ever forget—the fact that since the time of Christ, 40 million believers have been martyred for faith in Jesus Christ? In recent times, the total number of Christians killed for their faith is 300,000!

Perhaps too many of us Christians have been led to believe that Christianity is supposed to be nice—respectable, predictable, and smooth. We are deceived into thinking that being the people of God means lots of meetings and lots of blessings.

God's big purpose for leaving you on this earth is not to put you through a spiritual health spa regimen to make you feel better. Life on earth is war. And war is never nice.

But God's big purpose for leaving you on this earth is not to put you through a spiritual health spa regimen to make you feel better. He'll do all that in heaven in the twinkling of an eye. Life on earth is war. And war is never nice.

God says that Satan's world system is out to get us (John 15:18-19). He suggests that humans dedicated to the satanic counter-kingdom can destroy us. For example:

> A king will arise, insolent and skilled in intrigue. And his power will be mighty, but not by his own power. And he will destroy to an extraordinary degree and prosper and perform his will; he will destroy mighty men and the holy people (Dan. 8:23-24).

Why isn't all of Christendom humming with the excitement of finishing the task? Because it's not exactly going to be a breeze. Since it's global war, there are going to be casualties and body counts. Living out your part in God's great purpose won't be easy.

3. In light of God's purpose, what is the real meaning of the Christian life?

_____

_____

_____

Becoming a World Christian

World Christians are ordinary believers whose lives have been transformed by an extraordinary vision. As David Bryant puts it:

> World Christians are day-to-day disciples for whom Christ's global cause has become the integrating, overriding priority for all that He is for them. Like disciples should, they actively investigate all that their Master's Great Commission means. Then they act on what they learn.
>
> By taking three steps, we become World Christians. First, World Christians *catch* a world vision. They see the cause the way God sees it. They see the full scope of the Gap. Next, World Christians *keep* that world vision. They put the cause at the heart of their life in Christ. They put their life at the heart of the Gap. Then World Christians *obey* their world vision. Together, they develop a strategy that makes a lasting impact on the cause, particularly at the widest end of the Gap.*

4. What impact does becoming a World Christian have on a believer's lifestyle?

_____

_____

_____

Obeying the Vision

How does one obey the vision? *Going* is one way, but it is certainly not the only way. *Praying, giving,* and *sending* are the most accessible roles for most World Christians.

Prayer

The most powerful and direct avenue for obedience to the Great Commission is through prayer. By using this mighty spiritual weapon, the most ordinary of Christians has the opportunity to be directly involved in winning the nations. Harold Lindsell describes prayer this way:

---

* Bryant, D. (1979). *In the gap* (pp. 73-74). Madison: InterVarsity Missions.

Distance is no bar, space no barrier, to reaching the remotest place on earth. Nor is the power of prayer diminished by the distance between the person who prays and the person prayed for. Men and nations can and do have their destinies decided by God's praying people who, through intercessory prayer, wield power greater than the armed might of the nations of earth.*

5. Why is prayer the key to mission success?

_____

_____

_____

Few can go, but all can pray. Let us not be deceived into thinking that prayer is the lesser of the two roles. Prayer is still the most effective weapon there is for penetrating the last barriers to the gospel, for with it we pierce the darkened hearts of men and shackle the powers of Satan. As we consider this theme, we return to the writings of Bill and Amy Stearns.

❏ *Soldier Priests* **

Bill and Amy Stearns

God says to His people,

> "I have called you in righteousness... as a light to the nations, to open blind eyes, to bring out prisoners from the dungeon, and those who dwell in darkness from the prison. I am the Lord; that is My name" (Isa. 42:6-8).

Jesus spoke of the principle that you can't "enter the strong man's house and carry off his property"—to rescue the perishing—"unless [you] first bind the strong man." The wording in the original Greek here emphasizes the article "the"; Jesus is referring to a particular "strong man"—Satan. *Then*, Jesus said, you can "plunder his house" (Matt. 12:29). Now, Satan and his organized hierarchy of principalities, powers, and rulers of darkness are spiritual entities.

They are creatures of "the heavenlies." How can we, with our feet on the ground, "bind the strong man" to bring out prisoners (those under the bondage of Satan) from Satan's dungeon?

Christ entrusted to God's people the incredible priestly duty of agreeing together to bind and loose: "Whatever you shall bind on earth shall be bound in heaven; and whatever you loose on earth shall be loosed in heaven" (Matt. 18:18; see also Matt. 16:18-19). Our struggle, Paul clearly insists, is not against humans—flesh and blood—but against the powers that manipulate them in Satan's world system: "Our struggle is... against the rulers, against the powers, against the world forces of this darkness, against the spiritual forces of wickedness in the heavenly places" (Eph. 6:12).

---

* Lindsell, H. (1969). *When you pray* (pp. 52-53). Wheaton: Tyndale.

** Stearns, W., & Stearns, A. (1991). *Catch the vision 2000* (pp. 161-164). Minneapolis: Bethany House.

What do we do in this struggle? "Though we walk in the flesh, we do not war according to the flesh, for the weapons of our warfare are not of the flesh, but divinely powerful for the destruction of fortresses" or strongholds—even if the structure of those strongholds is buttressed on nothing more tangible than world-system ideas: "speculations and every lofty thing raised up against the knowledge of God" (2 Cor. 10:3-5). (The 70-year domination of millions under Communism should tell us what effect a satanically backed idea can have.)

Agreeing in prayer is, of course, a primary weapon:

- *Pray to pull down satanic fortresses over unreached people groups* (2 Cor. 10:3-4). Go ahead, vent your anger in prayer against the powers of evil that hold 12,000 people groups under the cruel, ugly, destructive god of this world. It's not fair! Life under the domain of darkness is not just. Innocent people are caught in its trap. If we accept their condition as "just the way it is," we've given in to the world- system's status quo. Someone has suggested that prayer is the ultimate rebellion against the status quo.* It's all right to be angry; refuse to accept the injustice, the horrible destitution, the preventable illnesses. And, as the poor widow persisted in presenting her case because of the injustice done her (Luke 18:1-8), persist in prayer until victories are won in the heavenlies.

Even if you can't work up your own anger against Satan's domain, take God's side in the matter. God's wrath against evil never cools.

Intercede—refusing to accept the way things are in the world. That is the very nature of spiritual warfare in prayer.

> *Intercede—refusing to accept the way things are in the world. That is the very nature of spiritual warfare in prayer.*

- *Pray for the saints involved in reaching the captives.* Listen to Paul's clear plea for prayer that closes his warning to put on the whole armor of God: "With all prayer and petition pray at all times in the Spirit, and with this in view, be on the alert with all perseverance and petition for all the saints, and pray on my behalf, that utterance may be given to me in the opening of my mouth, to make known with boldness the mystery of the gospel" (Eph. 6:18-19).

- *Pray for new laborers.* You've been looking at the fields that are ripened for harvest. Now "beseech the Lord of the harvest to send out workers into His harvest" (Matt. 9:38). Remember that the term for "send out" is more correctly translated "thrust out." It is the same word used when Jesus thrust out the money changers from the temple's Court of the Gentiles, the same New Testament term used for casting out spirits. Being "thrust out" may even be a bit uncomfortable for those God sends into His harvest. But pray!

6. *How do these three applications of prayer work together with strategic planning in missions?*

_____

_____

_____

_____

---

* Wells, D. F. (1979). Prayer: Rebelling against the status quo. *Christianity Today, 17*(6), 32-34.

Another weapon of our warfare in the heavenlies is a strong testimony—one that means business, that says we are willing to go to extremes in obedience to Christ. The blood-bought authority with which Christ directs His harvest of making disciples of all the nations (Matt. 28:18-19) empowers our testimony to break the grip of Satan, "who deceives the whole world." John writes:

> And I heard a loud voice in heaven saying, "Now the salvation, and the power, and the kingdom of our God and the authority of His Christ have come, for the accuser of our brethren [the meaning of Satan's name] has been thrown down…. And they overcame him because of the blood of the Lamb and because of the word of their testimony, and they did not love their life even to death" (Rev. 12:10-11).

Though a testimony may seem a vague weapon in spiritual warfare, accept it as fact: A surrendered life cleansed by the blood of Christ can break through Satan's barriers to bring light to the captives!

7. Why is a strong testimony of purity and righteousness an essential component of being a World Christian?

_____

_____

_____

Another weapon used to defeat Satan's minions is a combination of faithful prayer and fasting; Christ said that some powerful spirits of the counter-kingdom don't give up their rulership "except by prayer and fasting" (see Matt. 17:14-21).

A more obvious weapon is the sword of the Spirit, which is the Word of God (Eph. 6:17). It is an offensive weapon to be used against the forces of the evil one. Jesus used it skillfully in the incident recorded in Matthew 4:1-11. But it is important to note that abiding in the Word isn't just head knowledge of Scripture. No mere intellectual compilation of the Bible's information daunts Satan—he can quote Scripture too, and answer trivia questions about the Bible probably long before you can! The weapon that defeats the deception of the enemy is truth; and Christ said that the Word is truth (John 17:17). Let the Word of Christ dwell in you richly.

8. What does it mean to "abide in the Word"?

_____

_____

_____

Prayer, a strong testimony, and the indwelling Word of God are the Christian's greatest weapons in combating the spiritual forces of darkness. The Word is the eternal source, our testimony a fortress, and our prayers arrows launched at the enemy near and far. "God's army advances on its knees."

Serving as Senders, Mobilizers, and Welcomers

Commitment to God's cause will drive us to look for practical ways to support the effort. In the following article, Patricia Moore and Meg Crossman give an overview of the many ways World Christians can seek involvement in God's global cause.

❏ *Company of the Committed*

Patricia Moore and Meg Crossman *

"The share of the man who stayed by the supplies is to be the same as that of him who went down to the battle" (1 Sam 30:24, NIV).

David recognized a critical fact about warfare: support troops are as essential as those who go into battle. He ruled that their reward be the same. The Lord had earlier ordered that the Israelites were to divide the spoils between the soldiers who took part in the battle and the rest of the community who made it possible for them to go (Num. 31:27). No army, regardless of their strength, can long survive without support and supply.

All Christians are called to participate in the Great Commission, but not all are called to go out cross-culturally. A zeal for the spread of the gospel can be lived out in many ways. When we strategize to complete the task, the focus of our attention must go beyond missionary concerns at the front lines. It must extend to support and supply as well. Unless these support roles are filled, worldwide missions programs quickly grind to a halt.

Each person must discover which role God has equipped him to play effectively. Paul's examples of the interdependence of the body in 1 Corinthians 12 show the essential and unique part everyone fills. This is as applicable to God's worldwide plans as it is to a local church. Nothing is more energizing to the entire body than dedicated senders, mobilizers, or welcomers fulfilling their ministry with intensity, focus, perseverance, and sacrifice. Clearly, they too,

are full participants in the company of the committed.

Senders

…As you Philippians know, in the early days… when I set out from Macedonia, not one church shared with me in the matter of giving and receiving, except you only…. You sent me aid again and again when I was in need (Phil. 4:15-16).

Without a team of committed senders—both churches and individuals—no missionary will ever win his target people group.

Paul deeply valued his partnership with the Philippian believers who acted as senders—backing his missionary endeavors with prayer, concern, involvement, and provision, while they actively ministered at home. Paul and the church at Philippi thought of themselves as a team. Without a team of committed senders—both churches and individuals—no missionary will ever win his target people group. The U.S. Center for World Mission estimates that it takes a team of six to 30 active senders to make it possible for one person to go.

In the days of the Student Volunteer Movement, more than 100,000 volunteered to go to the field. Only about 20,000 actually got there, largely be-

---

* Patricia L. Moore is a leader in women's ministries in northern Arizona. She is the author, with Julie McDonald, of *Adventures in Giving*. Meg Crossman was the Executive Director of I CARE prison ministries for 10 years. She taught English in China and has led teams to minister on the Navajo Reservation. She currently serves as the coordinator of courses on *Perspectives on the World Christian Movement* in Arizona.

cause of a lack of committed senders. Senders are often unaware of the critical importance of their task. They usually do their work behind the scenes, isolated from one another. Thanks and public recognition seldom come the sender's way. Effective senders, therefore, operate on an inner conviction that their investments in the gospel grow out of God's specific call on their lives. They also recognize that sending requires as much discipline and commitment as going.

Clearly, in kingdom economy, investment precedes heart involvement, not the other way around.

Two key ingredients combine in the ministry of most senders: *generosity* and *intercession*. There is constant pressure in our culture to conform lifestyle to income, but senders strive to resist this. Many have chosen to adopt a lifestyle comparable to that of missionaries on the field, in order to free more income for support. Some dedicated senders are known to quietly give away half of their income or more for the spread of the gospel.

Prayer flows out of giving. In Matthew 6:21, Jesus said, "Where your treasure is, there will your heart be also." Clearly, in kingdom economy, investment *precedes* heart involvement, not the other way around. Those who invest in others' ministries find it natural to lift these supported needs and concerns to the Father in an ongoing way. Countless missionaries affirm that the resultant prayer is even more vital to their work than funding.

Senders' generosity of heart often includes other significant roles, such as research and supplies. One whole ministry focuses on shipping needed materials to the field. Others serve as backup to field workers by doing much-needed research in various realms. A group of computer experts in Florida has developed a ministry to use their skills both in training missionaries to use computers and in finding donated computers and software suitable for missionaries' special needs. Accountants, teachers, and business consultants use their proficiencies in their vacation time for mission undertakings, freeing up the full-time workers to do their mission specialties.

9. Explain the relationship between giving and praying.

_____

_____

_____

Mobilizers

The Lord said to Moses, "Make two trumpets of hammered silver, and use them for calling the community together and having them set out" (Num. 10:1-2).

Sending is not the only way to participate in the Great Commission from home base. Someone must sound the rallying call. Those who desire to see others trained, prepared, and released to ministry are known as *mobilizers*. Mobilizers stir other Chris-

tians to active concern for reaching the world. They coordinate efforts among senders, the local church, sending agencies, and missionaries on the field.

Awakening the church, providing the facts and the motivation for her to take joy in involvement, and encouraging her on her journey are the responsibilities of mobilization. In World War II, only 10 percent of the American population went to the war. Only 1 percent were actually on the firing lines.

However, for that to happen, the entire country had to be mobilized! Completing our task will call for serious, persevering mobilizers.

Mobilizers are energized by a desire to help people find their calling and enter into significant service. They are often networkers and trainers. Rather than focusing on a single ministry, they delight to make known a full spectrum of possibilities from which each person can choose. Often, they are involved in providing training, practical help, and encouragement, both motivating the church and helping her get underway.

Welcomers

> "The alien living with you must be treated as one of your native-born. Love him as yourself, for you were aliens in Egypt" (Lev. 19:34).

God prepared His own people to be sensitive to the needs of strangers by their sojourn in Egypt. Even His own Son lived as a refugee in Egypt. Welcomers are those stirred by the needs of ethnic groups who reside in the welcomers' home country. Welcomers seek opportunities to touch the lives of thousands of internationals who come to study, work, or emigrate permanently. They are especially strategic in reaching populations whose home countries restrict mission work.

Much of this ministry grows out of the gift of hospitality (Greek: *philoxenia*, meaning "love of strangers"). Welcomers befriend people, demonstrating the love of Christ in very practical ways. They may work with university students, diplomats, refugees, military personnel, or immigrants. Instead of viewing new ethnic groups as a threat, Christians see their coming as a strategic opportunity for love and witness.

Welcomers develop special strategies, appropriate to each group. A ministry in Chicago works with churches to present each new refugee family with a "Welcome to America" packet within a week after they arrive. Elsewhere, in a Chinatown setting, classes teaching English use Ann Landers columns. They read the advice to discuss American idioms and present Christian values (often by disagreeing with Ann!).

Effective welcomers learn all they can of the culture and language of their target people. Guest workers from Turkey are being reached in Germany. Christians in The Netherlands work with Indonesians who have relocated there. While they were students in Hungary, Mongolians were won to the Lord. Both language and cultural sensitivity contribute to these ministries.

Effective welcomers learn all they can of the culture and language of their target people.

This highly convenient and fruitful form of cross-cultural ministry also provides sensible connections for anyone preparing for field service. A small college-age team wanted to explore the possibilities for getting into a closed country in North Africa. They got to know as many students from that country as possible. When they were turned down for entry visas, the father of a student they had befriended was the key to getting them permission to enter for a year!

To discover whether sending, mobilizing, or welcoming best utilizes your gifts and abilities, simply try them out. Often, in reality, they will overlap and strengthen one another. One of the real advantages of these ministries is that you don't have to get permission from anyone to become involved!

10. *How do sending, mobilizing, and welcoming roles "overlap and strengthen" each other? For which are you best suited?*

_____

_____

_____

_____

_____

II. Teaming Up in the Local Church

Finding World Christians in your congregation to "team" with depends on your circumstances. If you are taking this course with others from your own church, it may be simply a matter of arranging to meet together for discussion, prayer, and encouragement. Your church may already have an active missions group. If you are the only one in your fellowship who has caught the vision, your personal mission challenge will be to communicate that vision to others. Begin to pray that God would give you others with whom to team.

There are two basic kinds of missions groups which function at the local church level—prayer groups and administrative committees. Prayer groups are the simplest kind of group to organize and lead. They take on the nature of a discipleship group as the World Christian leads others into *catching, keeping,* and *obeying* the vision. There are several ways to organize this kind of group. The suggestions which follow are easy to implement and will help keep the group fresh and dynamic.

World Christian Prayer Fellowship

The World Christian Prayer Fellowship is based on relational, weekly encounters. Commitment to each person in the group is built as the Lord builds commitment to His cause. One-hour sessions can be used, although more time can easily be utilized if available. The time may be distributed in the following suggested manner:

Opening (10 minutes)	• Introduce any new participants and present the agenda. • Praise the Lord together through the reading of a psalm or through singing choruses. • Commit your time to the Lord in prayer.
Missions Mini-Lesson (15 minutes)	• Present a mini-lesson (7 minutes) on a key concept you have learned in your study of *World Mission*. Use a Bible text or read a portion from *World Mission** (or other appropriate source) and comment on it. • Allow discussion of the lesson presented (8 minutes). • Offer prayer for application of the teaching to each one's life.

---

* We suggest you begin with Volume 1, *The Biblical/Historical Foundation,* and progressively present key concepts. Many mini-lessons can be prepared from each chapter.

Nation Focus (15 minutes)	• Present a geographic, political, economic, and spiritual description of a selected nation or unreached people.* • Pray for the needs presented.
Missionary Focus (10 minutes)	• Uphold missionaries from your church in prayer. Request information from your church's missions committee, or glean requests directly from missionary prayer letters or mission agency publications.
Testimony (10 minutes)	• Have one member of the group, who has been previously assigned, share a testimony from his or her "spiritual pilgrimage" (5 minutes). • Pray for the person and close the meeting (5 minutes).

The above outline is a proven format for a World Christian Prayer Fellowship meeting. The ideal size for the group is six to 12 members. Large groups should be split into smaller ones after the opening and missions mini-lesson. The system works best when responsibilities are shared on a rotated basis among members of the group. Figure 15-1 offers a practical model of a "Planning Guide" to help you organize your group. Make sure to keep a group roster with addresses and phone numbers.

Planning Guide for World Christian Prayer Fellowship			
Week: 1 Moderator: Ann Bishop		Week: 2 Moderator: Ann Bishop	
ACTIVITY	**PERSON RESPONSIBLE**	**ACTIVITY**	**PERSON RESPONSIBLE**
Opening	Ann Bishop	Opening	Ann Bishop

Mini-Lesson:
  WM, pp. 1-2 and 1-3
	Phil Bishop	Mini-Lesson:
		  WM, pp. 1-3 and 1-4
			Phil Bishop

Nation Focus:
  Afghanistan
	Fred Andrews	Nation Focus:
		  Albania
			Bill Peterson

Missionary Focus	Alice Smith	Missionary Focus	Mary Fowler
Testimony	Bill Peterson	Testimony	Fred Andrews

Figure 15-1

11. *Does your church have an organized missions prayer fellowship? If not, what would it take to organize one?*

_____

_____

_____

_____

* For the most complete and nearly inexhaustible resource for a Nation Focus, see Johnstone, P. (1993). *Operation world.* Grand Rapids: Zondervan. Available mail-order through O.M. Lit, 1-800-733-5907.

Missions Administrative Committees

The involvement of local congregations in world missions is fundamental to completion of the Great Commission. Without them, missions would be devoid of their primary resources: prayer support, personnel, and finances. The vast majority of local churches, however, do little or nothing for cross-cultural outreach. In North America, where the missions enterprise is most developed, it is estimated that less than 20 percent of the churches have a group (missions committee) to administrate their missions matters. Less than 5 percent have any kind of significant program which emphasizes missions to the whole congregation.

Why aren't more local churches involved? William Carey addressed that question 200 years ago:

> It seems as if many thought the commission was sufficiently put in execution by what the apostles and others have done; that we have enough to do to attend to the salvation of our own countrymen; and that, if God intends the salvation of the heathen, He will some way or other bring them to the gospel, or the gospel to them.*

Apparently, the excuses for non-involvement have not changed. Many church leaders dwell under the illusion that the spread of the gospel is sufficiently advanced that no further mission initiatives are required. Others see their local parish as their "mission field" and feel no compunction to apply the "uttermost parts of the earth" portion of the Great Commission to their ministries. Still others have rationalized through their theology that God will ultimately save those whom He wills and that their congregation's efforts are superfluous.

All of these issues have been addressed throughout the chapters of this study. God's mission purpose is central to the biblical message. He has and He will use His people to carry out His purpose. He has left us the mandate, the message, the model, and the power to act. He has also established a specific ministry in the church to "equip the saints" for this important work of service.

Ephesians 4:11 names five basic equipping ministers in the church—apostles, prophets, evangelists, pastors, and teachers. By interpreting this passage in terms of ministry function, rather than in terms of personalities or any particular hierarchy, it is easy to see how each ministry serves to fulfill God's purpose. The word *apostle* in Scripture is of Greek origin and denotes *one who is sent*. Apostle (or missionary) could be listed first in this passage because without sent ones, Christ's Great Commission mandate to the nations cannot be *initiated*. Each of the other ministries follows this one in fulfilling specific functions, such as bringing people to a point of spiritual conviction (prophecy), leading them to a knowledge of Christ (evangelism), helping them grow spiritually (pastoring), and bringing them to a full knowledge and understanding of the Word (teaching).

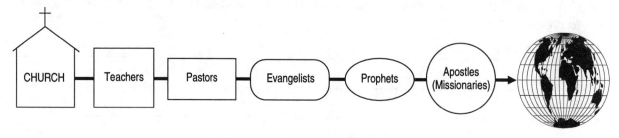

Figure 15-2. Missions, the Leading Ministry

---

* Carey, W. (1962). *An enquiry into the obligations of Christians to use means for the conversion of the heathens* (New Facsimile ed.). London: Carey Kingsgate Press. (Original work published 1792)

12. Why should missions be one of the fundamental ministries of each church?

_____

_____

_____

In order to mobilize and equip a local church for missions, the "apostolic" ministry needs to be activated. Each church needs a group of World Christians to administer a missions program. Such a group is often called a "missions committee." No organization has done more for the promotion and strengthening of these groups than ACMC (Advancing Churches in Missions Commitment). The following is excerpted from their brochure, *The ACMC Guide to Growing a Missions-Minded Church.*

❏ *Planting Ahead* *

World missions would die on the vine without local churches who think beyond local boundaries. Large or small, highly organized or loose-knit, well-funded or broke, your church's missions program plays a crucial role in filling that gap between you and the outside world.

Whether its progress in missions has been remarkable or restrained, every church would readily admit it could do better. And helping you to grow and improve is what this practical guide is all about.

When you plant a garden, you first take inventory of the materials you'll need: Do I have a suitable location? Plenty of sunlight and good soil? What plants will grow best in this climate? Is there a source of water nearby?

Much the same thought must go into "growing" a missions-minded church. Which individuals seem to be most concerned about missions? What efforts to evangelize—or support evangelization—have met with success? Is the church leadership open to change in this area?

Begin by sitting down with your pastor or missions coordinator to pinpoint where your church's missions program has been and where it's headed. List your observations on paper and study them carefully. Be as specific as possible. For example, calculate the percentage of church giving set aside for missions in the past year, or name the new missionaries sent out from your church in the past five years. You'll soon have a good picture of the "missions mindedness" level of your church.

13. Why is this first step important to the success of growing a missions-minded church?

_____

_____

_____

---

* *The ACMC guide to growing a missions-minded church.* Used by permission of ACMC, P.O. Box ACMC, Wheaton, IL 60189. For other missions committee resources, call 1-800-798-ACMC.

Your next step is to help organize the leadership. Pastors and lay leaders need to be encouraged to teach and preach about missions, to set the pace for the congregation. If you have a functioning missions committee, offer your assistance to them, meeting individually with each of the committee members to express your concern. But be sensitive to their feelings; listen, cooperate, and don't expect too much overnight.

Once a strong core of leaders has been developed, their vision for missions will inevitably be "caught" by other believers in your church. Only half the people in the world today have a reasonable opportunity to hear the gospel. Helping the congregation see their missions responsibility can be a creative, challenging ministry. Bulletin inserts, missionary prayer items, and exposition of key biblical passages are some of the tools which will stimulate the vision of your people.

After acquiring a genuine heart for missions, your church can develop a deeper understanding and stronger commitment to the task of world evangelization. Here are a few of the most important ways you can put its vision to work:

- Draw up a clear-cut missions organizational policy, one that embraces the unique framework and *modus operandi* of your church. Set specific goals against which your progress can be measured.

- Become acquainted with your missionaries and their needs. A compassionate, caring church will make a significant impact not only abroad, but also here at home. Your church's vision will be stretched to even higher limits as God provides the resources to support His programs.

- Encourage aspiring individuals in your congregation to seek long-term or short-term assignments with sending agencies. Maintain good working relationships with these agencies—they can be a rich source of ideas and advice.

- Above all, turn prayer into your primary tool for accomplishing the task that lies ahead. And take courage! Christ wouldn't have given you the command to "go and make disciples of all nations" without also promising to be "with you always, to the very end of the age" (Matt. 28:19-20).

14. What are the primary tasks involved in growing a missions vision in the local church and administrating it?

_____

_____

_____

_____

Church/Mission Partnership

The missions committee is responsible for communicating missions vision, keeping it fresh, and maintaining a high commitment in prayer, finances, and personnel for the mission enterprise. Over the years, methods have been developed which have proven effective in carrying out these ends. One of the best known and most practiced is the *Faith Promise Plan*. More than just a fundraising scheme, the Faith Promise Plan is a comprehensive plan for helping the congregation grow in faith and keeping it involved and excited about missions. In the following excerpt, veteran missions mobilizer Norm Lewis outlines the elements of this plan.

❏ *The Marks of a Faith Promise Church* *

Norm Lewis

If a church is looking for the best way to implement Faith Promise giving, there are three essentials:

1. *Hold an annual missions event.* Make this the most significant happening of the entire church calendar. Plan it well. Obtain qualified speakers. Teach the basic meaning of missions. Build it on the Bible. Have missionaries and appointees present. This is crucial for maximum spiritual impact.

2. *Set a missions goal each year.* A financial goal calls for commitment. Many churches suffer from aimlessness. A missionary event without a goal is pointless. The church can be like a car with the motor running but going nowhere. Sunday after Sunday the same routine unfolds. But set a missionary goal! All is changed. People are lifted, challenged.

3. *Use the Faith Promise Plan.* It is based both on money people have and on what they trust God to provide. Its focus is faith in the integrity of God and costly commitment by the believer. It encourages the giver to determine by prayer the sum he believes God will enable him to give on a regular basis during the year for world evangelization. Faith is its dynamic.

The promise is made to God; it is not a pledge to a church. There is no individual solicitation. The plan is spiritual, scriptural; it embarrasses no one. It encourages regular giving for world evangelization and tells the church in advance the amount available for missions for the coming year.

15. Why is faith such an important element in keeping the church motivated towards involvement in missions?

_____

_____

_____

_____

Current Trends in Church/Mission Partnerships

The faithful support of individuals and local churches has always been the "fuel" that drives evangelical missions. The term "faith missions" applied to many agencies describes this vital dependency on God's people in local churches for resources. These organizations usually depend entirely on voluntary contributions to carry out their ends. Although denominational missions often work with percentages of overall giving and may have a more stable budget, this giving is not always "automatic." All missions rely on working partnerships with churches.

Fifty to 100 years ago, these partnership relationships were fairly straightforward—agencies were an obvious necessity. A window to the world wasn't sitting in each living room, and jet planes weren't providing daily access to every country of the globe. Instant credit card transfers hadn't been invented.

---

* Lewis, N. (1992). *Faith promise: Why and how?* Available mail-order from O.M. Lit, 1-800-733-5907.

The pastor's week-long tour of the field was unheard of, and congregations were thrilled by slide shows of exotic places. Today's technology, however, puts the world at our fingertips. Fax machines, telephones, and electronic mail give us ready contact with our missionaries. Visits to the field are common, and the camcorder spontaneously records the happenings. With this new sense of power, some congregations are asking, "Why work through mission agencies at all? Can't we save money and maintain control by doing the job ourselves?"

Other issues also cloud the relationship. Accountability is one of the largest. Are mission agencies really getting the job done? Progressive vision, clear goals, and measurable objectives are not always evident. Communication seems to be reduced to continual appeals for funds. Missionaries' pastoral needs have at times been neglected, and churches feel their people are used, abused, and hurt. While espousing "partnership" in the task, mission agencies may be perceived by some as simply seeking people and money from churches.

There is no question that these problems need to be addressed by mission agencies if the agencies are to remain viable partners with churches. There are many good reasons why mission agencies and churches still need each other. In the following excerpt, Samuel Metcalf, president of Church Resource Ministries in Fullerton, California, points out why this partnership must continue.

❑ *Resolving Church/Mission Tensions* *

Samuel F. Metcalf

In 1973, Ralph Winter gave a landmark address to the All-Asia Mission Consultation in Seoul on "The Two Structures of God's Redemptive Mission." He argued that God's purposes have been carried out via two main structures—modalities (the local church) and sodalities (mobile, task-oriented agencies). He claimed that both are ordained by God,

> **The church in local form is only partially able to fulfill the Great Commission.**

legitimate, and equally "church." Their healthy interdependence is necessary for the progress of the gospel. He outlined a functional, or structural, understanding of ecclesiology that is critical if we are to grasp the current tensions with mission agencies and local churches.

In the November, 1990, issue of *Mission Frontiers*, Winter again addressed the issue of the local church's control of missions:

At the heart of the issue, regardless of its particular practical manifestation, lies an inadequate grasp of missiological structures and a lack of understanding of the historical and biblical dynamics that exist between local churches and mission teams sent out for specific purposes.

In light of Winter's thesis, I propose the following:

1. Local churches are not expected by God, nor do they have the structural capability, to carry out the missionary mandate by themselves. The church in local form is only partially able to fulfill the Great Commission. This is the clear pattern of the New Testament and the overwhelming verdict of history.

Local churches need agencies because agencies have:

• Vision and a narrow, task-oriented focus.

• Administrative personnel with long-term, career commitment.

* Metcalf, S. F. (1993, July-August). Resolving church/mission tensions. *Missions Frontiers Bulletin*, 28-29.

- Selectivity with personnel who join.

- The ability to respond rapidly to field opportunities.

- Expertise and professionalism in accomplishing their task.

2. Agencies are not expected by God, nor do they have the structural capability, to meet the missionary mandate by themselves. Agencies need local churches because churches have:

- Human resources.

- Finances and material aid.

- A broad base of intercessory prayer.

- Healing and training capabilities for personnel.

- Stability.

Historically, when local churches have dominated or controlled agencies, they thwart the agencies' efforts and, in severe cases, kill or render them impotent. If mission efforts are organized and sent under the supervision of one local church, they have the greatest chance for success when a separate entity is created (or contracted) to carry on this work.

> *If we are to continue to advance the gospel, the dynamic of healthy interdependence between local churches and mission agencies must increase.*

Local church and mission agency interdependence works best when leaders of both cooperate on the basis of shared values and vision. If we are to continue to advance the gospel, the dynamic of healthy interdependence between modalities and sodalities—local churches and mission agencies— must increase. Anything less will result in the kind of abortive, wasteful efforts that have periodically hindered the worldwide expansion of the church.

16. *Why is it important that churches and missions continue to work together in carrying out the missions enterprise?*

_____

_____

_____

_____

Mission agencies are an important bridge to the unreached. They have the long-term commitment to a focused, cross-cultural task, which a church can rarely sustain over time. They can often tap into a wider range of the body of Christ for critical human, spiritual, and financial resources. There is safety in this kind of diversity.

Shopping for a Mission

Let us assume you or your church are looking for a mission agency with which to team. How would you evaluate your options? In the following excerpt, Jim Reapsome, seasoned editor of the *Evangelical Missions Quarterly*, outlines a procedure which will help you ask the right questions.

❑ Choosing a Mission Board *

Jim Reapsome

Doctrinal compatibility

Before joining a team, you should know what it believes. Examine the published doctrinal statement carefully. Be sure that it fits your own convictions. Life on the mission field is tough enough without bashing your head against coworkers with whose doctrines you don't agree.

In your initial conversations with agency representatives, try to find out if the agency is broad or narrow in its doctrinal convictions. That is, do they strive for strong internal consistency around some low-key points, such as baptism, eschatology, church government, and relations with other churches and missions? Or do they allow for different opinions?

The agency may say it is "interdenominational," for instance, but over the years it may have developed some distinctives of its own. Find out what churches and major theological groups are represented among missionaries. Find out what the unwritten doctrines of the mission are—its traditions that have been elevated to orthodoxy. You can best do this by talking not only with recruiters, but also with veterans of the agency.

Compatible goals and objectives

You want a team that you not only agree with doctrinally, but also one with whom you can throw in your lot 100 percent because you share common goals and objectives. Find out what the mission's purposes are. Why does it exist? What is it trying to accomplish? How well has it been succeeding according to its own goals?

Try to get your hands on the agency's annual plan and its five-year plan. Is it going where you want to go with your life? Would you risk everything to reach these goals? As you understand your temperament, gifts, and goals, do they fit the mission?

Has the mission ever reassessed its purposes and goals? No organization can do well by standing pat on traditional goals. Is there a regular process for internal reevaluation and long-range planning? What new goals and strategies have appeared recently to show that the mission is adapting to changes around the world and in U.S. culture?

Policies and principles

These documents must be thoroughly checked and discussed with missions representatives. Question everything that you don't understand or don't agree with. Many missionary casualties arise because assumptions about missions policies were made prior to going overseas.

> *Never assume that for the sake of going overseas you will assent to some policy you don't agree with, and then fight it throughout your missionary career.*

These policies cover the basics of finances, field administration, mission government, personnel, rules of behavior, children's education, cars, retirement, insurance, and so on. Go over them with a fine-tooth comb. Ask reasons. Talk about applications. Are there exceptions? Try to assess the spirit behind the laws. Some missions are authoritarian; others are freewheeling. Find out in advance and see where you fit best. By all means, never assume that for the sake of going overseas you will assent to some policy you don't agree with, and then fight it throughout your missionary career.

Opportunities and scope for ministry

Look for a mission that invites and encourages you with the kind of opportunities you are looking for. Does their planning reflect creativity and active searching for new ways to effective ministry? Or do

* Reapsome, J. (1988). Choosing a mission board. *Evangelical Missions Quarterly, 24*(1).

you suspect you might feel cramped, or locked into traditional ways of doing things? Mission leaders should impress you with fresh ideas and with an enlarged vision for "new worlds to conquer," so to speak.

Track record where you want to serve

Check the fields where you might be headed. Are the people there upbeat, or do you find a steady dropout rate, people giving up in defeat? Do this field and the mission's ministry there show the undeniable marks of God's Spirit at work there? What about relations there, mission to mission, missionary to missionary, mission to church? Are they rife with problems and conflicts, or is there harmony, unity, interdependence, and trust? Beware of the field booby-trapped with dissension and locked into sterility and repetition of past mistakes.

Lifestyle

Probably the most difficult matter to probe is the lifestyle, or ethos, that develops around a mission. It is shaped over the decades by veterans and their traditions. Lifestyle grows around unwritten codes, not written ones. Put on your spiritual radar. How does the mission treat people? Do they put people ahead of programs? What happens to dropouts, for example? How does the mission care for its people when they come home on furlough, or when they come home for the sake of elderly parents, or for their children's education?

Is there a warm family spirit? Check out how missionary wives and children feel. How does the mission treat women, single people, those who may not fit the customary mold? Are there women in places of responsibility?

Choose a mission the same way you would a wife or husband. Go beyond the romantic attachment and poke around the family tree. See what kind of a personality your mission has. How does it respond to crisis? How does it show itself to the public? Ask a missionary, "If you had it to do over again, would you join the same mission?"

Written history

Start with current articles and reports in missions publications. Get your hands on as many missionary prayer letters as you can. If the agency is old enough, it should have a published history. Pore over its pages. You should come away with excitement and pleasure about the prospect of working with such a team.

Quality of people

Most of us are attracted to organizations because someone has ministered to us and because their people show top quality all around. That's the most impressive recommendation you can find—happy, satisfied, fulfilled people who know what they're about. They are confident about God's call and excited to be a part of His world mission. They are culturally aware, sensitive, and experts in their profession. You would find it a great privilege to work alongside them.

> *Look for a mission board that has the best people you can find—not perfect, to be sure, but those who serve as a model of the kind of missionary you would like to become.*

Find a mission like that. Listen to their people, not just from the pulpit, but in small groups. Grab them in informal settings and plague them with questions. If you sense you're being stiff-armed, make a note of that. If your questions, no matter how naive, are answered sincerely and profoundly, that's a welcome sign. Look for a mission board that has the best people you can find—not perfect, to be sure, but those who serve as a model of the kind of missionary you would like to become.

17. *Why is it important to thoroughly investigate the mission agency with which you or your church propose to work?*

_____

_____

_____

_____

III. Global Partnerships

Partnering in getting workers to the field is crucial, but it doesn't stop once they get there. Interagency partnerships are also a critical need, particularly if the church is to be planted successfully among unreached groups. In the following article, Luis Bush and Lorry Lutz present an overview of interagency partnership issues.

❑ *Testing the Waters* *

Luis Bush and Lorry Lutz *

The "Valley of Blessing," headquarters of the Antioch Mission, led by Rev. Jonathan dos Santos, a Brazilian pastor and visionary, is located in the verdant hills 35 miles from São Paulo, Brazil. Here missionary candidates from Brazil and other Latin American countries are trained to serve cross-culturally. Founded in 1975, the mission has sent out more than 45 missionaries to such faraway places as Israel, Angola, India... and Albania!

Facilities at the Valley are simple: cement block dormitories where a dozen students crowd into a room which should house four. Before the new dining hall was built this year, only a fraction of the staff and students could be seated at one time, which made mealtimes on rainy days a challenge. Every-

one lives "by faith," trusting God to supply their needs week by week.

But this is just the kind of missionary training Santos values. He knows the Brazilian church will not be able to provide high allowances, nor will the government allow transfers of large sums of money out of the country. "Brazilian missionaries already know how to live the simple lifestyle," Santos explains.

Coming from a position of powerlessness, as Jesus chose to do, might be just one of the unique advantages missionaries from the Two Thirds World have as they fan out across the world. Western values of advanced educational opportunities and financial

* Bush, L., & Lutz, L. (1990). *Partnering in ministry: The direction of world evangelism* (pp. 112-125). Downers Grove, IL: InterVarsity Press.

** Luis Bush grew up in Argentina and Brazil. He studied at the University of North Carolina and then earned a Th.M. from Dallas Theological Seminary. He pastored in San Salvador for seven years, was the director of the COMIBAM '87 conference in Brazil, served as President of Partners International, and is currently the Director of the AD 2000 and Beyond Movement.

Lorry Lutz and her husband, Allen, worked 20 years in South Africa as missionaries. She currently heads the publications department for Partners International. She has authored several books, including a novel, *The Soweto Legacy*.

and political power have often built a wall between the church and the missionary.

In spite of limitations of such resources, non-Western missionaries have grown from 13,000 in 1980 to 36,000 in 1988. Larry Pate, author of *From Every People*, projects that at current rates of growth, an estimated 86,500 missionaries from Two Thirds World countries will be serving cross-cultur-ally by 1995, and there will be almost 2,000 non-Western mission agencies by the year 2000. At present there are some 85,000 Western missionaries serving in foreign countries, but 42 percent of them are short-termers. Non-Western career missionaries are growing at five times the rate of Western missionaries and will surpass them in numbers before the turn of the century.*

18. What are some of the advantages Two Thirds World missionaries may have over their Western counterparts? What are some of the disadvantages?

_____

_____

_____

Will history repeat itself?

The leaders of these Two Thirds World agencies have not sprung up overnight. Many have attended the international congresses and consultations, have studied in the West, and have worked with Western missionaries. They've heard the partnership rhetoric and, indeed, are promoting it.

In an article for *Missionasia*, Filipino leader Dr. Met Castillo writes:

> The natural and logical outcomes of inter-linking the various Asian mission agencies and boards are concrete forms of mission partnerships. The vast number of unreached peoples in Asia and the complexity of the mission task, compounded by the chain of mission problems, call for the pooling of mission resources and personnel. But though there are many commendable instances of partnership in the West, Two Thirds World leaders can still point to the proliferation of Western mission agencies, more than 700 at latest count, and duplication of efforts. Rather than cooperating with existing bodies, Westerners continue to develop new independent mission organizations.

It will come as no surprise to learn that cooperation and partnership are just as difficult to implement among Two Thirds World agencies as they are in the West.

19. What alternatives are there to the proliferation of new Western missions?

_____

_____

_____

_____

* Pate, L. (1989). *From every people* (pp. 50-52). Monrovia, CA: MARC.

Will they partner with the West?

In his 1980 survey of Two Thirds World agencies, Dr. Larry Keyes asked to what degree these missions desired to cooperate with other Two Thirds World agencies and with the West. Mission leaders from all regions answered they would like to cooperate with others, but particularly with other non-Western agencies.*

Experience has taught these Two Thirds World mission leaders that Western missionaries tend to take control and that non-Westerners may too easily accept structures and teaching that are foreign in their society because of their poor self-image and/or lack of training.

Western missionaries tend to take control, and non-Westerners may too easily accept structures and teaching that are foreign in their society because of their poor self-image and/or lack of training.

Reacting to these dangers, Dr. David Cho, former president of the Asia Missions Association and the newly formed Third World Missions Association, declared:

> We must boldly remove the obstacles hindering Christian mission. We must remove all remnants of Western culture, Western colonialism, Western methodology, and Western thought from Asian theology, doctrine, churches, structures, and methods.**

Though Dr. Cho has expressed disappointment in the lack of cooperation on the part of Western missions, he values the gifts and abilities of Western Christian leaders. He asked Dr. Ralph Winter to share the platform with him at the very conference where Cho spoke on "De-Westernizing the Asian Christian Movement." His concern is to solidify and strengthen the Asian, African, and Latin American mission base, not "to form an anti-Western force."

His fear is rather that the Two Thirds World missions will lose their self-identity and become even less acceptable to the masses of people who have resisted the message of missions for so long. He stresses that Paul made it clear in his epistles that the church must be rooted in the culture and ethos of the people.

Wade Coggins, executive director of the Evangelical Foreign Missions Association (EFMA) for many years, recalls watching the tenuous steps of growth and partnership between Two Thirds World missions and their Western counterparts. While meeting with representatives of fledgling Brazilian missions in the mid-'70s, he realized:

> We weren't talking about the control of the mission over the church or the church's control of the mission. We were talking as people both committed to the concept of world evangelization. And that the old missions and the new missions ought to talk about what they could do together.

This was in contrast to most discussions between church and mission leaders in those days. Coggins said: "I realized that the way out of the church/mission dilemma that had been with us so long was an outward look."

But having lived through the church/missions tensions of the '60s and '70s, Coggins also understands the reticence of Two Thirds World agencies to trust us, for fear we'll take over and impose our methods and values. "Talking about partnership is easy," Coggins says. "We've come through the euphoria—'Man, this is marvelous.' The tough questions are ahead of us. Most of it's going to be two organizations sorting it out for themselves."

---

* Keyes, L. (1983). *The last age of mission* (p. 85). Pasadena: William Carey Library.

** Cho, D. (1982). The third force. In D. Cho (Ed.), *The official report of the third triennial convention of the Asia Missions Association.* Seoul, Korea.

And the task of educating the churches and missions candidates is far from over. Our ethnocentricity clings to us like a wetsuit, and the deeper the differences between cultures, the "colder" we seem to become.

One wonders at the audacity of an American college student going overseas for a short term "to train native pastors." It is this self-confidence and assurance that we have all the answers that frightens people like Dr. Cho.

20. *What are the main issues confronting partnerships between Western and non-Western missions?*

_____

_____

_____

_____

Western and non-Western agencies partner

In the mid-19th century, the Karen Christians in Myanmar (formerly Burma) formed one of the early non-Western mission agencies, the Bassein Home Mission Society. With help from the American Baptist missionaries, they sent Karen missionaries to work among the Kachins, a tribe living several hundred miles away.

More than 100 years later, John and Helen Dekker, missionaries with the Regions Beyond Missionary Union in Irian Jaya, encouraged the fledgling church among primitive Danis to take the message of Christ to neighboring and often hostile tribes. Within a few years, 65 Dani couples, fully supported by the gifts and prayers of Dani Christians, were in service. Though nobody even thought about formal partnership arrangements, Dekker provided the complementary encouragement, training, and counsel the Danis lacked.

With little cash income, the Danis needed to develop a means of funding their growing missionary force. Dekker introduced peanuts, and the income from the crop financed much of the church's missionary outreach. Without peanuts, the missionary effort would have been hopelessly strapped.

Today some Western mission agencies are developing more formal partner relationships with Two Thirds World agencies. For example, SIM has drawn up an agreement with the Indian Evangelical Mission and others to work together to recruit and support missionaries in Africa and Latin America where SIM serves.

The Indian missionaries are expected to raise funds and prayer support within India for outgoing airfare, baggage allowance, equipment needs, and so on, as well as furlough and medical expenses while in India. SIM arranges deputation for prayer and financial support for the balance of their needs, and while on the field the missionaries come under the direction of SIM.

Such co-sponsoring will become more and more urgent as the numbers of Two Thirds World missionaries grow. Larry Keyes discovered that 35 percent of these missionaries do not receive their promised salary. Part of the problem is due to poor administration and distribution and part to a need for better stewardship education in the churches.

A very real part of the problem is the lack of a strong financial base—in fact, bankrupt economies—in many of the countries where mission vision is growing fastest. And though Two Thirds World missionaries may "know how to live simply," according to Jonathan dos Santos, the cost of living may be much higher in the country of service than at home. A Brazilian missionary working among Muslims in

Germany could not live on his Brazilian allowance, no matter how simply he or she lived!

When the Iglesia Nazaret and El Escalon, two mission-minded churches in San Salvador, partnered to form the Salvadoran Evangelical Mission, the civil war was at its height. Over 40 percent of the population was without work, and the economy was in shambles.

But the SEM determined to send its first missionary couple to Spain to begin a church-planting ministry there. People gave sacrificially but could not pro-vide all that their missionaries, the Bustamantes, needed to live in Spain. They approached Partners International to form a co-sponsoring relationship, whereby donors in the United States matched SEM's contributions.

Such financial partnership not only enabled SEM to send the Bustamantes, but encouraged Christians to give sacrificially so that within a few years several other missionaries had been sent to an Indian tribe in Guatemala, and the first school for the deaf in El Salvador (a totally unreached segment of the population) was opened.

21. *What criteria should be used in putting together successful financial partnerships?*

_____

_____

_____

Other ways to partner

In spite of the difficulties and fear of repeating past experiences, Two Thirds World agencies realize that working together with Western agencies can better help them reach their mutual goal. Following are other forms of partnership which are emerging:

Training partnerships

As the Africa Inland Church Mission Board (AICMB) grew, the need for training African missionaries in mission strategy and methods became more urgent. Bible school and seminary training did not prepare their missionaries for the challenges of cross-cultural and church-planting ministries. Yet the AICMB did not have trained and experienced teachers to run such a school. So it turned to its parent organization, the Africa Inland Mission, to partner in establishing a missionary training school. The school remains under the leadership and control of the AICMB, but AIM missionary teachers help staff it.

As more and more non-Western missionaries volunteer to serve cross-culturally, creative training partnerships will have to develop in order to avoid sending inexperienced and untrained non-Western missionaries to repeat the same mistakes Western missionaries subconsciously made earlier.

But Western trainers will have to be willing to adjust their philosophies and methods to adapt to the cultures where they are teaching. To avoid repeating the North American models of Bible schools and seminaries, which have not necessarily been effective, a lot of hard questions have to be asked and a teachable spirit demonstrated.

As more and more non-Western missionaries volunteer to serve cross-culturally, creative training partnerships will have to develop.

Excellent training programs have developed in various parts of the Two Thirds World, and interchanges of faculty and students offer an exciting potential for the future of missions training.

On a less formal level, Jonathan dos Santos, pioneer in training Two Thirds World missionaries, responded to the urgent need for training in Eastern

Europe after the political changes allowed for freedom to travel and communicate. When he learned of the dearth of trained leadership for the Romanian Church, he offered to care for and train six Romanians at the Valley of Blessing if they could get to Brazil.

Research partnerships

Where will all these new non-Western missionaries serve? How will they avoid the endless duplications of the past, such as establishing a Baptist church, a Bible church, and a Presbyterian church in one small town?

The mission world has adapted the tools of research to discover where the churches are and where the unreached can be found. And agencies in the Two Thirds World are quickly taking advantage of the benefits of research as they plan their evangelism and church planting strategies.

Research is an area where Western agencies can make their expertise and equipment available, without the temptation to manipulate or interfere with the use of the data.

But research is expensive and exacting and requires sophisticated equipment if done on a large scale. Here is an area where Western agencies can make their expertise and equipment available, without the temptation to manipulate or interfere with the use of the data.

In the months preceding COMIBAM (Congress on Missions in Ibero-America), the continent-wide missions congress held in São Paulo, Brazil, in 1987, hundreds of researchers fanned out across Latin America asking questions to analyze the state of the church. Each country had its own COMIBAM committee which was responsible for finding researchers and for getting the data together.

But without the Global Mapping Project located at the U.S. Center for World Mission in Pasadena, California, these data could never have been analyzed and made available. With highly trained personnel and sophisticated equipment, Global

Mapping Director Bob Waymire and his associates were able to put all the major data on computerized four-color maps which visibly illustrated the concentrations of unreached people, the major language groups, and the evangelical population.

Working under tremendous deadlines, the COMIBAM team in Guatemala was able to deliver the "Atlas de Comibam" in time to be distributed to the more than 3,000 delegates at the conference.

This was indeed a partnership on a massive scale which yielded immediate and visible results and enabled each national group of churches to inspire and challenge their own constituencies and plan their mission outreach.

Other national research agencies, such as the Church Growth Research Center in Madras, India, and the Ghana Evangelism Committee in Ghana, partner with denominations and missions to help them plan their outreach programs.

Partnering through conferences

In May, 1990, the Latin American Consultation on Muslim Evangelism (CLAME 90) met in Miami, Florida. This consultation grew out of the Latin American church's growing interest in Muslim evangelism, as evidenced at COMIBAM. The Holy Spirit seemed to convict Christians in different parts of the continent that Latins could have a special advantage working among Arabs.

Because of 400 years of Moorish domination of Spain, Latin Americans share many of the same physical characteristics, cultural traditions, and even language similarities with the Arabs. Politically, Latin Americans hold no threat or historical animosity for the Arab nations.

Since COMIBAM, Latin American missionaries have gone to Pakistan, India, the Middle East, and Europe to work with Muslims.

CLAME 90 met to discuss the feasibility of sending 100 Latin American missionaries to the Arab world by the year 2000.

The conference was unique in its representation. Co-sponsored by the COMIBAM office in São Paulo, and Project Magreb, an indigenous Latin American mission in Argentina, a good proportion of the 95 delegates came from the Southern Hemisphere.

North America was represented by delegates from the Zwemer Institute and from Frontiers, both of which are involved in Muslim ministries and already work together closely at the U.S. Center for World Mission.

A number of leading Arab Christians from Middle Eastern and European countries added their insights to the conference. At the conclusion, one Arab brother stated: "This meeting is historical. This is the first time anybody has asked our opinion about coming to our part of the world, and we welcome it, and we welcome you, the Latins."

The lack of training to reach Muslims was recognized as one of the main obstacles, and training seminars across the continent were initiated. The North American delegates indicated their willingness to help where needed.

As a closing challenge, the Arab delegates commended the cooperative spirit and urged the Latins to send people who are "willing to make mistakes." But before sending missionaries, they want leaders to come and look over the situation, to know what training and ministries are already functioning, and to base their plans on what they've learned.

"Design a vision group," they recommended. "Send people on tours, and we will help them understand our situation and our people." This kind of partnering through conferences should certainly pave the way for more effective long-term partnering in future ministry.

22. Besides financial partnership, what other arenas present opportunities for partnership? What will be needed to make these succeed?

_____

_____

_____

Two Thirds World partnerships

On the other hand, the breakdown of long-term relations in missions has paved the way for new partnerships.

When the Indian government began denying visas to missionary medical doctors and other medical personnel, mission hospitals in India began closing down, for they had limited funds to hire national staff. It was at this time that the Emmanuel Hospital Association was formed, bringing together almost 20 Christian hospitals into a partnership for survival. The association offers administrative and financial assistance by serving as a channel for foundations and other agencies to provide funds.

John Richard, former executive director of the Asia Evangelical Association, believes, "It's one of the best patterns of partnership in my limited experience."

More and more Two Thirds World partnerships are emerging, as Christian leaders realize that chances of survival along with effectiveness increase as they close ranks.

> *The breakdown of long-term relations in missions has paved the way for new partnerships.*

Dr. Bong Rin Ro, dean of the Asia Graduate School of Theology, defines another reason for partnership in the area of theological education:

> We are trying to train Asians in Asia, within the Asian context, because of the high percentage of brain drain. Among Chinese from Taiwan, the brain drain has been 86 percent

in the last 20 years; among Indian theological students it has been about 90 percent.... For various reasons they don't go back. Asia has lost a large number of church leaders. We have 1,000 seminaries and Bible schools in Asia, but we don't have enough lecturers. To confront this need, the Asia Graduate School of Theology (AGST), a consortium of 17 graduate seminaries in four countries, was formed in 1984. Accredited by the Asia Theological Association, these schools offer four degrees, including the Doctor of Ministry. By banding together and allowing for interchangeable credits and exchange of students and lecturers, Asia Graduate School can offer degrees which are internationally recognized and of a high quality.

Through the cooperation among evangelical seminaries, we are able to offer this post-graduate school. Otherwise, not many people would recognize the post-graduate degrees offered by the individual schools.

In 1989, the Alliance Biblical Seminary in Manila, a member of the AGST, graduated its first doctoral students. The seven graduates came from Indonesia, Taiwan, the Philippines, New Zealand, and one from America—a missionary.

Dr. Ro recognizes that each Asian country has its own culture, and it would be preferable to study within the students' own cultural context. But he explains, "We can't afford to set up doctoral programs in each country. We don't have the professors or the research materials." However, he admits that the AGST program is more culturally relevant than a Western education because of the common ground shared by the Asian cultures.

23. What are some of the ways Two Thirds World mission institutions can partner with each other?

_____

_____

_____

Korean missionaries partner with Thais

It's this "invisible cultural link" which has drawn missionaries of the Korean International Mission to partner with the Church of Christ in Thailand in evangelism and church planting.

Koreans and Thais share the same Confucian/Buddhist background. They think similarly, believing that everything that happens has a spiritual cause. They share the virtue of conformity and filial respect ingrained for centuries. Thus the pastor carries enormous authority. Both cultures value the courtesy of saving face and seek to avoid offense by confrontation.

The Korean International Mission (KIM) began working in Thailand in 1956. But in recent years missionaries have sought to work in partnership with the Church of Christ in Thailand (CCT), which is an ecumenical body representing a number of denominations and parachurch agencies.

In preparation for working together, the joint committee planned a unique exchange program. A Thai evangelist was brought to Korea to study at the East West Center for Mission Research and Development for one year. Later a group of Thai Christian leaders attended the World Evangelism Crusade in 1980 and visited many Korean churches and projects. As a result, one of the Thai leaders established a prayer mountain for 24-hour prayer vigils and fasting, based on the Korean model he had seen.

KIM board members and Korean pastors visited Thailand for a week to see the work firsthand and get to know the people better, while the CCT executive committee visited Korea and also attended church growth seminars there.

Korean missionary Jung Woong Kim observed: "The more pastors, elders, and women leaders visit the mission field, the better the Korean church's understanding of the Thais and missionary work."*

Cultural imperialism is just as likely to tarnish Two Thirds World missionaries working in other cultures as it has Western missions.

Koreans are learning the meaning of *cha cha* ("slowly, slowly"), as they find church growth does not respond as rapidly in Thailand as it has in Korea.

Both Korean and Thai workers are recognizing some of the following principles that will have to be applied as Two Thirds World mission agencies around the world develop partnerships:

- Cultural imperialism is just as likely to tarnish Two Thirds World missionaries working in other cultures as it has Western missions. It should be remembered that North American missionaries share cultural roots with Europeans, but they are not immune from this accusation even there.

- Two Thirds World missionaries need to be wary of pride of accomplishment. For exam-

ple, the rapid Korean church growth and well-documented early-morning prayer meetings could cause Korean missionaries to look down upon churches in other cultures that do not experience these.

- Two Thirds World agencies and their supporting churches will have to understand the extent of the responsibility they assume when sending out missionaries, so that they are faithfully and consistently backed by finances and prayer. Some of the high rate of fallout among Two Thirds World missionaries is due to the lack of adequate and regular support from their home base.

- Constant shift of missionaries and changing strategies weaken the effectiveness of the ministry. Kim writes: "Missionaries change their areas and adopt different approaches, depending on the missionary's interest and concerns. There is often no connection between a missionary's work and his successor's."**

As Two Thirds World boards become more experienced, such problems should become less common. They will no doubt face many of the same obstacles Western agencies have faced. But hopefully they will learn more rapidly than the West has, that the right kinds of partnership will serve as cords of victory to strengthen their impact on the lost around them.

---

24. *What are some dangers of disregarding the experience and wisdom which Two Thirds World mission agencies could obtain through partnering with older Western agencies?*

_____

_____

_____

---

* Kim, J. W. (1985). *Third World mission/church relationship: A Korean/Thai model* (p. 163). Unpublished dissertation, Trinity Evangelical Divinity School, Deerfield, IL.

** Kim (p. 121).

It is a decisive moment for partnership. The Holy Spirit seems to be impressing this fact on the hearts of missions leaders around the world. In the following excerpt, Phill Butler, International Director of Interdev, documents this trend.

❏ *Partnership Is a Growing Movement* *

Phillip Butler with Clyde Cowan

Partnership in missions is an idea whose time is now. Consider the topics of the world's great missions organizations in recent conferences.

The Lausanne Movement, long a catalyst in cooperative efforts, emphasized partnerships at the historic conference in Bad Boll, Germany in 1992. Participants from 36 countries met there, and following the conference, the European Lausanne Committee called for a pan-European working conference on partnership.

The AD 2000 and Beyond Movement recently established a Partnership Development Task Force, chaired by Interdev's International Director, Phill Butler. The goal is to encourage practical cooperation and integration of ministry at the grass roots level for evangelism among unreached people. AD 2000 wants its specialized tracks and regional cooperation to bear fruit at the field level.

The Missions Commission of the World Evangelical Fellowship (WEF) focused its 1992 triennial meeting in Manila on the theme "Toward Interdependent Partnerships." Plenary sessions, working papers, and small group meetings all wrestled with the practical implications of partnership, especially in the growing number of alliances between Western and non-Western mission agencies.** WEF is promoting partnership of all kinds through its network membership in 75 countries, 500,000 churches, and 100 million evangelicals, as well as through its six major commissions.

In North America, ACMC (Advancing Churches in Mission Commitment) chose the theme "Renewal for Global Partnering" for its 1992 conference. The ACMC represents nearly 1,000 churches in the United States, and is on the cutting edge of missions strategy and helping local churches translate that into effective missions policies.

Besides all these, a Partnership Network is growing, linking innovators together for fellowship, information, and further training. Interdev contributes to this with its Partnership Effectiveness Program (a training course for Partnership Facilitators), regional meetings, and a newsletter called *Partnership Report*.***

Major donors, churches, foundations, and individuals are beginning to consider partnerships as a significant factor in giving. Many donors are asking mission agencies if they coordinate their efforts with others in their area. Such donors are clearly indicating they want the greatest spiritual return on their giving, through cooperative effort. No one wants to see his resources diluted through a duplicated project or one whose timing conflicts with another worthy project.

Churches want to be active partners. More and more churches on the leading edge of missions are seeking ways to become partners in the evangelism of specific people groups. They aren't content merely to supply resources of people, money, and prayer. They want to be active partners.

---

* Butler, P., with Cowan, C. (1993). *Partnership: Accelerating evangelism in the '90s* (pp. 14-16). Seattle: Interdev.

** For the WEF conference papers, see Taylor, W. D. (Ed.). (1994). *Kingdom partnerships for synergy in missions.* Pasadena: William Carey Library.

*** For information about these resources, contact Interdev, P.O. Box 30945, Seattle, WA 98103.

Strategic Evangelism Partnerships hold the brightest hope for reaching the 2 billion unreached people on earth. Of the many ways churches and missions can work together, this particular kind of partnership emphasizes the big picture, yet fits the details in place. It offers a comprehensive plan and coordination of resources, with the goal of seeing a viable national church developed among unreached people. It is an effective, strategic approach to fulfilling the Great Commission. The goal for Strategic Evangelism Partnerships is to reach the most people, in the shortest time, at the lowest cost, among people who have the least chance to hear of Christ.

25. In the drive to complete the Great Commission, why are Strategic Evangelism Partnerships so important?

_____

_____

_____

Summary

Becoming a World Christian begins with one's own commitment to Christ and His global cause. This commitment seems obvious, once one has been caught up in the vision of what God is doing and the exciting part Christians can play. The fact that not all Christendom is alive with this vision speaks to the "catch"—the call to sacrificial obedience. Becoming a World Christian demands that we give up our petty ambitions. It involves catching the vision, keeping it, and obeying it. Praying, giving, and sending are key ways most World Christians will get involved. Of these, prayer is the most strategic spiritual weapon. Basic to becoming a sender are giving and praying. Mobilizers and welcomers are two other proactive roles World Christians can take.

The involvement of the local church in missions is fundamental to the success of this enterprise. Two kinds of missions groups are needed—prayer fellowships and missions committees. The easiest to organize is the prayer fellowship. In addition, local congregations must understand the primary importance of the missions ministry and must implement such a ministry. This involves "growing" the vision and administrating it. Proven methods for doing this, such as the Faith Promise Plan, have been developed and tested over the years. Local churches should also consider partnering with missions in carrying out Great Commission objectives. Although tensions have arisen in partnerships, they must be worked through. A thorough assessment of a mission agency is encouraged as individuals and churches look to team up with a mission.

Partnership doesn't stop once workers have arrived on the field. Interagency cooperation is also fundamental to the success of mission ventures, particularly in reaching the unreached. Instead of proliferating missions, Westerners need to learn to use existing structures. Non-Westerners legitimately are looking for a fuller role when partnering with Western agencies and are finding the power available in cooperating with each other. There are many challenges and complex issues, but there is no doubt that partnership is on the Holy Spirit's agenda in these exciting days for world evangelization.

Integrative Assignment

1. *This study began in Chapter 1 with the Abrahamic Covenant. It ends with your own World Christian Covenant with God. Prayerfully consider your commitment to Christ's global cause. Agree with God about your participation in it. Don't be afraid to address what you expect of Him as you seek to fulfill His will in this. Write out your covenant, sign, and date it. Expect God to bless your commitment.*

2. *Using the suggestions from the ACMC article on "Planting Ahead" (pages 15-15 and 15-16), rate your church's involvement in missions. Based on this information, outline some concrete steps you can take to bolster or help grow the vision in your church.*

3. *Partnership is more than just a strategic issue. It has solid theological foundations. Outline a brief talk on partnership, using biblical and strategic arguments for its importance.*

Questions for Reflection

Becoming a World Christian calls for self-denial. This runs counter to the "me" philosophy that permeates modern societies. What did Christ have to say about discipleship? Meditate on passages such as Matthew 10:37-39, Luke 9:57-62, and Luke 14:25-35. Examine your own heart before God in light of these verses.

Subject Index

Author Index